How to Start Personal Histories & Genealogy Journalism Businesses

How to Start Personal Histories & Genealogy Journalism Businesses

✦

Genealogy Course Template, Syllabus, Writing & Marketing Guide

Anne Hart

ASJA Press
New York Lincoln Shanghai

How to Start Personal Histories & Genealogy Journalism Businesses
Genealogy Course Template, Syllabus, Writing & Marketing Guide

Copyright © 2006 by Anne Hart

ASJA Press
an imprint of iUniverse, Inc.

iUniverse books may be ordered through booksellers or by contacting:

iUniverse
2021 Pine Lake Road, Suite 100
Lincoln, NE 68512
www.iuniverse.com
1-800-Authors (1-800-288-4677)

ISBN-13: 978-0-595-38698-7
ISBN-10: 0-595-38698-9

Printed in the United States of America

Contents

1

How to Write a Genealogy Course Syllabus and Teach Online to Market Your Book

Here's how to open your own genealogy, family history journalism, or personal history business. This includes a genealogy course template and instruction on how to start and operate a home-based business working with personal and oral histories, genealogy, family history, and life story writing. You also learn how to interview people, what questions to ask, and how to put together a business and/ or a course or book on any aspect of genealogy around the world, journalism, writing, personal history, and life story writing.

Start your own course using the genealogy course template to inspire you to develop your own specialties and niche areas. Work with almost any ethnic group, and create businesses ranging from DNA-driven genealogy reporting services to family history, memoirs writing, or personal history videography services.

Use *social history* to find information such as female ancestors' maiden names that had not been recorded using hidden and niche areas of information, including ethnic, religious, and institutional sources such as widows' military pension applications. You'll learn how to write social history by using genealogy journalism resources, find hidden records, and market your own course or write your book or report in many different areas of personal history and genealogy journalism. Female ancestors' information also may be found in midwives' records, journals, or diaries and in later times, in prenatal records books.

Start your own business or set up a course and teach or train others to be genealogists or personal and oral historians. Write for historical, folkloric, or genealogy publications, specializing in writing eulogies for people or pets. Interview friends or family, and write obituaries for publications that have no staff obituary writer on board all the time. Assemble family history time capsules, keepsakes, or courseware and software. Record family history how-to lectures on audio CDs or

1

video DVDs. Teach life story journalism. Or write life stories as plays and skits. Do research for clients, libraries, and institutions. Learn what is appropriate to charge clients for personal history, genealogy research, or life story recording and writing services.

Make family tree charts with software or craft them in scrap books. Learn how to be an independent documentarian. Produce video and audio recordings such as DVDs for your clients or family. Develop genealogy and personal history classes anywhere. You'll make history. To start, first you need to create a course syllabus-either to teach beginners genealogy or to train professionals in other fields to use personal history techniques to find hidden information, or organize information for the reports you generate for your clients or family. Start your own business, club, franchise, or course.

One of the best ways to publicize and market your genealogy course and/or family history instructional book is to write a syllabus. Teach an online or in-person course related to the topic of your book. Require students to purchase the book. Teach the contents of the book in a how-to course. What's your hobby or field of expertise? My usual full-time working day emphasizes genealogy journalism and personal history research. My hobby combines visual anthropology and producing, viewing, and reviewing documentaries.

If your field relates to personal history or genealogy, here's how to write a syllabus to teach online (or in person) a genealogy course. You can train or teach at a variety of levels.

Starting your own classes and reserving a conference room in a library, church social hall, or community center don't require degrees or credentials, only expertise. Nothing lets you learn a subject better than if you have to teach it to beginners. If you don't like teaching face-to-face or training employees in a work setting, teach online from your Web site. Or apply to teach a course in something you can do well at online educational sites such as blackboard.com. Read online education publications such as the Virtual U Gazette. Check out GetEducated.com at: http://www.geteducated.com/vug/index.asp.

You learn more from your students' feedback than you ever learned from books in a variety of areas related to writing and publishing. The first step is to write a great syllabus that convinces others to hire you to teach a subject related to the information in your book. This technique works well with nonfiction, how-to or self-help books.

If your book is a novel, your course syllabus might emphasize plotting the novel or marketing and promotion. To sell your book in this type of class, you'd use each chapter to teach how to write "tag lines," emotions and behaviors in a novel, or portions of your novel as tools for fiction writers in the genre of your book—such as plotting the mystery or romance novel.

You'd use passages to teach consistency and transitions that move the plot forward and show how the characters grow and change or the romantic tension. A similar technique of "teaching the process" would be used if you wrote plays, poetry, or cinematic scripts. A syllabus helps you get hired and/or to recruit students so you can sell your book and teach a class or train a group of people either online or in person.

You can adapt this syllabus plan and format to the subject of your book in nearly any field. Instead of 'genealogy,' just substitute the concept and framework of your own book. Here's how to write a syllabus.

A short course may be taught online or arranged in any room available from a church basement to a library conference room. A seminar can last a few hours. A lengthy course can be planned for an entire semester at any level in adult education, for college extended studies programs, or at community centers. You need experience in your area of expertise, and a published book helps your credibility. If you're teaching a course in a community college or university for college credit you'd need a graduate degree. For public school you'd also need a teaching credential unless your expertise level is the equivalent. Teaching vocational education and using your book as instructional text is more flexible. You can teach in the extended studies (not for credit) department of universities and community colleges based on experience. Credentials in your field of work are helpful to get you hired, but without them, start your own course online or from an available room.

You can share a rented room to teach the course with other trainers or teachers. Least expensive is to teach at your Web site and sell your book online to students. At the end of the course, give them a certificate in the subject you've taught related to your book. Require students to buy your book, and use it throughout the course.

One of the easiest ways to get hired to teach a course is to offer one in genealogy and/or personal history, if you have done your research on how genealogists find their information. Since you have written a book, can you now call yourself an expert?

If genealogy, personal history, oral history, social history, anthropology, sociology, psychology, creative writing, early handwriting, or journalism interests you, a beginner's course in genealogy attracts people interested in where their ancestors came from and how they lived, ate, and played. Classes often fill up quickly.

People like to take courses where they can learn about themselves and their families' life styles. Genealogy courses work well online, at social, ethnic, and religious clubs, and at senior centers. So here's how to begin writing a syllabus for a genealogy course.

Your first genealogy course syllabus expands the four keys of genealogy research: identity, name, date information was recorded, locality, and kinship. How you organize, edit, and write a genealogy course syllabus often determines whether you'll be hired to teach a course in genealogy for beginners.

If you're a genealogist or want to promote your genealogy-oriented book or journalistic skills, teach a course in genealogy. Genealogy courses rely on verifiable details. Accidental or intentional alterations by scribes can dramatically affect information. Courses that go on year after year are evaluated by students as excellent.

Genealogists are concerned about accurate reproduction of texts or entry of information. For generations, most public family history entries were hand copied by government record clerks, clergy, and scribes deeply influenced by cultural, political, and theological disputes of their day.

Your syllabus can help students look for mistakes and intentional changes in surviving records. Can the original names be reconstructed? Genealogy course content also includes the social history of where and why these changes were made and how family historians go about reconstructing what might be the original names, relationships, and records as closely as possible.

Use your syllabus as a tool to outline your course. Students want an easy-to-follow syllabus. The *American Heritage Dictionary* defines the word 'syllabus' as an outline of a course of study. It's a table of contents with a schedule of topics, not a book proposal.

Your syllabus also needs to cover how to find records of hard-to-trace people, such as clergy. How would you direct students who want to trace nuns, priests, ministers, or rabbis?

Genealogy courses given in churches' social halls sometimes attract those who want to trace difficult-to-find genealogy records of clergy. Old books make excellent genealogy sources. Other primary sources to trace clergy or religious educators include College Alumni Records, The Clergy Lists, Crockford's Directories, Fasti Ecclesiae, Anglicanae, Parish Registers, Bishop's Records, Censuses, and County Directories.

GENEALOGY COURSE SYLLABUS TEMPLATE

A genealogy course syllabus for beginners includes answers to one of the most frequently asked questions: How do you find female ancestors and solve identity problems when maiden surnames didn't appear on the death certificates? Before you try to organize and write a syllabus, first list topics you'll cover in your syllabus.

Planning Your Syllabus

List all obvious items. Keep this list next to your blank syllabus page. Then list items often omitted from a syllabus for a beginning course in genealogy. Compare your syllabus with other genealogy course outlines that have received great student evaluations. Your clue is whether the course is repeated year after year. There are several copyrighted genealogy course outlines on the Internet to peruse. Use them only for comparison and motivation. Keep your syllabus unique to your own course. Make a list of resources to be used in your own course before you begin writing your syllabus.

Resources List
Social History (brief)
Genealogy sources created by women:

Diaries, journals, letters, postcards, family Bibles, heirlooms, artifacts, oral history, legislative petitions, atypical sources, published family histories, cemetery records, tombstone inscriptions or rubbings, church records, censuses, military records, hospitals, orphanages, institutions, sanitariums, passenger arrival lists, city directories, notaries' records, voter lists/registrations, pensions, widows' pension applications/civil war, orphans and guardianship records, land records, marriage records, medical records, Eugenics Record Office, (ERO), social data, midwives' journals, doctors' journals, asylums, divorce records, wills, probate, court records, school records, ethnic sources, codicils, ethnic/religious hospital records, naturalization laws.

After you compile this list, put it aside to refer to as you write your syllabus. Begin outlining the syllabus by starting with the course information, instructor information, text or reading materials, course descriptions, course calendar or schedule, and references or bibliography.

Each category would get a one or two-sentence description summarizing what will be covered in the course and what assignments are required of students. Keep your syllabus short—about three pages or less. The syllabus in a semester-long college level, 3-unit genealogy course meant for beginners and taught online or in person would look like this in its layout:

Syllabus

Course Number/Title: **Genealogy and Family History 1**
Name of School or College
Year and Month:
Department:
Credit Hours 3
Required Text
Days/Time
Instructor
Location
Prerequisite: None
Course Placement: Adult Education, Extended Studies, Community College, University Undergraduate level.

Overview
In Genealogy 1, students will learn special strategies for uncovering hard-to-find information about their ancestors. By the end of this course, students will become more versatile in using interdisciplinary skills for researching family and social history resources.

Course Description
Genealogy 1 is an introductory course in family and personal history research *methods* that includes learning interviewing and recording skills. This survey course covers the strategies of genealogical research in North America and introduces the student to the techniques of genealogical research around the world. Students able to read other languages may work on genealogical records in other languages if they can translate their findings, projects, or assignments to the class in English.

Research Methods
Students are introduced to a survey of all the methods used to identify individuals and their ancestors, including paper records, online searches, surname groups online, and DNA-driven genealogy resources.

Learning Objectives for Genealogy 1
At the end of this course, students will have learned the following skills:

1.   Students will be able to research the following resources:
     Original records
     Family histories
     Church records

Censuses
Passenger Arrival Lists
City directories
Family history libraries and genealogy sections of public and university libraries
Voter lists and registrations
Military records and pensions, widows' pensions
Land records and notary records
Marriage records
Medical records
Divorce records
Ethnic women and men
    African American
    Native American
    Jewish American
    European Immigrants
    Chinese and Japanese Immigrants in California

2. Methods for determining maiden names.

3. Solving identity problems in genealogy research

4. Methods for identifying women (midwives' records)

5. Genealogy as social history

   a. child bearing and raising in genealogy research

   b. children born out of wedlock and genealogy research

   c. women's work and genealogy records,

   d. property tax records

   e. religion and genealogy information

   f. women's reform movements, rights, and genealogy records

   g. merging social and family history in genealogy research

   h. documenting your own ancestor's history

6. Unpublished Genealogy Sources

7. Published Genealogical Sources

8. How to research population schedules

9. Probate and court records

10. Slave genealogy and schedules

11. Social history research and biographies

12. Property, Inheritance, Naturalization and Divorce laws for genealogists

13. Widows' pensions and applications-Acts and Laws, survey

14. DNA-driven genealogy, methods, resources, matrilineal and patrilineal research, surname groups and genetics associations

15. Online research resources

16. Checklist for genealogy research

17. Genealogical case studies

18. Articles and Bibliography

19. National Archives and Genealogy Research

20. How to read abstracted records

21. How to find and read microfilms and microfiche records

22. Military pensions—records in the National Archives

23. Searching records of the Veterans Administration

24. Published indexes to pension files and other aids

25. Genealogy journalism methods—interviewing and recording

26. Oral history, video and audio recording—what questions to ask.

How Students will apply the newly learned genealogy research skills:

1. Use the methods of scientific genealogical research.

2. Establish lines of descent for the person or family you select and develop a pedigree chart or family history tree of names and critical dates such as birth, marriage, and death for each ancestor on the family tree and/or pedigree chart.

3. Organize genealogy records.

4. Interview and record relatives or selected persons.

5. Research the past.

6. Use online technology to research or supplement written records and develop a pedigree chart or family tree.

Six Assignments and Projects: Due by End of 12-Week Course. (Insert Specific Due Dates) One assignment is due every two weeks.

1. Write a publishable 1,000-word researched family history/genealogy article and submit it to a publication.

2. Develop a list of 30 to 60 questions (chosen from a list of suggested questions to ask from the handout) to ask another person during a genealogy-oriented or life story-oriented personal or family history recorded interview.

3. Interview using critical and creative thinking skills one or more older adults and record on audio or video tape a half-hour to one-hour life story experience to submit to an oral history archive library. Obtain a signed release form from all persons interviewed to send the recording to an oral history library. Give all persons interviewed copies of the interview recorded on tape or disc, such as a CD or DVD.

4. Use written records and online resources/technology relevant to your personal interests or selected discipline. Genealogy has several areas of emphasis including archival records research, oral history, personal history, family history, video biography/life story recording, and DNA-driven genealogy/genetics for ancestry.

5. Understand opportunities, skills, and requirements for genealogy journalism and publishing concentrations.

6. Research the diversity of cultures in North America and other countries as related to how genealogy records have been maintained.

7. Find several new or hidden ways to find genealogy information on females whose maiden names (surnames) were not recorded in the usual records such as censuses and city directories. How would you find birth certificates of women?

Course Competencies:

1. Learn how to perform scientific genealogical research.

2. Fill out and expand a pedigree chart and family tree—first by hand and then using technology or genealogy software.

3. Collect sources and resource information and organize the sources using records, legacies, diaries, letters, or journals.

4. Understand the value of journaling and archiving journals, letters, and diaries.

5. Read an article on how to restore old diaries and photos.

6. Write and record as audio or video a life story to keep for future generations or to put in a time capsule. One copy would be text for reading and another recorded in any format, including text and photos, audio or video. Be aware technology changes, and a text copy on acid-free paper is required just in case the recorded format can no longer play.

7. Learn how to correspond with relatives or friends and what questions to ask when asking for genealogical information.

8. Fill out family group sheets for recorded information to be transcribed or kept in text form.

9. Read an article on genealogical identification, orphan trains, and family skeletons or hidden facts on everything from how a person's race or religion was listed to name changes. Understand how some pre-1948 housing laws and codes excluded certain groups from buying property in various areas and how some records were changed so people could buy homes. Research articles on this subject as related to genealogy records.

10. Understand the four keys of genealogy as research tools: identity, name, date information was recorded, locality, and kinship.

11. Research the American and/or Canadian trains when children were sent from the East to the West. These trains are separate from the orphan trains. Records with the children's names are in various archives. Find out where to find the records.

12. Learn organization, documentation, filing techniques.

13. Analyze, interpret, and present genealogy-related findings.

14. Keep a research notebook that cites each source of documentation.

15. Look at working files that organize genealogical documents.

16. Listen to a recording of oral history. Read an article on restoring or preserving keepsakes, heirlooms, photos, and scrap books that document family traditions.

17. Use oral history as a research method. Learn to record oral history in audio and/or in video using a camcorder or audio recorder.

18. Learn how items and traditions have been preserved by families, librarians, conservationists, archivists, or family and public historians.

19. Gather family folklore, recipes, superstitions, or traditions.

20. Record family rites of passage, celebrations, or traditions.

21. Search genealogy records on the Internet

22. Read published genealogy information online.

23. Survey genealogy published materials.

24. Enter family information and print-out computer-generated charts and family trees.

25. Learn how to use vital records, divorce and cemetery records, jurisdictions records, original records, Social Security Death Index records online, and specific localities searches of historical groups for an area. Look for transcriptions of original documents.

26. Understand handwriting changes and how to interpret early American handwriting. Translate documents recorded in early American handwriting.

27. Find out where to obtain court records used in genealogy research.

28. Use church data to fill in missing information.

29. Use newspapers in genealogy research

30. Trace ancestor's lives using a city directory.

31. Research information on the Family History Library, Salt Lake City, Utah. Locate the nearest Branch Family Center and research an ancestor or friend.

32. Learn to research immigration, emigration, and migration records, ships' passenger lists, Naturalization records.

33. Investigate the reason why your ancestor immigrated to America. Trace the migration patterns used. Use passenger lists and naturalization records and find out where these records are located.

34. Use land and tax records, school records, and ethnic records.

35. Research what records are available in the National Archives. Find out what military records are available to genealogists for research. Find out the addresses to write to for military, pension, and bounty land records.

36. Plan for and/or attend a genealogy-related seminar, research-oriented field trip, family reunion, or a meeting of a heritage, historical, or lineage association. Read an article on or view a documentary on a family reunion. Research what grants are available from various societies related to genealogy research.

37. Read an article on how to look at medical histories and genograms. A genogram is a schematic representation (drawing) of a family's medical history. A genogram describes the medical and/or genetic history of a family and includes family boundaries, attitudes, values, beliefs and related psychological history of family members.

38. Look at a Web site or surname group online researching DNA-driven genealogy for deep ancestry research. Read an article or handout on the psychological aspects of studying one's own family history. Start a genogram of your family. Does DNA-driven genealogy appeal more to anthropologists or to genealogists?

Libraries and Field Trips

Visit a library that has records related to genealogy and/or oral history research or archives. Record in your notebook in two paragraphs what you learned from the field trip and what most interested you there.

Method of Instruction

Class discussion, lectures, field trips, video documentaries, class participation, individual Internet computer research, collaborative projects, handouts, videos, and personal history recording projects is used. This course may be taught online or in person.

Evaluation

Class participation and completion of projects/assignments is due by the end of the course. Assignments are due by the due date specified in the handout.

Equipment

Access to the Internet, a personal computer and printer, a tape or other audio digital recorder or camcorder using either tape or DVDs, and a DVD or CD recorder/R/RW disk drive in your computer or other device that saves a computer file to a CD and/or a DVD. Save your recorded projects on DVDs or CDs. Instruction will be provided on how to save any recorded material to a DVD or CD. Technical help will be available.

Length of Course

Adjust the syllabus content and assignments to the length of your own course. Genealogy courses may run for a 12, 16 or 18-week semester in adult education unified school districts or in extended studies or community college classes.

◆   ◆   ◆

Ethnic Genealogy Web Sites

(Usually, there are several genealogy sites on the Web for each ethnic group.)
Acadian/Cajun: & French Canadian: http://www.acadian.org/tidbits.html
Afghanistan Genealogy: http://www.kindredtrails.com/afghanistan.html
African-American: http://www.cyndislist.com/african.htm

African Royalty Genealogy: http://www.uq.net.au/~zzhsoszy/

Albanian Research List: http://feefhs.org/al/alrl.html

Armenian Genealogical Society: http://feefhs.org/am/frg-amgs.html

Asia and the Pacific: http://www.cyndislist.com/asia.htm

Austria-Hungary Empire: http://feefhs.org/ah/indexah.html

Baltic-Russian Information Center: http://feefhs.org/blitz/frgblitz.html

Belarusian—Association of the Belarusian Nobility: http://feefhs.org/by/frg-zbs.html

Bukovina Genealogy: http://feefhs.org/bukovina/bukovina.html

Carpatho-Rusyn Knowledge Base: http://feefhs.org/rusyn/frg-crkb.html

Chinese Genealogy: http://www.chineseroots.com/.

Croatia Genealogy Cross Index: http://feefhs.org/cro/indexcro.html

Czechoslovak Genealogical Society Int'l, Inc.: http://feefhs.org/czs/cgsi/frg-cgsi.html

Eastern Europe: http://www.cyndislist.com/easteuro.htm

Eastern European Genealogical Society, Inc.: http://feefhs.org/ca/frg-eegs.html

Eastern Europe Ethnic, Religious, and National Index with Home Pages includes the FEEFHS Resource Guide that lists organizations associated with FEEFHS from 14 Countries. It also includes Finnish and Armenian genealogy resources: http://feefhs.org/ethnic.html

Ethnic, Religious, and National Index 14 countries: http://feefhs.org/ethnic.html

(Finland) Genealogical Society of Finland: http://www.genealogia.fi/indexe.htm

Finnish Genealogy Group: http://feefhs.org/misc/frgfinmn.html

Galicia Jewish SIG: http://feefhs.org/jsig/frg-gsig.html

German Genealogical Digest: http://feefhs.org/pub/frg-ggdp.html

Greek Genealogy Sources on the Internet: http://www-personal.umich.edu/~cgaunt/greece.html

Genealogy Societies Online List: http://www.daddezio.com/catalog/grkndx04.html

German Research Association: http://feefhs.org/gra/frg-gra.html

Greek Genealogy (Hellenes-Diaspora Greek Genealogy): http://www.geocities.com/SouthBeach/Cove/4537/

Greek Genealogy Home Page: http://www.daddezio.com/grekgen.html

Greek Genealogy Articles: http://www.daddezio.com/catalog/grkndx01.html

India Genealogy: http://genforum.genealogy.com/india/

India Family Histories: http://www.mycinnamontoast.com/perl/results.cgi? region=79&sort=n

India-Anglo-Indian/Europeans in India genealogy: http://members. ozemail.com.au/~clday/

Irish Travelers: http://www.pitt.edu/~alkst3/Traveller.html

Japanese Genealogy: http://www.rootsweb.com/~jpnwgw/

Jewish Genealogy: http://www.jewishgen.org/infofiles/

Latvian Jewish Genealogy Page: http://feefhs.org/jsig/frg-lsig.html

Lebanese Genealogy: http://www.rootsweb.com/~lbnwgw/

Lithuanian American Genealogy Society: http://feefhs.org/frg-lags.html

Melungeon: http://www.geocities.com/Paris/5121/melungeon.htm

Mennonite Heritage Center: http://feefhs.org/men/frg-mhc.html

Middle East Genealogy: http://www.rootsweb.com/~mdeastgw/index.html

Middle East Genealogy by country: http://www.rootsweb.com/~mdeastgw/ index.html-country

Native American: http://www.cyndislist.com/native.htm

Polish Genealogical Society of America:http://feefhs.org/pol/frg-pgsa.html

Quebec and Francophone: http://www.francogene.com/quebec/amerin.html

Romanian American Heritage Center: http://feefhs.org/ro/frg-rahc.html

Slovak World: http://feefhs.org/slovak/frg-sw.html

Slavs, South: Cultural Society: http://feefhs.org/frg-csss.html

Syrian and Lebanese Genealogy: http://www.genealogytoday.com/family/ syrian/

Syria Genealogy: http://www.rootsweb.com/~syrwgw/

Tibetan Genealogy: http://www.distantcousin.com/Links/Ethnic/China/ Tibetan.html

Turkish Genealogy Discussion Group: http://www.turkey.com/forums/ forumdisplay.php3?forumid=18

Ukrainian Genealogical and Historical Society of Canada: http://feefhs.org/ ca/frgughsc.html

Unique Peoples: http://www.cyndislist.com/peoples.htm Note: The Unique People's list includes: Black Dutch, Doukhobors, Gypsy, Romani, Romany & Travellers, Melungeons, Metis, Miscellaneous, and Wends/Sorbs

Genealogy, (General):

Ancestry.com: http://www.ancestry.com/main.htm?lfl=m

BMD Certificates, London, England, UK: http://www. bmd-certificates.co.uk/

Cyndi's List of Genealogy on the Internet: http://www.cyndislist.com/

Cyndi's List is a categorized & cross-referenced index to genealogical resources on the Internet with thousands of links.
DistantCousin.com (Uniting Cousins Worldwide) http://distantcousin.com/Links/surname.html
Ellis Island Online: http://www.ellisisland.org/
Family History Library: http://www.familysearch.org/Eng/default.asp
http://www.familysearch.org/Eng/Search/frameset_search.asp
(The Church of Jesus Christ of Latter Day Saints) International Genealogical Index
Female Ancestors: http://www.cyndislist.com/female.htm
Genealogist's Index to the Web: http://www.genealogytoday.com/GIWWW/
Genealogy Web: http://www.genealogyweb.com/
Genealogy Authors and Speakers: http://feefhs.org/frg/frg-a&l.html
Genealogy Today: http://www.genealogytoday.com/
My Genealogy.com: http://www.genealogy.com/cgi-bin/my_main.cgi
Scriver, Dr. Charles: The Canadian Medical Hall of Fame http://www.virtualmuseum.ca/Exhibitions/Medicentre/en/scri_print.htm
Surname Sites: http://www.cyndislist.com/surn-gen.htm
National Genealogical Society: http://www.ngsgenealogy.org/index.htm
United States List of Local by State Genealogical Societies: http://www.daddezio.com/society/hill/index.html
United States Vital Records List: http://www.daddezio.com/records/room/index.html or http://www.cyndislist.com/usvital.htm
How to Start Personal Histories & Genealogy Journalism Businesses

"Every life story has four seasons and twelve stages, like the months in a year. The four seasons are infancy, childhood, adulthood and grace-age."

—*How to Write Plays, Monologues, or Skits from Life Stories, Social Issues, or Current Events (for All Ages). ISBN: 0-595-31866-5*

2

How to Do Genealogical Searches Online for Family History & Ancestry. Searching Techniques and Resources: Early New England Settlers

Plenty of genealogy software is on the market that allows you to make a wide variety of tables and charts of family trees. But how do you trace the genealogy of one of your male descendants? Here's a sample you can follow regarding how the research is done, step-by-step to achieve results.

Sample:

How to Trace the Genealogy of One Line of Male Descendants from Deacon Stephen Hart, b. 1605, Essex (Early New England Settler 1631).

Who Was This Early New England Settler?

Deacon Stephen Hart arrived in Massachusetts Bay Colony on November 2, 1631, according to some records, on the ship called the 'Lyon.' However, the following passengers came in 1631 aboard the *William and Francis* (from the London Rolls Office): Gamlin, Harris, Hart, Hayward, Hill, Levins, Mannering, Norton, Olliver, Perkins, Smallie, Thomas, Whetson, Woodford, and Winslow.

Deacon Stephen Hart is listed in the Court records as a resident of New Towne (Cambridge) MA for 7 January 1632/33. By 1636, he moves to what is now

Farmington, Connecticut. Also, see The Winthrop Society site at: http://www.winthropsociety.org/doc_newtowne.php.

Using DNA-Driven Genealogy:

By Genealogy Records and by a DNA Y chromosome DYS 37-marker test.

How many Y-chromosome DNA tests show which Hart males are related to one another and to a common ancestor? How far back can that ancestor be traced with actual genealogy records?

E-Letter from Bryan Sykes:

From: Bryan Sykes
To: Anne Hart
Sent: Wednesday, December 01, 2004 4:28 PM
Subject: Re: Thank you for starting us to search for English ancestors

Dear Anne

Well I suppose that's what academics are for. I'm so thrilled that my research has led to something useful. It certainly didn't seem so at the time.

On a serious vein, what has happened in 'genetic genealogy' is extremely unusual. Blue sky scientific research has opened up a field which is now being championed by yourself and others. The research that counts is now being done by enthusiastic practitioners—mainly unpaid. It is the return of the long forgotten 19th century paragon—the amateur scientist. I feel a ponderous and pompous article coming on!

Best wishes—and a very happy Christmas.

Bryan

See also: The Connecticut Historical Society Museum collection includes a hornbook (CHSM# 1954.11.0) owned by Rev. John Hart of Farmington (1682–?). See: http://www.chs.org. research museum collections.

Tracing Back the Ancestors of Homer Vincent Hart: The Techniques of Researching.

The Hart Genealogy 1605-1938

Research Techniques and Sources: Using a Y Chromosome DNA Test

After the genealogy records were researched, then we added a Hart surname group project, and also a Y-chromosome DNA test of 37 DYS markers from Family Tree DNA. See some DNA sequences. Do they match yours? We already had the genealogy records in a direct line to Deacon Stephen Hart, b. 1605.

On the following page note the 37-marker Y chromosome DNA Test table from Family Tree DNA. See: http://www.familytreedna.com. The haplogroup is R1b. This table is one example of what DNA-driven genealogy test results look like. Men who receive these types of results want to interpret them in plain language and learn what the letters and numbers mean as far as ancestry and/or geographical possible origins or migrations in the distant past. Only males have Y chromosomes.

Women would get their mtDNA (matrilineal) line tested as the mtDNA passes from mothers to daughters. The Y chromosome passes from fathers to sons down through many generations for perhaps 500 years or more before mutations could be found—although some minor mutations may occur before that time. MtDNA (mitochondrial DNA) passes from mothers to daughters for thousands of years before a mutation may be found. There's always the exception.

Males with the same surname may want to compare Y chromosome results to see whether they share the same male common ancestor who lived generations ago. Many people share similar genealogy records, such as the descendant of early New England 17th century settlers seen in the table you can view at one of my Web sites at: http://www.hart_family_genealogy.htm. They get tested also to find out whether they are biologically related to one another and possibly to the common ancestor.

A genealogist also can help clients understand what the results mean geographically and as related to deep ancestry or whether a group of people with the same surname (last name) share the same Y chromosome or similar markers on a DNA test to see who might be descended from a common ancestor who lived generations ago.

At the Hart genealogy Web site tracing one line only, you can see that one of the males of our family can trace his ancestry by DNA testing of the Y chromosome to see how many other males tested for Y chromosome sequences that also have the same surname and same genealogy 17th, 18th, and 19th century paper records readily available in USA archives compare. They had their Y chromosome DNA tested to see whether they are possibly related to an ancestor who lived 12 generations ago who was born around 1605.

The Hart Surname DNA-Driven Genealogy Project:

The Hart DNA Project at: http://www.worldfamilies.net/ is collecting & studying DNA data on participants of the HART surname project. The purpose of these tests is to distinguish the relationships between the various lines.

Most have gone as far as possible with traditional methods of research (courthouse records, bible records, etc.). There are theories about how the lines mesh, but DNA testing could put research on the right track, showing which lines are related, and which are not.

Deacon Stephen Hart, born about 1605 in Essex England, was the progenitor of many Harts now living in North America and other parts of the world. The book on Stephen Hart and his descendants was originally published in 1875 to document all Harts then known to be descendants of Stephen Hart.

Stephen Hart is believed to have immigrated to New England on the ship 'The Lion' (Lyon) around November 2, 1631. The ship left London and headed for New Towne (Cambridge). Some group participants have documented their ancestry to Deacon Stephen Hart. (Also see the Winthrop Society at: http://www.winthropsociety.org/.)

The first participant who took the 37 marker test results could benefit others that are trying to prove their connection to Deacon Stephen Hart. That group is looking for DNA sampling from any male, in a direct line of documented descent. A possible DNA signature of Deacon Stephen Hart's descendants could be found. There are other Harts, not related to Deacon Stephen Hart, such as those related to John Hart, of New Jersey, signer of the Declaration of Independence.

◆   ◆   ◆

Back to Genealogy Records

Stephen HART

(Stephen Hart, born in 1568 is the father of Deacon Stephen Hart born in 1605.)

• **BIRTH: 1568**

Family 1 :

1. **Elizabeth HART**

2. **Richard HART**

3. **Stephen HART**

4. **Christopher HART**

5. **Ann HART**

6. **+Stephen II HART**

Source: http://www.howellresearch.com/d0042/g0000051.html - I97866

+Stephen II HART (Deacon Stephen Hart, born 1605, Essex, England)

Migrated to New England in 1632 on a ship called the Lyon.

See RootsWeb at www.rootsweb.com, where you'll find a genealogy of the Harts descended from Stephen Hart and a biography at The Dunne & Allied Family's Site at: http://worldconnect.rootsweb.com/cgi-bin/igm.cgi?op.

Also see: 1. Frederick Adams Virkus, ed., "Immigrant Ancestors", Genealogical Publishing Co., 1942, p.36.2. Steve Condarcure, "Steve Condarcure's New England Genealogy," http://newenglandgenealogy.pcplayground.com/. Also research these Web site resources: http://armidalesoftware.com/issue/full/ Thaler_1067_main.html - FN1 and http://www.armidalesoftware.com/issue.

Also see to get started the Web site at: http://newenglandgenealogy.
pcplayground.com/f_142.htm - 80

HART, Stephen
b. 1605 Braintree, Essex, England
d. MAR 1682/83 Farmington, CT.
Family:

Children:

   HART, Sarah
   HART, John
   HART, Stephen
   HART, Mary
   HART, Mehitable
   HART, Rachel
   HART, Thomas

The father of Deacon Stephen Hart also was named Stephen Hart. Resources note: 1. STEPHEN[1] HART was born sometime between 1550 and 1591, and died between 1604 and 1701. [1] Child. His son became Deacon Stephen Hart, born 1605, Essex, England.

Consider that the first Stephen Hart would have been old enough to have a son born in 1605 when researching his birth date. How many other Stephen Harts were there before him related in a direct line? What was Stephen Hart's great grandfather's name?

So far research shows that Deacon Stephen Hart's son, John Hart was born in 1630 in England and died in Farmington, CT on December 15th 1666. He was the son of Deacon Stephen Hart and his wife Sarah, born in England. When Deacon Stephen Hart came to New England, John was about two years old.

Deacon Stephen Hart was born around 1605. Stephen and Sarah Hart had at first, three children, John, Sarah, and Stephen[3]. So we have 'grandpa' Stephen Hart, his son, Deacon Stephen Hart, and his surviving son, Stephen3 or Stephen, the third.

There also are listed in genealogical records the other surviving children. Stephen the third's son, John Hart, was born 2 APR 1655 in Farmington, CT. Stephen was (the third) son of Deacon Stephen Hart. And that Stephen also had a son named John.

(This family line is descended from "John, born in Farmington, about 1655, baptized April 2d, 1655, saved from the fire, he being that night at Nod," according to the 1875 book on the Hart family published online at: http://users.rcn.com/harts.ma.ultranet/family/andrews/p043.html.

The fire occurred on December 15, 1666. The surviving child, John Hart, was only eleven years old in 1666. He was away from the house at the time. See the Web site at: http://newenglandgenealogy.pcplayground.com/f_142.htm - 81 for some of these resources and information. Also see other Stephen Hart Web sites mentioned on this site for more research on those events. Here is what is noted about some family members as to the year 1666. Other children also survived.

The children of the oldest son, John Hart, who didn't survive, include Deacon Stephen Hart's oldest son, born in 1630, named John, and John's wife, Sarah, as well as some of the children of John Hart, also named Sarah and Stephen. The other John Hart, the eleven-year old grandson of Deacon Stephen Hart, did survive as he was out of the area that night—at a place called 'Nod.' Deacon Stephen Hart also had other surviving children. Here is what the genealogy records state:

Sarah,
d. 15 DEC 1666 Burned to death
Family:

Spouse: HART, John
b. ABT. 1630 England
d. 15 DEC 1666 Burned to death
Parents:

Father: HART, Stephen

Children:

HART, Sarah
b. ABT. 1653 Farmington, CT.

d. 1666 Burned to death
HART, John (John Hart, grandson, survived)
HART, Stephen
b. JUL 1657 Farmington, CT.
d. 1666 Burned to death

In 17th century New England, for a male settler to serve in public office and be declared a citizen, he first had to join the Congregational church before he could be declared "a free man." In court records 1633 of New Towne (Cambridge) and after 1636, in Farmington, CT, Deacon Stephen Hart serves in public office and also serves as a soldier in the Pequot War (1634-1638) where he is awarded "a soldier's lot" of land. He owns a large estate in Farmington and another home and surrounding area nearby, called 'Nod.'

John Hart, born in 1655, married Mary Moore, who was born 15 SEP 1664 Farmington, CT. They had Isaac Hart [1] 27 Nov 1683 and a son also named John Hart in born in 1684 in Farmington, CT. They also had other children named Sara, Matthew, Samuel, Nathaniel, and Mary. The birthdates and Web links of information for each child are at the Dunne and Allied Family's site at: http://worldconnect.rootsweb.com/cgi-bin/igm.cgi?op=GET&db=dunne1&id =I08416.

Those children of John Hart are: Isaac[2] Hart b: 27 NOV 1683, John HART b: 1684 in Farmington, CT, Sarah HART b: 11 DEC 1687, Matthew HART b: 7 DEC 1690, Samuel HART b: 18 SEP 1692, Nathaniel HART b: 14 APR 1695, and Mary HART.

MARY[3] HART (Stephen[2], Stephen[1]), daughter of (2) Stephen[2] HART, was born in 1635 in Berlin, Connecticut[2], and died on 10 Oct. 1710[2]. She married in 1658, (VF-1) JOHN LEE[2], who was born on 6 Aug. 1620 in Essex Co., England[2], and died on 8 Aug. 1690 in Farmington[2]. Child: See (VF-1) John LEE. Also see the Web site at: http://armidalesoftware.com/issue/full/Thaler_1067_main.html - N3. Note resources: 1. Frederick Adams Virkus, ed., "Immigrant Ancestors", Genealogical Publishing Co., 1942, p.36. 2. Steve Condarcure, "Steve Condarcure's New England Genealogy", http://newenglandgenealogy.pcplayground.com/.

Our family's line comes from John Hart's (b. 1655) first-born son, Isaac[2] Hart, born Nov. 27th 1683, son of John[2] Hart, b. 2 Apr 1655 in Farmington, CT .

Stephen Hart is the grandfather. Isaac Hart married Elizabeth Whaples on the 24th of November 1721 in Farmington, Hartford, CT. Elizabeth was born 15 Aug. 1697.

Isaac Hart's son is Job Hart, born 3 Jan. 1730/31. Our family descends from Job Hart. Isaac Hart's children are named: Ebenezer, Isaac, Elizabeth, Mercy C. and John, all born between 1722 and 1734. Job Hart married Eunice Beckley 20 Mar. 1755. Job Hart and Eunice Beckley had twelve children. Their first child was a boy named (alternate spellings) Jabez (Jabish) Jaluish Hart, born 1 Jan. 1757.

Our Hart family descends from Jabez (Jabish) Jaluish Hart. Job Hart's children born between 1758 and 1775 include: Jabez (Jabish) Jaluish, b. 1757, Canadua, b. 1758, Job, b. 1759, Harvey, b. 1760, Lucretia, b. 1762, Eunice, b. 1763, Joseph, b. 1765, Simeon, b. 1766, Reuben, b. 1768, Comfort, b. 1771, Hepzibah, and Betsey, b. 1775.

Jabez (Jabish) Jaluish Hart married Jemima Brace, b: 25 Oct. 1762, and Jabez (Jabish) Jaluish Hart had nine children. His first-born, a son named Harvey Hart was born Apr. 9 1784. Our Hart family descends from Harvey Hart. Jabez (Jabish) Jaluish Hart's nine children include in order of birth year: Harvey, b. Apr 9, 1784, Tryphena, b. Dec. 23, 1785, Theadoria, b. Dec. 15 1787, John, born Oct. 20, 1789, Demas, b. Nov. 25 1791, Cyrus, b. Nov25, 1794, George, b. July 4, 1797, Eunice, b. May 10, 1799, and Frederick b. Aug 6, 1802.

Harvey Hart married Polly Jackson on April 3, 1792. They had six children. Our Hart family descends from their second born, William Hart, b. Oct. 17, 1810. Other children include Martha M. Hart born Nov. 7, 1811 in New York, and the others including John, b. June 17 1812, Eunice, b. Sept. 10, 1819, Catherine, b. July 24th 1821, and Chauncy, born Sept. 3, 1826.

William Hart—b. Oct. 17, 1810, son of Harvey Hart.
William Hart married Zillah Thompson. Zillah Thompson was born on Apr. 29th 1810. William and Zillah had six children. Our Hart family descends from George Washington Hart who was the fourth in birth order. George Washington Hart was born in 1839. Other children include Harvey, born Sept. 11, 1831,

Chauncy Benion Hart, born Dec. 1, 1834, Elizabeth Hart, born in 1836, Mary Cecelia, born April 3, 1841, and Jeremiah.

George Washington Hart married Adelina (Addie) Hydenberk) on June 4, 1874. Addie was born in 1849. In the 1900 census the family was living in Hudson, Michigan. George's children include Homer, a son born in November of 1875, a daughter, Dora, born in Dec. 1877, Walter, a son born in May of 1883, and Arthur, a son born in Apr. 1886. George Washington Hart's son, Homer Vincent Hart, is the man from whom our Hart family descends.

William Hart—1810–1889, Son of Harvey Hart (1784–1856). Married Zillah Deuel Thompson. William Hart was the son of HARVEY HART, Victor, Ontario County, N. Y., who was the eldest son of Jabish Hart, of Kensington, Conn., and subsequently of Victor, N. Y., and his wife, Jemima (Brace), born [April 9], 1784, at Stockbridge, Mass. Jabish married Polly Jackson. For more information, see Alfred Andrews book at: http://users.rcn.com/harts.ma.ultranet/family/andrews/index.shtml At that site you'll note that information on Harvey Hart and some of his descendants has been supplied to the Hart site by David Downes.

Jabish (Jabez) Hart's Children are the following, according to Alfred Andrew's book on the Web, being the eighth generation from Deacon Stephen Hart:

374. William, born [October 17, 1810 in Victor, Ontario Co., N.Y.]
375. John, born
376. Martha, born
377. Eunice, born
378. Chauncey, born

So William Hart (1810-1889) had a son named George Washington Hart, who is our paternal great grandfather. George's son was Homer Vincent Hart, Senior, who had eight children, one of whom was his son, Homer Vincent Hart, junior (1911-1989) my husband's dad. Theoretically, all of these male descendants from early New England settler, Deacon Stephen Hart, b. 1605, should have the same or very similar Y chromosome DNA—R1b. So DNA tests, anyone?

◆   ◆   ◆

Genealogy Techniques Used

Homer Vincent Hart & Wife: Vera Dell Palmer—Family Roots. Homer is a descendant of Stephen Hart, b. 1605, and his wife Vera Dell Palmer is a descendant of Walter Palmer, b. 1585. This couple is our family's grandfather and grandmother. Here are the techniques and records we used to track the couple back to their founding families in Massachusetts, Connecticut, and Michigan from 1632. Homer was born in 1875 in Michigan and married Vera Dell Palmer (b. 1881) in 1908 in Hudson, Lenawee County, Michigan.

Starting with Homer, senior, our family's grandfather:

1 Homer Vincent Hart, Sr. b: 15 October 1875 in Medina, Lenawee, MI d: 17 June 1945 in Hudson, MI.
+Vera Dell Palmer b: 17 January 1881 in Hudson, Lenawee, MI m: 15 October 1908 in Hudson, Lenawee, MI d: 23 September 1975 in Adrian, MI.
We went back one generation to our family's paternal great grandfather, George Washington Hart's 1918 newspaper obit:

Next:

We researched the male line of the surname 'Hart' of known relatives for the Hart family. For Vera Dell Palmer, who married Homer Vincent Hart in 1908, we searched the male Palmer line starting with her father, Langford Wright Palmer back to Walter Palmer. Langford Wright Palmer descends from Gershom, who is Walter Palmer's sixth child from his second wife, Rebecca Short. Here is the technique used. The Dunne and Allied Family's index at www.rootsweb.com also shows the spouses and children of each of the Harts. (Note the names of living relatives have been left off this Web page to preserve privacy.)

◆   ◆   ◆

You can look at the Descendants of Stephen Hart Web site at: http:// users.rcn.com/harts.ma.ultranet/family/harts. The biography at that Web site explains the highlights of Stephen Hart's life, his wife and children, the town, the environment, his home, and the events of his life as one of the early settlers. One of his children named John married Mary Moore. From John Hart and Mary Moore descend the various branches of the Deacon, Stephen Hart. If you search the records in Essex, England, you'll find the ancestors of Stephen Hart moving in time backwards from his birth in 1605, if you can find the records earlier than 1605 in the area of Essex.

At the Descendants of Stephen Hart Web site, you'll see the scanned old book presented with a new technology. The contents of the book "Stephen Hart and his Descendants," by Alfred Andrews are reproduced at the Web site. The pages online have been amended with corrections and additions that many have sent to Richard Hart. http://users.rcn.com/harts.ma.ultranet/family/harts/DeaStephen Will.shtml. It is thought that he arrived in Plymouth on the ship called the Lyon in 1632 coming from Essex, England. Essex is just east of London. You also can view the site above showing Deacon Stephen Hart's will.

Stephen Hart, born about 1605, was the progenitor of many Harts now living in North America and other parts of the world. The book on Stephen Hart and his Descendants originally was published in 1875 to document all Harts then known to be descendants of Stephen Hart. According to a paper by John Corley, "Emigration to New England on 'The Lyon' in 1632," prepared in 1984 by the Braintree and Bocking Heritage Centre, Braintree, Essex, England, "Emigrants on 'The Lyon' sailed in 1632 with the Rev. Thomas Hooker's 'Braintree Company' on board. It has been said that the ship carried only 350 passengers. However, many names are missing from the list in The Lyon.

This is partly due to the fact that several were members when only the head of the household was mentioned. Also others omitted went as servants. In 1635 two servants worked their passage for a John Brown. Another version written in The Planters of the Commonwealth by Charles Edward Banks, pp. 99-102 introduces a passenger list with a sailing date of June 22, 1632 going from London and arriving at Boston on September 16, 1632. The Banks passenger list mentions that William Pierce Lyon only brought 123 passengers—fifty children. More information on the Lyon and its passengers is at the "Passenger Lists for the Lyon" Web site at: http://www.whipple.org/docs/lyon.html

So how does this relate to my husband's paternal great grandfather, George Washington Hart, born in 1839 in Hudson, Michigan or George's son, my husband's grandfather, Homer Vincent Hart born around 1875 in Hudson, Michigan who married Vera Dell Palmer, a direct descendant of Walter Palmer who also arrived on the sister ship "The Four Sisters" and also again in 1632? I begin by tracing back from Hart, Homer Vincent (1911–1989)—male, b. 27 JAN 1911 in Hudson, MI to his father also named Homer Vincent Hart (1875/6-1920) also from Hudson, MI.

Notes

Searching for the Wives' Maiden names?

See: http://newenglandgenealogy.pcplayground.com/f_142.htm - 86

This Genealogy Data Page will also get you started in your research of spouses because it also lists the women who married many of the 17th-19th century early New England Hart males who lived in Farmington, CT. (The site lists many other names of people who lived in those eras.) For instance, Mary Moore, the wife of John Hart is listed with her mother's maiden name as well as her father's name.

MOORE, Mary
b. 15 SEP 1664 Farmington, CT.
d. 19 SEP 1738
Parents:

Father: MOORE, Isaac
Mother: STANLEY, Ruth

Family:

Spouse: HART, John
b. ABT. 1655 Farmington, CT.
d. 11 NOV 1714 Farmington, CT.
Parents:

Father: HART, John
Mother: Sarah,

Children:

    HART, John
    HART, Isaac
    HART, Sarah
    HART, Matthew
    HART, Samuel
    HART, Nathaniel
    HART, Mary

See the 19th century published genealogy book on the Hart family branches which is now online at:

http://users.rcn.com/harts.ma.ultranet/family/andrews/p043.html.

Excerpted below is information on the particular lineage of this family of one particular Hart branch, descendants of the Capt. John Hart born in 1655, the third generation from Deacon Stephen Hart.

"JOHN HART, of Farmington, eldest son of Deacon Stephen Hart, of Braintree, Eng., Cambridge, Mass., Hartford and Farmington, Conn., born in England, married Sarah. They resided in Farmington, where he was made a freeman by the General Court, at their May session, 1654. Sarah, his wife, joined the church at Farmington, Oct. 19th, 1653; he was admitted to the church April 2d, 1654.

He was one of the first settlers of Tunxis, and bought his house lot of the original owners, and among the list of the eighty-four proprietors of 1672, is numbered the "Estate of John Hart." At the October session of the General Court, in 1660, a committee was raised to examine "Thirty Mile Island," with the view of settlement, when John Hart, of Farmington, was elected one of said committee.

His sad and untimely death occurred on this wise, viz.: his house, which was located near the center of the village, was fired in the night by Indians, and he and all his family, with the exception of his eldest son, John, who was that night at Nod, or Northington, since called Avon, looking after the stock on a farm they owned there, perished in the flames. What aggravated the public calamity was the burning of the town records, at the same time. The General Court made diligent search among the Tunxis tribe for the incendiaries, but this neither restored life nor records. This fire occurred in 1666."

"[This fire may not have occurred as described here. Research by David Mauro published in the July/August 1997 issue of Hart Historical Notes seems to show that no Indians were involved. Dr. C. Bickford of the Connecticut Historical Society is quoted: "The 19th century accounts of Farmington contain a lot of fiction. With-out any corroborating evidence to support Andrew's story, I had to conclude that it was without substance."

There may have been a fire of unknown origin, though. From the "Hart Family History, Silas Hart, His Ancestors and Descendants." by William Lincoln Hart, 1942, Alliance, Ohio, page 17:

"The Rev. Samuel Danforth, pastor of the first church in Roxbury kept a diary, and under the date of February 11, 1666 (O.S.) appears the following entry: "Tidings came to us from Connecticut how that on ye 15th of 10M66 Sergeant Hart, ye son of Deacon Hart and his wife, and six children were all burned in their house at Farmington, no man knowing how the fire was kindled, neither did any of the neighbors see ye fire till it was past remedy. The church there had kept a fast at this man's house two days before. One of his sons being at a farm, escaped the burning."

BRANCH OF JOHN HART FOLLOWS, THEIR CHILDREN BEING THIRD GENERATION.

8. Sarah, born in Farmington, about 1653, baptized Oct. 23d, 1653, burned to death in 1666.
*9. John, born in Farmington, about 1655, baptized April 2d, 1655, saved from the fire, he being that night at Nod.
10. Steven, born in Farmington, July, 1657, baptized July 19th, 1657, burned to death in 1666.

* Regarding *9, John, born in Farmington: (Capt. John Hart)

"CAPT. JOHN HART, of Farmington, eldest son of John Hart and Sarah, his wife, (who were burned to death by the burning of their house, in 1666,) born in Farmington, about 1655, and baptized there April 2d, 1655, married Mary, daughter of Deacon Isaac Moore, of Farmington, and both were admitted to the church there Nov. 24th, 1656. He was one of the appraisers of his uncle, Stephen Hart's estate 1689.

"In May, 1695, he was confirmed by the General Court ensign of the Farmington train-band, and in October, 1703, was Commissioned lieutenant, and subsequently promoted Captain. He was for four successive years (1702-5) a deputy from Farmington to the General Court, and was appointed in May, 1705, one of the auditors of the Colony.

When his father's house was burned by the Indians, he was absent from home, and thus providentially saved to be the progenitor of a numerous posterity. The offices and honors thus bestowed upon him indicate that he stood high in the community. Capt. John Hart died in Farmington, Nov. 11th, 1714, aged 60 years; his wife died Sept. 19th, 1738, aged 74 years."

THEIR CHILDREN, BRING THE FOURTH GENERATION.

11. John, born 1684, baptized Nov. 27th, 1686, married March 20th, 1706, Esther Gridley.

12. Isaac, born baptized Nov. 27th, 1686, married Nov. 24th, 1721, Elizabeth Whaples.

13. Sarah, born baptized Dec. 11th, 1687, married Feb. 15th, 1705, Ehenezer Steele.

14. Matthew, born 1690, baptized Dec. 7th, 1690, married Jan. 10th, 1725, Sarah Hooker.

15. Samuel, born baptized Sept. 18th, 1692, married Dec. 5th, 1723, Mary Hooker.

16. Nathaniel, born baptized April 14th, 1695, married Dec. 3rd, 1719, Abigail Hooker.

17. Mary, born married John Leffingwell, Esq., of Norwich, Conn.

Also see the line of Isaac Hart at: http://users.rcn.com/harts.ma.ultranet/family/andrews/p045.html - n12

"ISAAC HART, of Farmington and Kensington, second son of Capt. John and his wife Mary (Moore), baptized Nov. 27th, 1686, in Farmington, married Nov. 24th, 1721, Elizabeth Whaples. They lived on Hart street, next west of. Worthington Village, sometimes called lower lane. The house is still standing, 1873, with the upper story projecting over lower. It is related of him that when at work in Farmington meadows, he observed a bear coming into the lot; he seized his pitchfork and mounted his horse hitched under a tree, and pursued the bear and killed it."

"This anecdote is related by his great grandson, of Candor, N. Y. He was a deacon in Kensington church, and died Jan. 27th, 1770, aged 84 years. Elizabeth, his widow, died Nov. 14th, 1777. He is said to be one of the early settlers of "Great Swamp Society." In 1753, April 27th, he headed a petition to the General Assembly for a division of this society, and the result was a new society, called New Britain in 1754, now, 1874, the town and city of New Britain."

THEIR CHILDREN, BEING THE FIFTH GENERATION,

24. Ebenezer, born Nov. 27th, 1722, married Martha .

25. Isaac, born 1724, married Ann Mather, of New Britain.

   Elizabeth, born July l2tb, 1726, died Jan. 24th, 1726-7.

26. Mercy, born April 4th, 1729, died March 29th, 1786, aged 57 years.

27. Job, born Jan. 3d, 1731-2, married March 20th, 1755, Eunice Beckley.

28. John, born 1734, married, Hepzibah, died March 23d, 1803.

29. Lois, born 1744, married Hezekiah Judd, died August 13th, 1825, aged 81 years.

See Job's genealogy information at:
http://users.rcn.com/harts.ma.ultranet/family/andrews/p052.html - n27

He was admitted to the Congregational Church in Worthington, Feb. 9th, 1775, soon after its organization. He died Feb. 1st, 1776, and on the 10th of March, 1789, Samuel Hart and Zachariah Hart, of Berlin, were appointed by the Court of Probate, District of Farmington, distributors of the estate of Isaac Hart, late of Berlin District—John and Anna Hart being the administrators. They set to Levi, the eldest son, a double portion, viz: £130 1s 6d.

THEIR CHILDREN, BEING THE SIXTH GENERATION.

67. Levi, born, baptized Aug. 24th, 1765, married Martha Hart.

Lorana, born, baptized Feb. 8th, 1767, died young.

68. Lydia, born baptized June 4th, 1769, married, Sylvester Gridley.

Isaac, baptized Aug. 11th, 1771, died 1772.

69. Chloe, born 1774, married Samuel Gridley.

70. Isaac, born posthumous, baptized March 9th, 1777, lived single in Hart street, Worthington.

27. Kensington and Berlin, Conn.

"JOB HART, Kensington, third son of Isaac Hart, of the same place, and his wife Elizabeth (Whaples), born Jan. 3d, 1731-2, at Kensington, married March 20th, 1755, in Newington, by Rev. Joshua Belden, Eunice Beckley; both admitted to the church in Kensington, Dec. 19th, 1756, and from thence to the church in Worthington, at its formation. He removed to Stockbridge, Mass., about 1781, and was received into the church there in 1782, and Eunice his wife in 1792."

THEIR CHILDREN, BEING THE SIXTH GENERATION.

71. Jabish, born 1756, baptized Jan. 2d, 1757, married, Jemima Brace.

72. Candace, baptized Feb. 8th, 1758, married Roswell Barnes, Oneida, N. Y.

73. Job, born baptized March 11th, 1759, married 1784, widow Rachel Ball.

74. Harvey, baptized Dec. 28th, 1760, died of consumption, single, Dec. 3d, 1780, aged 21 years.

75. Leverett, born, baptized June 27th, 1762, died single.

76. Eunice, born baptized Oct. 80th, 1768, married, Abijah Williamson, Victor, N. Y.

77. Joseph, born, baptized March 17th, 1765, married, Beulah Warner.

See Jabez's information at:
http://users.rcn.com/harts.ma.ultranet/family/andrews/p069.html - n71

JABISH HART, of Kensington, eldest son of Job Hart, of same place, and his wife, Eunice Beckley, was born, 1756, at Kensington, and baptized there Jan. 2d, 1757. He married Jemima Brace. They removed to Victor, Ontario Co., N. Y., about 1785. She was admitted to the church in Stockbridge, Mass., 1782, and died May 23d, 1823. He died Dec. 20th, 1832, aged 76 years.

177. Harvey, born April 9th, 1784, married Polly Jackson.

178. Tryphena, born Dec. 23d, 1785, married Boughton, of Bloomfield, N.Y

179. Theodocia, born Dec. 15th, 1787, married Cyrus Jackson.

180. John, born Oct. 20th, 1789, married Betsey Clyne.

181. Demas, born Dec. 13th, 1791.

182. Cyrus, born Nov. 25th, 1794, died Dec. 9th, 1821, aged 27 years.

183. George, born July 4th, 1797, died Aug. 6th, 1802.

184. Eunice, born May 10th, 1799, died, 1836.

185. Frederic, born Aug. 6th, 1802, married, Sept. 8th, 1825, Sylvia Rowley.

See Harvey's information at:
http://users.rcn.com/harts.ma.ultranet/family/andrews/p098.html - n177
177. Victor, N.Y.

HARVEY HART, Victor, Ontario County, N. Y., eldest son of Jabish Hart, of Kensington, Conn., and subsequently of Victor, N. Y., and his wife, Jemima (Brace), born [April 9], 1784, at Stockbridge, Mass.; married Polly Jackson.

[Information on Harvey Hart and some of his descendants has been supplied to Richard Hart by David Downes.]

THEIR CHILDREN, BEING THE EIGHTH GENERATION.

374. William, born [October 17, 1810 in Victor, Ontario Co., N.Y.]

375. John, born

376. Martha, born

377. Eunice, born

378. Chauncey, born

After William Hart, this family's line continues with William's son, George Washington Hart, b. 1839, Homer Vincent Hart Senior, b. 1875, and Homer Vincent Hart junior b. 1911. (The many living relatives are left off this genealogy to respect their privacy.)

For a look at all the Hart family genealogy prior to 1875, the book is online at: http://users.rcn.com/harts.ma.ultranet/family/andrews/p039.html

◆   ◆   ◆

More Notes & Sources:

Sources:

Also see similar information below at:
http://www.bankert.org/genreport/p26.htm.

    1. Robert Charles Anderson The Great Migration Begins, 869-873.

    2. Register of the Society of Colonial Wars.

In another genealogy listing, Deacon Stephen Hart was born circa 1599 in England.[1] His second wife is listed as Margaret. There's no mention in that source for Margaret's surname. Margaret is mentioned as a widow 1678.[1] It's interesting that Margaret is listed as the widow of two previous husbands—Joseph Nash and Arthur Smith, which would make Stephen Hart Margaret's third husband. In that listing at the Bankert genealogy Web site, Stephen Hart is listed as having died between 16 March 1683 and 31 March 1683 in Farmington, Hartford Co., Conn., at about age 84.[1]

When you check out the source for immigration to Cambridge before 1632, Stephen Hart's name appears in Cambridge. Back in 1634, Cambridge was called Newtown. Stephen Hart is listed as of May 14, 1634 as being a Freeman. He works as a Deacon in the church of Reverend Thomas Hooker, according to the Bankert Web site, which lists the source on Stephen Hart as the book titled The Great Migration, by Robert Charles Anderson, and Register of the Society of Colonial Wars. It's notable that Stephen Hart's military service is listed as serving in 1637 under under Mason in the Pequot Indian War.[2]

A decade passes before Stephen Hart appears in Public Office: between 1647 and 1655 . He becomes one of the first representatives at the General Court, and again in 1660. Stephen Hart also is listed as the founder/proprietor: Hartford, CT in 1635 and of Farmington, CT in 1650.

The Bankert Web site lists Stephen Hart's birth date in Braintree, England as about 1599. Other sources list Hart as being born in Essex in 1605, and another source lists him as being born in Ipswich in 1602. (Braintree is in Essex.) About 1632 Stephen Hart is listed in t Cambridge (formerly Newtown), Massachusetts.

He's noted as being one of the fifty-four original settlers. According to the Bankert Web site, Stephen Hart might have been a brother of Edmund Harte of Weymouth and Westfield Massachusetts. Edmund Harte is listed in New England at the same time. Could all the 17th century New England Harts have been related if they appear close by at the same period of time?

Thomas Hooker worked with Stephen Hart. He lived in a house across the street from Thomas Hooker. Also, Stephen Hart worked as a deacon of Reverend Thomas Hooker's church in Cambridge, MA and moved with Thomas Hooker in 1635 to Hartford, Conn.

By 1639, Stephen Hart continued as Deacon and then became the original proprietor of the church. Hart's name appears on the founders' monument in the Center Church burial ground in Hartford, CT. It has been said that Hartford got its name from a crossing of the Connecticut river that Stephen Hart discovered, known as Hart's Ford.

Other sources note that Hartford could have been named after the English town of Hertford. Stephen Hart served as a soldier in the Pequot Indian War in 1637. Based on his military service, Hart soon earned a lot in Soldier's Field, located in Hartford, Connecticut.

Children of Deacon Stephen Hart:

> Sarah Hart+ (c 1624–1697)
>
> John Hart+ (c 1630–1666)
>
> Stephen Hart (c 1634–18 Sep 1689)
>
> Mary Hart+ (c 1638–10 Oct 1710)
>
> Capt. Thomas Hart (c 1640–27 Aug 1726)
>
> Rachel Hart (c 1642–a 1689)

◆   ◆   ◆

Additional Notes & Sources:

Notes received from Richard Hart which he received from David Downes in 1999, on George Washington Hart include the following research:"GEORGE WASHINGTON9 HART (WILLIAM8, HARVEY7, JABEZ JABISH6, JOB5, ISAAC4, <<CAPTAIN>> JOHN3, JOHN2, <<DEACON>> STEPHEN1)was born March 30, 1839 in Victor, Ontario, NY, and died January 02, 1918 in Lincoln Street, Hudson, Mich.He married ADELINA EMMA HEYDENBERK June 04, 1874 in Hudson, Lenawee, MI, daughter of JOHN HEYDENBERK and ELIZABETH KETTLE. She was born November 30, 1848 in Medina, Lenawee, MI,and died February 20, 1920 in Hudson, Lenawee, MI.

Notes for GEORGE WASHINGTON HART: Burial Maple Grove Cemetery, Hudson, Michigan, McEldowney and Sons Lenawee County Directory 1897, general farm PO, Medina res. 1/2 m n w 1/2 n 1 n w, sec 33 Hudson,Twp." Sources: 1920 Census Maryland, Washington County (Hagerstown) Film 1,820,676 ED no 152 Sheet No. 12 Line 64.

"Children of George Washington Hart: 1. HOMER VINCENT HART, SR., b. October 15, 1875, Medina, Lenawee, MI; d. June 17, 1945, Hudson, Lenawee, MI. 2. DORA ELIZABETH HART, b. July 26, 1877, Hudson, Lenawee, MI; d. February 04, 1962, Chelsea, MI Methodist Home. Dora Elizabeth Hart is buried at the Maple Grove Cemetery, Hudson, Michigan. She worked as a school teacher in Dist No 3, Norton District, p.o. and res. Geo W Hart, Hudson Twp. 3.WALTER THOMPSON HART, b. May 15, 1883, Medina, Lenawee Co., Mich; d. April 07, 1919, Massilon, Ohio. WALTER THOMPSON HART worked in steel mills in Massilon,Ohio. He's buried in Maple Grove Cemetery, Hudson, Michigan. 4.ARTHUR LASON HART, b. April 1886, Medina, Lenawee County, MI; d. April 28, 1947, Paw Paw, Van Buren, MI; m. ELIZABETH ROCKWELL, September 1912, Hudson, Lenawee, MI."

Homer Vincent Hart, Sr.

HOMER VINCENT HART, SR. generation 10 from Deacon Stephen Hart, (GEORGE WASHINGTON 9, WILLIAM8, HARVEY 7, JABEZ JABISH 6, JOB 5, ISAAC 4,<CAPTAIN> JOHN 3, JOHN 2, <DEACON> STEPHEN 1) was born October 15, 1875 in Medina, Lenawee, MI, and died June 17, 1945 in Hudson, Lenawee, MI. He married VERA DELL PALMER October 10, 1908 in Hudson, Lenawee, MI, daughter of LANGFORD WRIGHT PALMER and MARY HIGLEY. She was born January 17, 1881 in Hudson, Lenawee, MI, and died September 23, 1975 in Adrian, MI.

Census

Homer Vincent Hart was only four years old when he appeared on the 1880 census place taken at Hudson, Lenawee, Michigan. The source information is Family History Library Film number 1254591. NA Film Number T9-0591, page number 262A. His father and mother's birthplace is listed as Michigan. Homer Vincent Hart married Vera Dell Palmer in Hudson, Lenawee, Michigan on Oct. 15, 1908. Homer Vincent Hart and Vera Dell Palmer reared eight children: including Margaret Dora, b. 1909, Homer Vincent, b. 1911, John George, b. 1913, Robert Langford, b. 1916, and Richard Kenneth, b. 1918. The names of the rest of the children who are still living will not be mentioned on this public Web site.

From Homer Vincent Hart, Junior, born in 1911, our family descends. Note there is Homer Vincent Hart (senior) born around 1875/6 and his son, Homer Vincent Hart (junior) b. 1911—d.1989. Homer Vincent Hart, Senior and Vera Dell Palmer had eight children. Some are still living. So their names will not be made public or entered in this genealogy page to preserve their privacy.

The grandchildren also will not be included here as it is my policy never to write information about or make public the names of living people. If you're one of the living people who wishes to be included, then you need to send me in writing a letter of permission. Otherwise, it's in the best interest of those living not to have their names made public on a Web site. I did not include my husband's name or any other descendants who are living.

Homer Vincent Hart, born in 1911 in Hudson, Michigan is my husband's father. Homer Vincent Hart passed on in 1989. So going back generation by generation and finding the son that each male grand parent is descended from leads back to Stephen Hart. The source up to 1875 is Elaine Hart Kerskie of Victor, Ontario Co., NY, book 1940 Genealogys & Vital Records. Other sources could be the various government and military indexes online, especially for more recent dates.

As for Homer Vincent Hart, Senior, the 1910 census lists Homer's age as 34. He's in West Grants Pass Precinct, Josephine, Oregon with his wife Vera. This puts his birth date as about 1876. The 1900 census has a birth date for Homer as November 1875. (The 1900 census showed him then as age 24.) This Homer Hart born in MI in 1875 or 1876 has a sister named Dora. Homer Vincent Hart and Vera Dell had a child named Margaret Dora born in 1909.

According to the 1910 census "Family 23. Hart, Homer V. 34 M2 MI MI MI…Vera Wife, 29, M2, 1 child 1 living. MI MI OH…Margaret. Daughter. 9/12 OR MI MI. Palmer, Langford W. Father-in Law, 60. MI NY NY…Harold Brother-in-law 22… MI MI OH.

In the census of 1910, there's a listing "1910 Hudson, Lenawee, MI. Hart, George W. 71, NY NY NY. Langford Wright Palmer is living with his daughter and her husband, Homer Hart. Margaret is a toddler. Other people in the household are listed as Addie E. 61, MI NY NY…Arthur L. 24 MI NY MI (Fireman), and…Dora E. 32 MI NY MI (teacher, public school).

In the 1900 census at Lenawee, Hudson, Michigan, family 172: Hart, George is listed as being born in 1839 61 m25 NY NY NY. His wife is listed as Addie, No. 1849, age 51. m24…4 children…4 living MI NY NY. Children include: Homer, Son born Nov. 1875, 24, MI NY MI. Dora is listed as the daughter, born Dec. 1877, age 22, MI NY MI. Walter, a son was born May 1883, 17, MI NY MI. Arthur a son was born April 1886, age 14 MI NY MI.

So that verifies the line of Harts starting with Deacon Stephen Hart, born 1605, Essex, England, directly related from the males to Homer Vincent Hart, born in 1911 in Hudson, Michigan, the father of my husband. Birthdates and names of his parents are on my husband's birth certificate. I can look up the 1880 census from http://www.familysearch.com where it lists Homer as a four-year-old with his dad, George. Now that I've found the links back to Stephen Hart and Walter Palmer, what will the DNA tests show? Will the Y-chromosome go in a line back to the founder? Can anyone actually be found who wants to take a DNA test to link genealogy with genetics?

In 1870 George is not in the census in Michigan. The year of the 1870 census there are no Harts in Lenawee county. He could be with his parents. Looking up George Hart, there were many born in NY around the same date. So the next step would be to see whether Homer Vincent Hart's 1911 birth certificate lists his parents birth dates. Since George Hart died after 1910, there could be an obituary in the newspaper that might mention the names of his children. If the death certificate is researched, it would probably have his parent's names, but if he's from New York, it might be difficult to find that line of research.

Another channel to research would be when George W. Hart applied for a Civil War pension. The place to look is the Civil War list to query about Michigan information—where to go to send away for data. Many applied for pensions, but on one pension application, records report that George W. Hart applied for a Civil War pension on April 26, 1889. The application number was #700929, cert: # 731396. Could that be him?

Another excellent Web site address might be http://awt.ancestry.com/cgi-bin/ igm.cgi?op=GET&db=dunne1&id=I08612. Or I could try http://awt. ancestry.com/cgi-bin/igm.cgi?op=GET&db=dickdutton&id=I147864.

Regarding Homer Hart's father, George W. Hart (George Washington Hart), the first step would be to find out which unit would be in the Lenawee, Hudson, Michigan county. There also was a George W. Hart that filed for a pension. With so many George Harts in the Civil War, it had to be narrowed down to George Washington Hart of Hudson, Michigan who is the father of Homer Vincent Hart born around 1875. In the 1880 census Homer was four years old.

The 1880 US census notes that Homer Vincent Hart is the son of George Washington Hart, born Nov. 30th 1839. In another online index I later found out George died Feb. 25th 1920. Back on the 1880 US census, George's wife and children are listed along with the city in which they live (Hudson, MI). The next step is to turn to the Dunne and Allied Family's index at www.rootsweb.com. It shows George Washington Hart is the son of William Hart, born Oct. 17th 1810 who died Nov. 16th 1889.

Note: William Hart was his second born, having been born on 10/17/1810. But all his siblings are listed as having been born after 1810. So there either needs to have been a seventh sibling born before 1810, or William was not the second born. Anyone have a good source on the correct dates or birth order regarding William Hart?

William Hart's father was Harvey Hart, born April 9 1784. Harvey Hart's dad was Jaluish Hart, born Jan 1, 1757. And Jaluish (Jabish) Hart's dad was Job Hart, born Jan.3, 1730/31. Job Hart's dad was Isaac Hart, born 27 Nov. 1683.

Note: Regarding Harvey Hart: Information from Richard Hart notes, "An alternate birth date for Harvey's birth date is listed as Apr. 9, 1784 and his marriage is listed as Apr. 3, 1792. If this were correct, he would only be 8 years old at the time of his wedding, which is probably not right. Also the time between his wedding date and his first child is 18 years, again a bit suspicious. Based on Harvey's birth date and the births of his children, I might expect that Harvey and Polly were married about 1809 or 1810." Anyone have other dates for these events?

Sergt. Isaac Hart found in the Marriage Index: Connecticut, 1635-1860. Isaac Hart married Elizabeth Wheples on: Nov 24, 1721 in: Farmington, Hartford, CT. Information is found in the Family history library microfilm roll info: microfilm reference number: Roll number: 1315116 items 3 and 4 . Isaac Hart's father was John Hart, born on April 2, 1655 in Farmington, CT. And John Hart's father was Stephen Hart born in 1605 in Essex, England. Stephen Hart was a church Deacon. A biography is presented at the Descendants of Stephen Hart Web site at: http://users.rcn.com/harts.ma.ultranet/family/harts/.

There is also a biography in the volume titled: New England Families, Vol. III page 1549. The page reads: "Deacon Stephen Hart, the immigrant, was father of John Sr., coming from Braintree, county Essex, England, to Cambridge, Massachusetts, in 1632, and to Hartford in 1636, finally locating in Farmington, where he died in 1682-83 aged seventy-seven." Also see Family History of Central NY, Vol. I, page 485-8 that shows the family story of this line. Online, you can check out the name Stephen Hart and his descendants back to George Washington Hart from the Roots Web site http://worldconnect.rootsweb.com/cgi-bin/igm.cgi?op=GET&db=dunne1&id=I08612.

Also check out the RootsWeb.com Web site at http://worldconnect.rootsweb.com for other searches. My piece of the puzzle was to verify through the 1910 census whether the names matched with the descendants of Homer Vincent Hart who married Vera Dell Palmer in 1908. The last piece in the puzzle focused on verifying that this was the same Homer Vincent Hart who lived in Josephine, Oregon in 1910 with his wife, Vera and baby daughter, Margaret, who was a familiar relative to my husband when he was a child. Margaret was born around 1909. Various other relatives are mentioned in the census as living with the family.

My husband, the child of Homer Vincent Hart, born in 1911 is the son of Homer Vincent Hart born in 1875/6 as listed in the census of 1880, 1900 and 1910. A birth date of 1879 is listed in the Family History Library, Salt Lake City. That Family History Library records his marriage in 1908 in Michigan. So Homer Vincent Hart's dad is the George Washington Hart who applied in 1889 for a pension for service in the Civil War on April 26, 1889, the same year in which George Washington Hart's own dad, William Hart passed away on Nov. 16th 1889.

Homer Vincent Hart married Vera Dell Palmer in 1908 in Hudson, Michigan. My husband remembered their daughter, Margaret when he was young. By the time the 1910 census is taken, Homer Hart's family is living in Oregon with their daughter, Margaret and other members of the family mentioned in the census, including the father-in-law, Langford Wright Palmer. George W. Hart is living back in Michigan.

George Washington Hart is descended from Stephen Hart, born in 1605 who also is the early Cambridge, New England settler from 1632. George Washington Hart's son, Homer Vincent Hart, born in 1875/6 married Vera Dell Palmer in Hudson MI in 1908 according to records at the Family History Library, Salt Lake City, UT and census records.

The Palmers are easy to find and trace back to Walter Palmer by researching online the Walter Palmer Society. Vera is descended directly from the sixth child of Walter Palmer named Gershom, born in 1644. Now, the genealogy task is to trace back for the Hart family. Yes, this is an adventure. How about a DNA-driven genealogy time capsule? Thank you, Crystal from MyWebTree for guiding me by email to the 1880,1910, and 1900 census online which verified the recognizable names.

Are you related to Vera Dell Palmer and/or Homer Vincent Hart?

Vera Dell Palmer is related to Walter Palmer (1585-1661) born in Yetminster Parish, England. Walter's mother was Elizabeth Carter. Walter died in Stonington, CT in 1661. Vera Dell Palmer is descended from Walter Palmer through his son, Gershom Palmer 1644-1718, from his second wife, Rebecca Short, whom he married in 1633. Genealogy links to all these Palmers may be found on the Walter Palmer Society Website. The Walter Palmer Society Web site is at http://www.walterpalmer.com/ or at: http://www.walterpalmer.com/WPS.wbg/wga87.html - I20605. According to the Walter Palmer Society's Web site, Walter Palmer, as a Separatist Puritan, in an effort to seek religious freedom, on April 5, 1629 sailed from Gravesend England on a boat called "Four Sisters"—one of six ships; the others being the Talbot, Lyons Whelp, George Bonaventure, Lyon, and The Mayflower.

Walter arrived in Salem, Massachusetts on June of 1629 and settled in Charlestown Massachusetts with his five children and Abraham Palmer, perhaps his brother. Vera Dell Palmer's father was Langford Wright Palmer, born January 20th 1851 in Dover township, MI. From Langford Wright Palmer, moving back in time by generations, each male Palmer is linked eventually to Walter Palmer, born in 1585, who had 12 children, five from his first wife and seven from his second wife, Rebecca Short. When seeking sources, start with the original books used as sources and birth certificates as well as searching similar resources online. Military records and the census also help locate people over time.

To continue the genealogy, here is a sample of the children of Homer Vincent Hart that links to Vera Dell Palmer from the Walter Palmer Society Web site. If you're related to a Palmer, check out the Walter Palmer Society Web site. It will lead you to your other relatives as well. It's incredible how many people are direct descendants of any one of the twelve children of Walter Palmer who lived in Massachusetts and Connecticut in the 17th century, and spouses with most birthdates, death dates, and marriage dates are included on the site. I highly recommend the site to search for anyone who might be related to, descended from, or married to a Palmer at any time in history on this side of the world.

Our family's original ancestor this side of the world was Walter Palmer whose mother was Elizabeth Carter, born in Yetminster Parish, England in the mid-1500s. Walter Palmer's genealogy Web links with our family's descendants are found at the Walter Palmer Society's Web site at: http://www.walterpalmer.com/WPS.wbg/wga29.html - I6787

Walter Palmer's son, Gershom Palmer, 1644-1718, born in Seacuncke, Plymouth Colony, Antient Rehoboth, was the sixth child of seven from Walter

Palmer and his second wife, Rebecca Short. Gershom Palmer married Ann Denison, and had a son, George Palmer, the fifth of ten children born in 1678 who died in Stonington, Connecticut in 1728. George Palmer married Hannah Palmer in 1710 and had five children. The second child was Zebulon Palmer, born in 1714. He married Comfort Fairbanks in 1743 in Stonington, CT. Zebulon Palmer had a son also named Zebulon Palmer (junior) born in 1740. He was the third child of three.

Zebulon (junior) married Deborah York in 1743 at Stonington, CT. Zebulon Palmer and Deborah York had Jairus Palmer, the sixth child of seven born in 1758. Jairus Palmer married Sarah Spencer and had a son also named Jairus (junior) who was born the 18th of November, 1785 in Voluntown, CT, married Sarah Eells in 1808. Their son, John Celestine Palmer, was born in Ira, New York on June 18th 1824, the seventh of eight children.

John Celestine Palmer married Martha Ann Smith in 1849 in Ira, Cayuga Co., NY. The couple's first child, a son, born on January 20th 1851 in Dover township, Michigan, was named Langford Wright Palmer. John Celestine Palmer and Martha Ann Smith had four children. Langford Wright Palmer married Mary Permelia Higley in Medina, Michigan. They had three children, Percy Earl Palmer in 1876, Vera Dell Palmer in 1881, and Harold D. Palmer in 1888. Vera Dell Palmer was our family's grandma and link to the original Walter Palmer born in 1585.

Vera Dell Palmer was born January 17th 1881 in Hudson, Michigan. Vera Dell Palmer married Homer Vincent Hart on October 15th, 1908 in Hudson, Michigan. Homer Vincent Hart was born in Hudson, Lenawee, Michigan in 1875/6. The Family History Library in Salt Lake City lists the birth date as 1879 on one record that contains the date of marriage to Vera Dell Palmer in 1908 in Hudson, MI.

Each 1880, 1900, and 1910 census list his birth date as 1875/6 or list his age as 51 in 1900 or 61 in the 1910 census. Vera Dell Palmer and Homer Vincent Hart had eight children. The names of the children who are no longer living are: Margaret Dora Hart, Homer Vincent Hart, John George Hart, Robert Langford Hart, and Richard Kenneth Hart, all born between 1909 and 1918. Their second child, born on January 27th 1911 in Hudson, Michigan also was named Homer Vincent Hart (junior).

Homer Vincent Hart (junior) born in 1911, d. 1989, married Hazel Ridenour. Homer Vincent Hart (junior) and Hazel Ridenour had two children born in the 1930s. (Never put the names of living people online in a genealogy site as privacy must be preserved.) One of those two is my husband of many decades. That's the genealogy connection. At last I can visualize a long line of people lined up in a row representing each century and each branch joining a tree growing from a rock by the seashore.

Genealogy has revealed in a time capsule how my husband connects to both Stephen Hart and Walter Palmer, according to the surname list at the Walter Palmer Society Web site link at: http://www.walterpalmer.com/WPS. wbg/wgasurs.html. Check your own name as there are hundreds of names and links descended from Walter Palmer. Yes, we are all part of history anywhere in the world. This really is an adventure and a journey. Let's make time capsules that link all of us through the generations. That's what intergenerational life stories are all about.

The list starts with Stephen Hart and Walter Palmer arriving in sister ships, "The Lyon" and "The Four Sisters" in the new world which links the genealogy records back to Walter Palmer's mother, Elizabeth Carter in 1585 England. (I wonder whether he or his mom or dad of the same name ever experienced a Shakespeare play-live?)

Stephen Hart and Walter Palmer find themselves in Massachusetts around 1632 and then in Connecticut a few years later. Who would think that hundreds of years later that one of the male children descended from the male children of Stephen Hart would marry the one of the female children descended from one of the male children of Walter Palmer after so many generations?

Through Walter Palmer's son, Gershom Palmer, each son in each generation finally links to our family grandma, Vera Dell Palmer. The male lineage would continue through Langford Wright Palmer's brothers. The female link joins Vera Dell Palmer to Homer Vincent Hart. So there should be lots of relatives out there. Vera Dell Palmer's father was Langford Wright Palmer, born in 1851. Her mother was Mary Permelia Higley, born in 1853. Vera Dell Palmer was born Jan. 17th 1881 in Hudson, MI. She married Homer Vincent Hart Oct. 15, 1908 in Hudson, MI. The children of Vera and Homer born in Hudson, Lenawee, Michigan are Margaret Dora, born 1909, Homer Vincent, born 1911, John George, born 1913, Robert Langford, born 1916, and Richard Kenneth, born, 1918.

Genealogy projects can be an adventure in historical research and a journey in a time capsule. New projects could also include DNA-driven genealogy, old photos, and information about those relatives who served in various wars such as the Revolutionary War in the 18th century, the Civil War, or similar historical events and how they relate to records and/or photos or paintings of various ancestors. All these names and dates are part of keepsake albums that may be put into a time capsule and sent to future generations from any or all branches of this lineage. Visualize how many descendants must exist of all the children.

Each generation had anywhere from twelve children in the earlier generations to three to five children by the early to mid-19th century. Those children who survived began branches of the same tree. So there must be quite a number of descendants of Stephen Hart or just John Hart, his surviving son who had seven children. Our Hart family lineage comes from Isaac Hart. The other children have branches also, and these are more genealogy projects to explore. Like archaeology, DNA-driven genealogy may be another journey in time.

Primary Sources:

Elaine Hart Kerskie of Victor, Ontario Co., NY, book 1940 Genealogys & Vital Records.

FTM Genealogical Library, New England Families, Vol. III page 1549.

FTM Genealogical Library, Compendium of American Gen., Vol. VII, page 49.

FTM Genealogical Library, Families of Early Guilford, CT Vol. I, page 605.

FTM Genealogical Library, Family History of Central NY, Vol. I, page 485-8.

Compendium of American Gen., Vol. VII, page 49 says: Capt. John Hart (1655-1714), he alone of his father's family escaped being burned to death, Dec 15, 1666; Capt. Colonial troops in Queen Anne's War. 1703; dep. Gen. Ct. 4 yrs; m Mary Moore (d1738). There's confusion as there are many John Harts descended from the earliest John Hart, and the sons of Capt. John Hart have many descendants, some also named John Hart among others. Also, there's no way to know whether the story about the fire or who set it and who survived as written on the Internet is clear. So you have to go to the primary sources to find out what happened or could have happened.

Sergt. Isaac Hart found in:

Marriage Index: Connecticut, 1635-1860.

Married: Nov 24, 1721 in: Farmington, Hartford, CT.

Family history library microfilm roll info: microfilm reference number

Roll number: 1315116 items 3 and 4.

1880 US Census, Hudson, Lenawee, Michigan. The US 1880 Census is searchable at: http://www.familysearch.com.

Application for Civil War Pension, April 26, 1889. The application number was #700929, cert: # 731396. 1900 US Census, Hudson, Lenawee, Michigan.

1910 Census, Hudson, Lenawee, Michigan.

1910 US Census, West Grants Pass Precinct, Josephine, Oregon.

Walter Palmer Society Web link at:
http://www.walterpalmer.com/WPS.wbg/wgasurs.html.

Family History Library, Salt Lake City Utah (birth and marriage records).

US Social Security Death Index 30 September 2000. Family Search [TM] Web site at: http://www.familysearch.org/Eng/Search/SSDI/individual_record.asp?recid =383184892&1d.

Descendants of Stephen Hart Web site is at:
http://users.rcn.com/harts.ma.ultranet/family/harts.

"Deacon Stephen Hart's Will" site at:
http://users.rcn.com/harts.ma.ultranet/family/harts/DeaStephenWill.shtml.

"Passenger Lists for the Lyon" Web site at:
http://www.whipple.org/docs/lyon.html.

The Dunne and Allied Family's index at www.rootsweb.com

The Dunne & Allied Family's at: http://worldconnect.rootsweb.com/cgi-bin/
igm.cgi?op=GET&db=dunne1&id=I08416.

For your own genealogy searches documents and records searching could include
court and medical records, census searches, notary records of land and home
transfers in various nations, schools, orphanages, hospitals, institutions, schools,
farm land grants, and even pet licenses. Working with libraries and even university training programs for librarians also may be helpful. There also are the oral
and personal history associations and message boards.

Books:

Banks, Charles Edward, The Planters of the Commonwealth 1620 1640, (1930).

Morgan, Edmund S., The Puritan Dilemma, The Story of John Winthrop, Little, Brown & Co., Boston, (1958).

The New England Historical and Genealogical Register,

Boston.

Paget, Harold, Bradford's History of the Plymouth Settlement, Mantle Minis-
tries, San Antonio, (1988).

Paige, Lucius R., History of Cambridge, Boston (1877).

◆   ◆   ◆

Associations Helpful for Your Research Interests:

National Genealogy Society
http://www.ngsgenealogy.org/

Association of Personal Historians
http://www.personalhistorians.org/

Oral History Association
http://omega.dickinson.edu/organizations/oha/

There's an email group and mailing list for Deacon Stephen Hart's descendants or those interested in Deacon Stephen.

To learn more about the Deacon Stephen group, please visit

http://groups.yahoo.com/group/DeaconStephen

Hart Family Genealogy: Descendants of Deacon Stephen Hart, b. 1605, Essex, England, arrived in Massachusetts, 1632, later settled in Farmington, CT.-1660s.

Stephen Hart's former house in MA later was turned into Harvard University's bookstore warehouse.

Ancestors are Stephen; John; Capt. John; Isaac; Job; Jabez; Harvey; William, George W.; Homer V., sr; Homer V., jr; present generation.

Homer Vincent Hart Senior and Vera Dell Palmer, 1908. Grandmother and Grandfather Hart taken on the day they announced their engagement. Taken in the woods on the George Washington Hart farm, Hudson, Lenawee County, Michigan.

1948—First Hart Family Reunion-Descendants of Stephen Hart (male lineage) b. 1605 and Vera Dell Palmer (female lineage) descendant of Walter Palmer b. 1585.

◆   ◆   ◆

George Washington Hart's Newspaper Obituary—Local Newspaper, Hudson, Lenawee County, Michigan—Jan 2, 1918 is written on the news clip that you can read as I posted it at http://www.newswriting.net/ hart_family_genealogy.htm. However, as another source, The book written by Elaine Hart Kerskie of Victor, Ontario Co., NY, published in 1940 titled:

Genealogys & Vital Records, **gives the date of George Washington Hart's passing as 25 FEB 1920. His birth date is given as 30 NOV 1839, whereas the
news clip obituary lists his birth date as March 30th, 1839. Note that sometimes baptism and birthdates were listed alternatively. In the book, Genealogys & Vital Records, it is the date of George's wife, Addie Hydenberk, death
that is listed as 2 JAN 1918. The couple's marriage date is listed in the book
as 4 JUN 1874.**

**The town of Hudson, Michigan was very small, with about 2,100 inhabit-
ants. There were many farms, and even today, it's still has a small population.**

Also, there are two spellings of Addie Hydenberk. The book lists one spelling as
Addie WYDENBECK. Another source lists Adelina Hydenberk, which is the
most frequently listed spelling. The death certificate of Homer Vincent Hart
senior, son of George Washington Hart, lists the spelling of his mother's name as
Addie Hydenberg, born in Medina, Michigan. George Washington Hart's birthplace is listed as New York, probably Victor, NY. Homer Vincent Hart is listed as
a civil engineer who worked for the Hardie Mfg. Co. Homer's birthplace is listed
as Hudson, Michigan. His birth date is listed as Oct. 15, 1876. Research published newspaper obituaries and similar articles found in newspaper library
archives and on microfilm, microfiche and on genealogy or history-related Web
sites, or in the historical records of family history libraries. Published news or
obituary articles for your relative or client may have been digitized or sent to a
genealogy library, particularly if the town was very small with one local newspaper.

More Notes:

MARY[2] LEE (John[1]), daughter of (1) John[1] and (RA-3) Mary (HART) LEE, was
born on 14 Aug. 1664 in Farmington, Hartford[1], was christened in Farming-
ton, Hartford, and died on 15 Feb. 1715/6 in Waterbury[1]. She married in
Farmington, Hartford, on 28 Dec. 1682, (AIS-2) STEPHEN UPSON[1], son of
(AIS-1) Thomas and Elizabeth (FULLER) UPSON, who was born in 1655 in
Hartford, Hartford, Connecticut, and died on 5 Nov. 1735 in Waterbury. [2, 1].
Children: See (AIS-2) Stephen UPSON at the Web site: http://armidalesoftware.
com/issue/full/Thaler_1066_main.html - N1

Resources: 1. Steve Condarcure, "Steve Condarcure's New England Genealogy", http://newenglandgenealogy.pcplayground.com/. 2. The Church of Jesus Christ of Latter-day Saints, "Ancestral File (R)", Copyright (c) 1987, June 1998, data as of 5 January 1998.

Hart-surnamed people also directly related to the Mary Hart who married John Lee (Mary Lee Hart) may also be distantly related to the late Princess of Wales, Princess Diana. Additional recommended reading includes: American Ancestors and Cousins of the Princess of Wales, by Gary Boyd Roberts, Baltimore, 1984. W. Addams Reitwiesner, Reference 29. How the Harts are related to the late Princess Diana is through the Mary Hart who married John Lee.

Mary Hart was the daughter of Stephen Hart (Deacon Stephen, b. 1605). Mary Hart married John Lee. Mary was born around 1631 in England. John Lee was born about 1620 in England. They married in Farmington CT. See: MARY[3], b. in 1635 in Berlin, Connecticut, d. on 10 Oct. 1710; m. (VF-1) JOHN LEE in 1658.

Lee is directly related to the late Princess Diana. So any children of Mary Hart through John Lee are related to the late princess Princess Diana. And Mary Hart's brother was John Hart, whose 11-year old son, the John Hart born in 1655 in Farmington, CT, is the direct male descendant of the males in this family. That John Hart, the grandson of Deacon Stephen Hart, begat one line of the Harts documented here.

Relationships to Stephen Hart:

Some of their descendants:

Direct Descendants of Stephen Hart—to—Princess Diana—13 generations from Stephen Hart to Prince William via Mary Hart

1 Stephen Hart
...+Unknown
2 Mary Hart
...+John Lee
3 Tabitha Lee
...+Preserved Strong

4 Elizabeth Strong
...+Joseph Strong
5 Benajah Strong
...+Lucy Bishop
6 Joseph Strong
...+Rebecca Young
7 Eleanor Strong
...+John Wood
8 Ellen Wood
...+Frank Work
9 Frances Eleanor Work
...+James Boothby Burke-Roche
10 Edmund Maurice Burke-Roche
...+ Ruth Sylvia Gill
11 Frances Ruth Burke-Roche
...+Edward John Spencer
12 Diana Frances Spencer
...+Charles Prince of Wales
13 William Prince of Wales.

Sarah Hart to Humphrey Bogart

1 Thomas Porter
...+Sarah Hart
2. Ruth Porter
...+Samuel Smith
3 Nathaniel Stanley
...+Sarah Smith
4 John North
...+Esther Stanley
5 Isaac Humphrey
...+Esther North
6 Jonathan Humphrey
...+Rachael Dowd
7 Belmont De Forest Bogart
...+Maud Humphrey
8 Humphrey Bogart (1899-1957)
...+Lauren Bacall.

See Also: The History and Genealogy of the Gov. John Webster Family of Connecticut at: http://www.langeonline.com/Webster/webster1.html

Also see at the Webster site mentioned above material on Rev. Thomas Hooker's Journey from New Towne to Connecticut. Stephen Hart moved from New Towne to Connecticut with this group or company. See: The Colonial History of Hartford (1914) by—The Rev. William DeLoss Love, Ph.D., of Hartford, CT . He documented these pioneers that located their house lots on the north side at that time, namely, Elder William Goodwin, John Steele, William Westwood, Thomas Scott, Stephen Hart, William Pantry, John Barnard, William Butler, William Kelsey, Nathaniel Ely, Nicholas Clark, Richard Webb, Richard Goodman, Edward Elmer, Mathew Marvin, Thomas Stanley,—sixteen.

Tracing the Female Lineages Descended from Deacon Stephen Hart

As you know, Deacon Stephen Hart's grandson, John b. 1655, had many children. Each family descended from those children who reproduced. Each generation descended from Stephen Hart had between 6 and 9 children or more per generation until relatively modern times. Many survived, both males and females. The books on Hart descendants usually list the names of the wives and also sometimes the wives' fathers.

If the mtDNA of each wife of a descendant of Stephen Hart was tested, each wife would have a different sequence passing her mtDNA to her daughter. Only the males with the same surname would pass on their Y chromosome markers to the next generation of males with the surname, Hart.

Here is a list of the maiden names of the wives of Hart descendants from only one lineage—Stephen-John-John-Isaac-Job-Jabish-Harvey-William-George W.-Homer Vincent Sr.-Homer Vincent Jr. The wives' maiden names (until around 1875) are listed in the Andrews book which also is online. The CD would have updated information.

Multiply this list of wives' maiden name from only one lineage by having six to nine children per family. Then think of Hart's daughters and the various husbands they married. Imagine how many other lineages there are to trace.

If you wanted to know Deacon Stephen Hart's mtDNA, you'd have to first find out the name of his mother and all daughters and grand daughters descended from only her female line to the present looking at mother to daughter.

If you didn't know Stephen's mom's name and line of females descending from her, you wouldn't be able to find her mtDNA unless you found a lineage descended from female cousins of Stephen Hart who were descended from Stephen's mom's sisters or grandmother's sisters.

It might be easier to find women descended from his first wife, Sarah to trace his daughter's mtDNA. To find out all women descended from his first wife, Sarah, you'd trace all women descended from Stephen's wife, Sarah, such as Stephen Hart's daughter Mary Hart who married John Lee. One of her daughters was Tabitha Hart.

Or trace daughter also named Sarah Hart who married Thomas Porter. If other daughters reproduced females, you'd follow their lineages to the present to find out the mtDNA or the female lineage DNA of Stephen Hart's first wife. Here's a list of the wives' maiden names of just one lineage descended from Deacon Stephen, our male family's lineage.

Stephen Hart—Elizabeth, nicknamed Sarah

John–Sarah

John—Mary Moore

Isaac—Elizabeth Whaples

Job—Eunice Beckley

Jabish—Jemima Brace (Revolutionary war period) (Moves from

Farmington to Victor, NY 1785)

Harvey—Polly Jackson

William—Zillah Deuel Thompson

George Washington Hart—Adelina (Addie) Hydenberk

Homer Vincent Hart Sr.—Vera Dell Palmer

Next two generations after Homer Vincent Hart have living family members.

Now to trace all the wives from their maiden names, you can test the mtDNA of each woman's female relatives. Their mtDNA will always be different unless they are descended from the same female ancestor. For example, in case Stephen Hart's first wife, Sara, had a particular mtDNA sequence, she would pass it on to her daughter, Mary Hart who married John Lee.

Mary's daughter, Tabitha Hart, and any other daughters would have that same mtDNA looking only at the female line. It would be passed down 12 generations or more from mother to daughter. Somewhere out there, Stephen Hart's mother's mtDNA and his first wife, Sarah's mtDNA have been passed to different women that exist today.

Some women today carry the same mtDNA as either Deacon Stephen's mom or Deacon Stephen. Other women carry a different mtDNA sequence which would be the same mtDNA as Stephen Hart's first wife Sarah. Start tracing his first wife's daughters and their daughters. You'd also see whether any children were born from his second wife, the widow of Adam Smith.

To find out Stephen Hart's mtDNA, we would look only at his mother's mtDNA. We'd check all women descended from mother to daughter from Deacon Stephen Hart's mother. Her name may have been Elizabeth Symons of Devon, if we're looking at the correct name of the mother of Stephen Hart. First, we'd have to be sure which females are descended from his mother. What was his mother's actual name?

It probably would be easier to locate descendants of his first wife which would have passed to his daughters and to their daughters and great grand daughters. Happy tracing.

Teaching Family History Online

How do you open a family history or genealogy journalism business? As an independent contractor, how would you teach family history online, by correspondence, or in-person? How would you organize your classes, writing, or research, find a suitable space for gathering groups, or record personal histories and life story highlights? Would you prefer to do public speaking in person or on radio and TV, or write for family history magazines and local newspapers and answer genealogy questions for clients for a fee?

Magazines often pay researchers $10 or more to answer each genealogy-related question. You'd research one question per reader or have your own clients for a set fee.

How would you write your genealogy, personal history, or genealogy journalism *course syllabus*?

You could start a *genealogy boot camp* for helping campers develop intergenerational life stories and family history projects. Your history and creative writing camp could be intergenerational—where teens work with older adults. Or each age group could work separately on genealogy topics.

At a set time, all age groups might meet and *learn to write skits or plays from life stories, history, news, or other current and past events* as part of a summer *social history or creative writing boot camp.*

Adult education programs, college extended studies curricula, libraries, ethnic associations, life long learning programs for retired adults, and intergenerational writing camps offer personal enrichment courses. Also look at the various private store-front learning centers such as the Learning Annex. These community-based education businesses or institutions offer courses in *genealogy-related* topics. Start with the oral history archives and libraries found at numerous universities, regional historical societies, and public archives collections.

You could focus on virtual educational programs online. Organize family history research events, including planning, location, publicity, and logistics. Specialize in genealogy research, family history journalism, or video biographies and time capsules.

Teaching online as a business is called distributive education. To start, pick a niche area of genealogy. Almost every city has adult education and extended studies courses offered at community colleges, unified school districts, universities, community centers, park recreation districts, private schools, and lifelong learning programs. Find your niche. I was contacted by the gerontology departments of community colleges and by the communications departments of several universities to offer writing courses.

The writing courses led to teaching video biography production—recording highlights of life stories or narrated experiences on DVDs for older adults, and courses on how to write the slice-of-life 7-minute 1,500 word vignette. That led to courses on how to write skits, monologues, and plays from the significant life events of older adults, and related courses. Finally, several books emerged from these family history niches.

What's Your Genealogy Niche?

To write a course outline in family history, you start with a niche or special area. Online you can offer a class in Census research, an adoption investigative course, or offer Native American or African-American genealogy research, Middle East genealogy, hidden resources for finding women's maiden names, historical medical, hospital, dental, elementary school, or prison records genealogy, or searching notary and court records using online resources.

You can offer services to genealogists such as transcribing oral history tapes, typing manuscripts, indexing or editing genealogy books, scanning photos, duplicating, restoring old diaries and books, making family prayer boxes, teaching digital scrap booking online, or taking a tour abroad with a group of genealogists.

Such tours go in search of court, school, and property records in various countries. The online part of a tour business can be the reservations, publicity, marketing, event planning, speaking, and organizing.

The Virtual University Gazette, at: http://www.geteducated.com/vug/oct01/ newcont1001.htm is a free distance educational newsletter that offers free advertising in its jobs-wanted section for those who want to be hired to teach any type of courses.

Most genealogy courses are filled by the time the course starts. Those offered online at present are usually sponsored by professional associations and directed at people interested in genealogy or oral history as an occupation. Those offered in person at present are usually sponsored by adult education programs within community college districts or by churches and private groups.

To make money teaching family history online, you need a popular niche. Who is your intended audience? If you have a specific group such as the descendants of early New England settlers, Native Americans, African Americans, adoptees, or any other ethnic or religious group, go to their club meetings and ask them what type of online course they need most.

You'll get a list of topics. Choose a topic according to your research in what is most in demand. Then write a course outline so that the course can be worked into a required course or elective already offered by the school such as a history, writing, speaking, or communications course within an existing department. For those without a master's degree and teaching experience, in any subject, instead of teaching in a university, you'd target the extended studies departments of colleges and adult education programs or private personal enrichment schools. You don't need a degree or credential to teach family history courses online.

Customize, tailor, and cater to an individual's niche. There's room for a wide variety of popular topics in any online course. Your course outline actually is a home-based business plan emphasizing teaching research techniques, writing, speaking, or multimedia strategies online.

You'll need a Web site on which to teach such as Blackboard.com located online at: http://www.blackboard.com. You can buy space at Blackboard.com for a small fee each year and teach all your courses from Blackboard's sites. Or teach at your own Web site. You don't need any type of special education or credentials to buy space at Blackboard.com and put up your family history course online. It's thoroughly professional.

You'll have to find your own students by your own publicity, flyers, or online promotional efforts. According to Blackboard's Web site, "Blackboard.com[SM] is a course Web site creation service that enables instructors to add an online component to traditional classes or teach an entire course on the Web.

"You can quickly and easily create your own course Web site to bring your learning materials, class discussions, and tests online. It's easy to get started. The service is free for the first 60 days, or may be activated for one year for a modest fee. Blackboard.com also features an extensive course catalog, from which learners can access a course their instructor has set up or search for distance learning courses."

Blackboard offers a limited number of reduced cost registrations. If you teach in adult education or for one of the extended studies programs for a university community college district, or unified school system's adult education program, usually the school already has a Web site where you'll teach.

If you don't want to work for an existing school that already uses Blackboard.com, then you can buy space at Blackboard and upload your own course, working entirely as an independent online teacher. Use your own Web site if you have one. Or use Microsoft's Outlook Express to create newsgroups and teach through email and newsgroups.

The choice is yours depending on your education and experience with uploading course material to Web sites. If you're hired by a university to teach elective courses, the school usually trains you free on how to post your course and syllabus to their Website at Blackboard.com.

If you're independent and want to buy space at Blackboard.com, the site shows you how to post your course material or syllabus. Each time a university hired me to teach a specific course online, I had to go through a month or two of online training in how to post my course material, write a syllabus, and use Blackboard.com.

Selling Your Online Course

Any student who takes your online genealogy course will need a syllabus and course outline. You need to write course materials. My personal history course is at: http://www.newswriting.net/personalhistorycourse.htm. It's a text-based course and also on video and/or audio at http://www.newswriting. net/writingvideos.htm. You can charge a fair price for your courses. Some extended studies courses at community colleges charge students about $50-$80 for a short online course in genealogy. Facilitators teaching an online course are paid a percentage, commission, flat fee, or as an independent contractor. Keep your course about five weeks or less and affordable.

Most people who take genealogy courses online will not spend the same amount as they would for a 3-credit/unit university online course that runs five weeks. You can repeat the course as long as there's demand. Some courses do better if they are one-day seminars. For a seminar, you could make the price affordable, about $20-$40.

Check out the prices of adult education courses in your unified or community college school district for non-credit courses and personal enrichment offerings. Some are free to older adults. Other courses have materials fee. The teacher is paid by the unified school district offering adult education courses to older adults or to anyone for a fee. Other adult education fees run about $60-$80, particularly for longer courses that can run up to eight weeks. Cost varies with locality.

What you need before talking to anyone is a course outline and syllabus with course materials to market your course to schools or programs. You need to pitch, show, and sell existing educational programs the value of your course.

Most adult education program designers or administrators ask you to mail them your course outline and syllabus, along with a resume and list of experience in your field.

Having speaking experience in genealogy actually is teaching experience. Joining a genealogy speaker's group helps to add to your experience. Target extended study courses open to all ages that charge a fee per course. The facilitator or instructors in these types of courses are paid a percentage of the fees charged to the students.

Join Historical and Genealogy Associations

Take online courses offered by the historical and genealogical associations. Join one or more of the genealogy specialties associations. In addition to the Association of Professional Genealogists at: http://www.apgen.org/, there are associations for genealogy writers such as the International Society of Family History Writers and Editors at: http://www.myfamily.com. You can join the Historical Novel Society, at: http://www.historicalnovelsociety.org/USA/schedule.htm and the Genealogy Speakers Guild at http://www.genspeakguild.org/.

To make contacts with oral historians, start with the personal history libraries situated on university campuses. One great oral history library, the Bancroft Library, http://bancroft.berkeley.edu/, is located at the University of California, Berkeley. The oral history libraries are where you make contacts, network, and find clients. The Association of Personal Historians has a Web site at: http://www.your-life-your-story.com/aph-upclose.html. The American Historical Association's Web site is at: http://www.historians.org/pubs/Free/ProfessionalStandards.htm.

For recording oral history, try the Oral History Association. Its Web site is at: http://omega.dickinson.edu/organizations/oha/pub_eg.html. They have an excellent pamphlet titled, Oral History Evaluation Guidelines. They publish *the Oral History Review*. See: http://omega.dickinson.edu/organizations/oha/pub_ohr.html.

Some of these professional associations offer classes, such as the Association of Personal Historians http://www.your-life-your-story.com/aph-upclose.html.

What Subjects Are Most Popular to Teach Online in the Personal History and Genealogy Fields?

1. Practical time management for genealogists.

2. Managing work projects.

3. How to produce quality genealogy client reports. Different types of family history reports and how to prepare them. Tips for creative, practical reports. Techniques of writing a genealogy report.

4. Standards in genealogy publications.

5. How to make time capsules for future generations.

6. DNA-driven genealogy—where history records end. How to open a DNA-driven genealogy reporting service.

7. How to do record searches, lineage construction, and problem solving in family history projects.

8. Billing issues for family historians.

9. How to educate clients online in genealogy/family history. Listing objectives. Communication is sharing meaning.

10. Enhancing the working relationship between client and genealogist.

11. How to read Census reports and information.

12. Investigating adoptions and the genealogy of orphanages and orphan trains.

13. How to set up speakers panels on family history for conventions, meetings, and conferences. Planning events for family historians.

14. How to plan reunions online, in person, and by satellite networks.

15. Teen or senior citizen genealogy camp. Creating a family history computer summer camp for researchers.

16. Schooling, certification, and professional standards for genealogists and family historians.

17. How to handle clients, peers, vendors, and suppliers in the genealogy, family history, and DNA-driven genealogy fields. How to motivate suppliers. Getting credibility, responsibility, and respect in your field from peers and clients. How to negotiate and how to bargain, the difference. Handling client's demands for specific research answers. Dealing with rush orders when you need time to research.

20. Taking clients on genealogy tours where records are available. How to plan a tour and include yourself free.

21. Unclaimed property searching. Missing heirs and adoption research. Finding heirs for unclaimed property. Fee structures, what to charge, and what the competition is like. How to network and work a room.

22. How to write for scholarly journals and popular magazines on different aspects of genealogy or family history. Slanting to the publication. The different ways to write for scholarly journals vs. popular publications.

23. How to be a Personal Historian or Oral Historian.

24. Transcribing oral history tapes or audio files.

25. Releases and legal forms you need to obtain before interviewing people and recording them.

26. Marketing genealogy and family history research, writing, and speaking.

27. How to become a professional public speaker on genealogy or family history, oral history, and personal history topics.

28. Marketing plans, priorities, prices and billing, niche and atypical markets, hidden markets for genealogists, packaging services, and labeling services. How to set up a family history business online. Inventor taking of your skills and defining goals.

29. How to teach genealogy online and where to find jobs or set up businesses and find clients. Handling contracts and fees. Your expenses. Using financial software, and running your genealogy business. Your genealogy business plan.

30. Publicity for genealogists/family historians. How to use TV and radio publicity to charge higher fees. How to design flyers an brochures, get speaking engagements, and position yourself as number one in demand. Where to get your own expertise, portfolio, and reputation or credibility enhanced in the media. How to mentor others and what professional growth is available for you.

31. Self publishing through print-on demand publishers.

32. What genealogists need to know about written agreements, fees, terms, confidentiality, and publication. How to estimate the magnitude of what you're researching. What to look for in agreements with sub-contracts. For genealogy writers, what you need to know about copyright and writing for publication.

*Source: Association of Professional Genealogists at:

http://www.apgen.org/conferences/pastpmcs.html

Audio MP3 educational lectures for writers and personal historians are at: http://www.newswriting.net/writingvideos.htm

List of published books for life-long learning also is at http://www.newswriting.net/id1.htm

Audio MP3 educational lectures for writers and personal historians are at: http://www.newswriting.net/writingvideos.htm

List of published books for life-long learning is at http://www.newswriting.net/id1.htm

Some old Hart family photos from 1908-1948 are shown at http://www.newswriting.net/hart_family_genealogy.htm, including the historic 1908 picture of Vera Dell Palmer and Homer Vincent Hart, senior, son of George Washington Hart, on the day they became betrothed at George Washington Hart's Michigan farm. Vera is shown again in a 1948 Hart family reunion photo posted on the site. The purpose is to depict a 12-generation lineage that kept in touch between 1631 and the present.

There are thousands of descendants of Deacon Stephen Hart. Families were large in those days. At some Hart family reunions more than 200 people from the Palmer_Hart lineage appear, and there are many other lineages in addition to the descendants of Walter Palmer (1583) who married the descendants of Deacon Stephen Hart (1605) approximately, which represents one line of many Harts. The inspiration and motivation intended is to encourage other families to have reunions of descendants, especially to discuss genealogy and record highlights of life stories of various ancestors. It's fun, and of historic value for everyone.

◆   ◆   ◆

Bibliography

See: the book: *Stephen Hart and His Descendants* by Alfred Andrews, first published in 1875. It's online at: http://users.rcn.com/harts.ma.ultranet/family/andrews/index.shtml

It's also available in rare book stores and on a CD from the above Web site.

Also see: *Dramatizing 17th Century Family History of Deacon Stephen Hart & Other Early New England Settlers: How to Write Historical Plays, Skits, Biographies, Novels, Stories, or Monologues from Genealogy Records, Social Issues, & Current Events for All Ages* by Anne Hart. ISBN: 0-595-34345-7, Publisher: ASJA Press, iUniverse. Phone toll-free 1-877-288-4737, http://www.iuniverse.com

This paperback book is about how to write skits and plays or other material from his life story, genealogy resources and bibliography, and chapters on how to write for the family history field, including searching other family histories in other areas, and how to teach family history online. This book includes how to write skits, plays, novels, biographies, and genealogies of all types of people, how to interview for personal history and creative genealogy projects, and searching Stephen Hart's roots following one lineage from his grandson, John, b. 1655, includes names of spouses and children for one lineage: Deacon Stephen Hart, John Hart, John Hart (grandson), Isaac Hart, Job Hart, Jabish Hart, Harvey Hart, William Hart, George W. Hart, Homer Vincent Hart (senior), Homer Vincent Hart (junior). Twelfth generation is living and not mentioned in book.

The focus is on how to write, edit, dramatize, package, promote, present, publish and launch personal histories, autobiographies, biographies, vignettes, and eulogies: launching the inspiration-driven or design-driven life story and detailing your purpose. It is a step-by-step guide to writing historical skits, plays, or monologues for all ages from true life stories, genealogy records, oral history, DNA-driven anthropology, social issues, current events, and personal history of early colonial era settlers. Put direct experience in a small package and launch it worldwide.

You could emphasize the early New England 17th century settlers and their diaries of family life, food, clothing, marriage, spirituality, customs, or significant life events, migrations, work, lifestyle, or turning points. Write your life story or your ancestor's or favorite historical person in short vignettes of 1,500 to 1,800 words. Write a longer novel or a short play for school audiences. Write a children's book with illustrations. Write a skit, a monologue, or a play based on genealogy, family history, or significant events. You can focus on relations between families, or early settlers and Native American tribes or on personal family history, marriages, and inter-family issues.

3

Tracing Baltic Genealogy

To look to the future, you begin by scanning the past—electronically and ethnographically. For the Baltic Sea nations, there's an excellent site on Basic Registers in the Baltic countries at: http://www.kada.lt/regno2001/presentations.php.

Finland

The Finnish American Heritage Center (FAHA) has the distinction of housing the most comprehensive Finnish-American archival collection in the world. The mission of the FAHA is to collect and preserve the multifaceted history of North American Finns. Check out its archive with more than 20,000 items at the Finnish American Heritage Center at: http://www.finlandia.edu/fahc.html, including old newspapers. Excellent sources of information on individuals are newspaper articles on Finnish-Americans.

In the past, the law of inheritance focused Finnish genealogy on legal matters. Special provisions made genealogical research necessary. Today, you also can start your ancestor search with the Genealogical Society of Finland at: http://www.genealogia.fi/indexe.htm. It's in English and includes articles on the Finnish communities in various US cities, including grave markers.

The site also offers links to church records, parishes, libraries, family indexes, research directories, societies, mailing lists, other genealogical societies, photo galleries, biographical indexes, abbreviations, and personal names. The site also has a database on men who didn't report for military service without reason. Check out their article on Karelians. The Genealogical Research Agency Radix is situated in Turku, Finland, but its activities cover the whole of Finland.

Also contact The Institute of Migration at: http://130.232.32.230/index.php. Click on the site's English translation icon. The Institute of Migration researches, compiles, stores, and documents ethnic research and migration materials relating to Finland's international and internal migration and serves as a major resource site for genealogists. Another excellent online database is the Finnish Genealogy site at: http://www.canadianfriendsoffinland.ca/genfin.htm. For information on Finnish immigration to the USA, try the Suomen Sukututkimusseura at: http://www.genealogia.fi/. The site is in Finnish. It also lists cemeteries where ancestors from the Finnish immigrations to the USA are buried.

These cemeteries include the following areas in the USA: Savo Cemetery (Savo Township, Brown County, South Dakota); Finnish Apostolic Lutheran Cemetery (Savo Township, Brown County, South Dakota); Toledo Cemetery (Toledo, Lewis County, Washington); Eglon Cemetery (Kingston, Kitsap County, Washington); Winlock Cemetery (Winlock, Lewis County, Washington). Lisätty hautausmaaluetteloita (USA): St. Paul's Lutheran Cemetery, Moe Township, Douglas County, Minnesota; Holmes City Lake Finnish Apostolic Lutheran Church Cemetery, Moe Township, and Douglas County, Minnesota.

You can find genealogy articles and links at the Sukututkimus Web site at: http://www.engr.uvic.ca/~syli/geneo/. Also see the article on *Changing Uses of Genealogical Research in Finland* at: http://www.genealogia.fi/emi/art/indexe.htm. Also try the Scandinavian and Nordic Genealogy site at: http://www.cyberpursuits.com/gen/scandlist.asp. See the Evangelical Lutheran Church of Finland site at: http://www.evl.fi/english/. The Swedish Finn Historical Society is at: http://sfhs.eget.net/welcome.html, since so many Swedes migrated to Finland. The Finns on the Titanic site is at: http://www.migrationinstitute.fi/index_e.php.

You'll find an excellent article on Finnish surnames at: http://www.genealogia.fi/emi/art/article104e.htm. For example, an excerpt from the article states, "The most prevalent form has been the shortening of the Finnish patronymic, usually by clipping either a prefix or suffix. This process abbreviated the surname in the interests of American phonology yet retained for it an unmistakable Finnish identity. Thus, by dropping the prefix, Kaunismäki, Kauramäki, Koivumäki, Myllymäki, Palomäki, Lamminmäki, Rautamäki, Peramäki, Hakomäki, Kortesmäki, Hautamäki, Niinimäki, Katajamäki, etc., became simply Maki;[2] or then again, by deleting the suffix, Mäkelä, Mäkinen, Mäkitalo, Mäkivuori, etc., were similarly transformed into Maki." The article explains in footnote [2] that, "The Finnish vowels ä and ö are inevitably rendered jo this country as the English a and o. The Finnish v and w are interchangeable."

Also see the publication, *American Speech. A Quarterly of Linguistic Usage*, Volume XIV, p. 33-38, 1939. A patronymic is a personal name based on the name of one's father. A personal name based on the name of one's mother is a matronymic. The present trend in Finland is from Swedish to Finnish patronymics.

Read the article titled, Surnames in Finland on the threshold of the new millennium by Sirkka Paikkala at: http://www.genealogia.fi/nimet/nimi82s.htm.

According to Kate Monk's Onomostikon at: http://www.gaminggeeks.org/Resources/KateMonk/Europe-Scandinavia/Finland/Surnames.htm "Originally Finns had only one forename followed by a patronymic taken from the genitive form of their father's first name with the suffix 'poika'—son, or 'tytär'—daughter. For example, Jussi Pentinpoika—Jussi, Pentti's son, or Ulla Pentintytär—Ulla, Pentti's daughter."

There's a Web site researching the Saari surname at: http://members.aol.com/dssaari/saarinam.htm and a tutorial on Finnish surnames along with farm names. The Finnish surname Korela Web well-researched site is at: http://www.cs.tut.fi/~jkorpela/korpela.html.

You can consult the Population Register Center of Finland, or look at the Web site of the international Porvoo Group that seeks to support the deployment of electronic identity in Europe. The Porboo Group's site (in English) is at: http://www.vaestorekisterikeskus.fi/vrk/home.nsf/pages/20710B02C6C5B894C2256D1A0048E290.

According to its Web site, "The Porvoo Group is a pro-active, European-level electronic identity 'interest group', widely recognized as a significant and relevant contributor to informed public dialogue in this area."

To register a child born in the United States (to Finnish parents/ Finnish parent) to the population registry in Finland, the parent would ask the Finnish Embassy in Washington DC or the Consulate General in New York or Los Angeles (http://www.finland.org/doc/fi/usamap/ to send the parent a "birth registration" form.

Also see the pdf file titled, *250 Years of Population Statistics in Finland* by Mauri Nieminen, Statistics Finland, Population Statistics, Työpajakatu 13, Helsinki, Finland. The Web site is at: http://www.stat.fi/isi99/proceedings/arkisto/varasto/niem1020.pdf. For other population statistics, also see Register Based Statistics Production, Statistics Finland, by Riitta Harala. The site is at: http://www.stat.fi/tk/ys/roundtable/sefdrha.html.

Development of electronic government transactions in Finland site is at http://europa.eu.int/idabc/en/document/966/334. The site notes, "Many transactions between the government and its citizens are largely automated using databases and electronic data transfer." In 1998, the Finnish *government* decided to create a generic system for electronic identification, data transfer encryption and digital signatures for electronic transactions. The Population Register Center offers PKI-based certification services, where a citizen can buy an electronic identification card the size of a credit card. The private key and certificates are installed on the smart card, see http://www.fineid.fi/.

Finnish Genes and Genealogy

Check out the Discover magazine article, *Finland's Fascinating Genes, Learning Series: Genes, Race, and Medicine [Part 2]*, According to the article, "The people in this land of lakes and forests are so alike that scientists can filter out the genes that contribute to heart disease, diabetes, and asthma," by Jeff Wheelwright, DISCOVER Vol. 26 No. 04 | April 2005 | Biology & Medicine.

The UCLA study also might help you learn more about your Finn-American medical heritage. For example, Karelians from Eastern Finland and Karelia are being compared in studies to people from Western Finland to see whether or not there are any genetic predispositions in the Eastern Finns and Karelians compared to the Western Finns. The article notes that Karelians and Eastern Finns with short arms and legs may have genes for different genetic predispositions compared to Western Finns with longer arms and legs, but all this is currently under study. Gene hunters described in the spring 1999 UCLA magazine article at: http://www.magazine.ucla.edu/year1999/spring99_03.html and http://www.magazine.ucla.edu/year1999/spring99_03_02.html state that Leena Peltonen, of the world's foremost geneticists, helped to put Finland on the map as a global powerhouse in genetic research. She hopes to do the same for UCLA.

Finland has a small population, isolation, and less immigration than other European nations. The government kept meticulous tax records. As a result, Finland has medical records on individuals that go back more than three hundred years. With carefully written medical and genealogical records, it's one way to trace familial health and ailments as well as family surnames. According to the UCLA 1999 magazine article, "Finland also has a system of free, high-quality health care in which patients trust their doctors and are highly willing to participate in medical research."

According to the UCLA magazine article, "In the 20 years that she has been studying genetic defects, Peltonen has identified no fewer than 18 genes related to such common disorders as multiple sclerosis and schizophrenia as well as more obscure diseases like AGT, a rare and horrific brain disorder found almost only among children in Finland."

In 1998, Peltonen localized the gene for familial combined hyperlipidemia, or FCHL, in a group of Finnish families. According to the UCLA magazine article, "the condition leads to the early onset of coronary-artery disease, which remains one of the leading causes of death in the industrialized world."

Check out the UCLA Human Genetics Web site at: http://www. genetics.ucla.edu/home/future.htm. Or if you're in the Los Angeles area, you can hear guest speakers presented by the Department of Human Genetics, David Geffen School of Medicine at UCLA. In your own area, go the many free lectures on genetics open to the public and learn what scientists are talking about in the fields of human genetic variation, population structure, or temperature sensation.

How can you (as a general consumer) apply what scientists have learned yesterday to benefit humanity today? For example, Peltonen's findings on FCHL coincided with a study by UCLA geneticist Jake Lusis, who localized the same gene using a mouse model. "The two scientists, who only learned of each other's research when each published a paper in the same issue of Nature Genetics, are now working together," according to the UCLA magazine article of 1999 titled *Gene Hunter*. You'll find the entire article on the Web site at: http://www. magazine.ucla.edu/year1999/spring99_03.html.

Check out this 1999 article as well as the more recent April 2005 issue of *Discover* magazine article which also describes Peltonen's more recent work at UCLA in genetic research and particularly with Finnish genes. You'll find that the Internet's Web can act as a springboard to motivate you as a consumer with no science background to read about what is being done in the evolving field of genetic testing.

If several scientists can collaborate, so can a world of consumers. Your goal would be to find out how to interpret and apply the results of any genetic tests to improve your quality of life and health. You don't need a science degree to move into new areas. Scientists are doing this daily.

Consumers need to observe the proliferation of information available online and in libraries. Federal research and the Human Genome Project have been mapping human genes since 1990. Ever since the human genome code was cracked in 2000, a flood of publications, articles, books, DNA testing companies, DNA testing kits, and DNA-driven genealogy services proliferated. What's offered as a result of testing is information. For every gene hunter, there is or could be a consumer seeking practical applications of such research.

Genetics is about preventive medicine. As a consumer, you've got breadth. Scientists have depth. They are only beginning to collaborate with one another and get the breadth that general consumers always had without much science knowledge. Genetics is a horizontal expression of a vertical desire. The consumer represents the horizontal breadth of knowledge.

The scientist's hierarchy sits amidst the vertical tower of scientific terminology. It's about language and communication as much as it's about science. Consumers want tests interpreted in plain language so they can readily apply the results to change their lifestyle.

Do scientists working in different disciplines really collaborate with one another? They have to now that the consumer is involved in the practical side of genetics—information dissemination. Collaboration means understanding how to interpret your test results and apply the research to what nourishes your body.

Finnish and Baltic Genealogy Research Starting Points

List of Items to Research:

For more information on Finnish ethnology and ethnography, see the Information Center (Centre) of Finno-Ugric Peoples. The Web site is at: http://www.suri.ee/index.html.

At the Web site you can learn about the "The Fenno-Ugria Foundation, established by a group of Estonian scientists, politicians, economists in Tallinn in 1927 with the aim of supporting the organizing of Finno-Ugric cultural congresses and promoting relations between Estonia and other Finno-Ugrian peoples."

Click on the link to the Finno-Ugric Peoples' Consultative Committee. There are links to its statutes and rules. Members include the following ethnicities: Erzyas, Estonians, Finns, Hungarians, Ingrian Finns, Ingrians, Karelians, Khants, Komis, Mansis, Maris, Mokshas, Nenetses, Permian Komis, Saamis, Tver Karelians, Udmurts, and Vepsians. Observers include: Livonians, and Setos.

Start with Dates

1. Dates: Several hundred thousand Finnish immigrants arrived in the USA between 1880 and 1920, settling throughout the country.

2. Look for census documents with names, dates, and places when personal history information from relatives runs dry. Trace women's as well as men's lineages by looking at birth, marriage, and death certificates.

3. Family Bibles provide notes and names. Ask living relatives for any information, photos, or other memorabilia.

4. Ask for naturalization papers and petitions for the intention to be naturalized as well as final papers after naturalization.

5. Visit cemeteries and ask from sexton's records.

6. Were any letters kept from older relatives or from Finland or any other former country? Many Finnish people came to Finland from Sweden or had Swedish names.

7. Do you have any old passports?

8. Get maps and find addresses of churches. Contact churches for a Parish Membership Transfer Certificate. In Finnish, it's called a Muuttokirja. If your ancestor belonged to a Swedish-speaking parish, ask for in Swedish a Utflyttnings betyg.

9. In the US, use city directories and census for various decades for data on birth, marriage, and death information or addresses in the case of city directories. These vital records are indexed by state, but were originally recorded by city or town. You'll find these city or town records indexed by county. In the US, marriage records were the earliest to be indexed. The western states didn't organize birth and death records until the beginning of the 20th century.

10. Contact your State Department of Health and your State Vital Records Office. Ask to purchase a certificate. If you need various years searched, the offices usually charge a fee. Some states have privacy laws.

11. Look for various states' and counties' microfilm and microfiche copies of vital records at the Family History Library in Salt Lake City. The library's Web site is at: www.familysearch.org. Or write to them at: Church of Jesus Christ of Latter-Day Saints the: Family History Library, 35 N West Temple, Salt Lake City, UT 84150. Phone (801) 240-2331.

12. Learn to read old handwriting. Before 1920, most vital records in the US were kept in hand-written ledgers. If you're searching in Finland, you'd need to find someone who reads Finnish unless you can take a language course at least to get reading ability. In the US, the handwritten indexes are typed onto a certificate.

13. How many ways were your ancestor's named spelled? Clerks who have to type certificates reading from misspelled handwritten entries and poor writing

may take a long time. At least at the Family History Library, copies of the originals may already be on microfilm or microfiche and easily printed out.

14. Search the census records. Those records may have the names of members of a family unknown to living descendants. Also names on pages just after or just before the name you want may also be relatives. Certain censuses list everyone in the household. US Federal Census records for 1880, 1900, 1910 and 1920 do list everyone in the same residence.

15. In Finland, you can access the national registry. In the US, Finnish immigrant names (and names of other nationalities) are microfilmed and available in the genealogy sections of some local libraries, State Libraries/ Archives, university libraries. First try the Family History Library in Salt Lake City, Utah and LDS branch libraries. Then look at the files or books with genealogy names on loan from the National Archives.

16. On census records, look for full names, ages, genders, relationships, number of children, name of the mother, the state or country of birth for the head of household and the name and country of birth for the parents, year of immigration. You'll also find categorized whether the immigrant is an alien, petitioned or naturalized. You'll find the head of household's occupation; language spoken if not English. If you need phonetic indexes, use the partial Soundex index. It's available for the years1880 and 1910. A complete Soundex index is available for the years 1900 and 1920.

17. What indexes are most likely to contain the records of Scandinavian, particularly Finnish immigrants? It's the various state Censuses. Check them on microfilm at the Family History Library, Salt Lake City, Utah. Most Finns went to Minnesota, Michigan, North and South Dakota, Colorado, and Wisconsin. Some went to Canada. **The Family History Library** lists the following **Censuses**:

1. Minnesota: 1875, 1885, 1895, 1905. Complete.

2. Michigan: 1884 & 1894. Only a few counties' records exist.

3. North Dakota: 1915 & 1925. Complete.

4. South Dakota: 1885 & 1895. Partial census. 1905, 1915, 1925, 1935, 1945. Complete. State Historical Society.

5. Colorado: 1885.

6. Wisconsin: 1875, 1885, 1895, 1905. Complete.

At the Family History library, you also can check the Canadian Census records as they have them on file open to the public for the years 1881, 1891 and 1901. Canada also put an individual's religion in the Census, whereas the US didn't include any affiliation.

18. Visit courts to find old US naturalization records processed before 1906. Look for your ancestor's Petition for Naturalization and/or Intention for Naturalization. This petition contains the name of applicant, country of origin/ monarch to whom allegiance was previously owed, and date of application. Check the records by county.

19. After 1900, numerous counties added more data on each applicant. Also after 1906, the district courts included places of birth, dates, physical descriptions, when and where the applicant first entered the US, the port; occupation, spouse, and children. Photos and comments went into the various district courts handling naturalization. Gradually, the county courts handed naturalization processing over to the district courts.

20. New England towns kept records as well as district courts. There's a master index dated from 1791–1906 for Maine, New Hampshire, Vermont, Massachusetts, Connecticut and Rhode Island.

21. Check county draft registrations for the World Wars. You have 3,000 counties to paw through, but luckily only two or less draft boards—unless your relative lived in a large city. Registration for World War 1 required US citizen and foreign males living in the US to register for the draft on three specified dates. Look for registrations for the draft on June 5 1917, September 12 1917 and September 12 1918. The birthdates of the men fell between 1873 and 1900.

22. What you're searching for are the registration forms. On these forms you'll find listed full name, birth date, birth place, citizenship, residence, age, occupation, employer, name of relative and address of relative to contact in case of emergency, some physical description, signature, date and any other registration number(s).

23. Finnish immigration to the US at its highest count coincided with World War 1 draft registrations. If you locate the registration cards or forms, at least you'll have a birth date and place of birth.

24. You'll know whether the ancestor had US citizenship at that time or was classified as an 'alien' living in the US. Since the applicant had to put down who to contact in case of emergency—usually a relative, you might be able to track the name of a parent or wife and that relative's address.

25. Then you can turn to a city directory as well as a census to compare the information for that date. When you see someone's city of birth on a registration card, you have a lead when visiting that place in whatever country to track down other descendants. For example, if the city listed is in Finland or Sweden (or any other country) you can visit that town and begin research at the local parish.

26. Church records of marriages offer new information. Before visiting the National Archives of the particular country, first track what microfiche or microfilm copies are retained in the Family History Library, Salt Lake City, Utah (or any of the Family History Library branches).

27. Check US passport applications. They are available to the public up to the year 1925. Scandinavian, particularly Finnish immigrants may have obtained passports to visit the old country.

28. If you are searching for passport applications for other countries, the US Federal Government began issuing passports in 1790. Many 18th century residents visited their former country, particularly England and Western Europe. Passports actually were not required to go back and forth to the 'old' country until World War 1 began.

29. When you check out passport history, in 1900 information on passport applications required full names, birth dates, places of birth, dates of entrance to the US, date of naturalization, physical descriptions of hair and eye color, destinations. You even had to explain why you were going to another country and had to list spouses, children, where you worked, and provide photographs. So you can see all this historical information up to the year 1925, which is now public information.

30. Use information on passport applications to locate church parishes in the old country. For other religions, check records of religious schools and houses of worship with the information obtained from 1790 to 1925 passport applications.

31. Indexes: For Finland and Sweden, check the index for 1906-1925, unless you know your relatives came from Sweden with an early immigration to New England or Virginia.

32. A few Swedes settled in New England in the 17th century. In checking Finnish names, the index lists applicants by the first two alphabet letters of a last name. However, the Finnish passport applications index lists the year of application and passport number. The index leaves out the person's address and state. To save time, all these indexes mentioned above for Finland already have been microfilmed at the Family History Library, Salt Lake City, Utah.

33. Look for maps of parishes. In the parishes—Scandinavians and Finnish peoples registered vital records with their home parish of the Lutheran Church. Records date from the late 17th century. You can obtain microfilmed records from the mid 19th century from the parishes. What you're looking for is the *Rippikirjat*. Translated, you want to see the "Main Books," also known as the "Communion Books." These are Lutheran Church records that began to appear early in the 17th century.

34. Indexing: The "Main Books" are organized by *farm name* first with the name of the *owner of each farm* listed second followed by any other resident of the farm listed by relationship. Each farm is then indexed by the name of each *village*, and the records are accurate, particularly for the 1600s.

35. Other parish records. You'll see registration for births, baptisms, confirmations, banns, marriages, membership transfers, parish minutes, deaths, burials, and detailed information on parish business. Once through that, you have the military and court records that have been microfilmed in Finland.

36. Don't forget tax and property records, notary records on farm ownership, and whatever else has been microfilmed and then transferred to electronic databases. Check to see whether any census data has been put on smart cards or in electronic databases.

37. Research the records of other religious groups living in Finland. Was your Finnish ancestor a member of the Russian Orthodox Church in Finland or the Finnish Jewish community? Jewish community records in synagogues and religious schools date back to the mid 19th century.

38. Recorded Finnish Jewish history began in the first half of the 19th century. Jewish soldiers (called cantonists) that had served in the Russian Army stationed in Finland continued to live in Finland. Note any Finnish residential records that followed the decree of 1858, under which discharged Russian soldiers and their families, without regard to their religion, were encouraged to live in Finland. On Jan. 25, 1782, the government passed a special regulation so the Jews could possess synagogues in Stockholm, Göteborg, and Malmöhus.

39. Many Jews had Swedish names. In 1862 a law concerning passports was enacted in Finland. Note that a few retired Jewish soldiers and sailors from Sweden and Russia lived in Finland. Some adopted Finnish names, and others kept their Swedish, Germanic, Yiddish, or Russian surnames. See the Helsinki Jewish Community's site at: http://www.jchelsinki.fi/home.htm - hometext and The Jewish Encyclopedia for Finland site at: http://www.jewishencyclopedia.com/view.jsp?artid=147&letter=F. The sites are in English.

40. During the Finnish-Russian War of 1939-40 (the Winter War), Finnish Jews fought alongside their non-Jewish fellow countrymen.

41. During the Finnish-Russian War of 1941-44, in which Finnish Jews also took part, Finland and Nazi-Germany were co-belligerents. Despite strong German pressure, the Finnish Government *refused* to take action against Finnish nationals of Jewish origin who thus continued to *enjoy full civil rights* throughout the War. There are many anecdotes from this period, concerning, among others, the presence of a Jewish prayer tent on the Russian front under the Nazi's noses and the food help given to Russian-Jewish POWs by the Jewish communities of Finland. See "A Short History of Finnish Jewry" Web site at: http://www. jchelsinki.fi/history.htm. Also view the Jewish Community of Helsinki, Finland Web site at: http://www.jchelsinki.fi/home.htm - hometext.

42. Russian Orthodox Church records also have some Finnish members. About one percent of the Finnish population follows the Russian Orthodox faith. In addition, thousands of Karelian (Eastern Finnish) immigrants moved into Finland when Karelia in Eastern Finland became part of Russia. There also are some Estonians living in Finland. Most Finns belong to the Lutheran Church. Also look at records of other religious groups and military service records. Read the records in various houses of worship.

43. Microfiche information on Finnish records dating to 1900 is at the Family History Library, Salt Lake City, Utah. Lutheran Parish Records microfilmed at the Family History Library listed below are available at the Family History Library, Salt Lake City, Utah for the following Finnish surnames:

	Kannus/ Yli-kannus	Kivijärvi
Bötom/ Karijoki	Karijoki/ Bötom	Kjulo/ Köyliö
Eno	Karjala/ Mynämäki	Korsnäs
Forssa	Karjalohja	Kuhmo(oinen)
Ilmajoki	Karkkila	Kuopio
Joroinen/ Jorois	Karinainen	
Jorois/ Joroinen	Karleby/ Kaarlela	Kuortane
Jämsä Kaarlela/	Karuna/ Sauvo	Kurikka
Karleby	Karvia	Kymi
Kalajoki	Kauhajoki	Kälviä
Kangasala	Kauvatsa	Kärsämäki
Kangaslampi	Kemi (rural)	Kärkölä
Kangasniemi	Kivennapa	Köyliö/ Kjulo
Laihia	Lapua Larsmo/	Lohja
Laitila/ Letala	Luoto	Lohtaja
Lammi	Lavia	Loimaa/ Metsämaa
Lapinlahti	Lemi	Loppi
Lappajärvi	Lempäälä	
Lappee	Leppävirta	Lundo/ Lieto
Lappfjärd/	Lestivirta	Luoto/ Larsmo

Lapväärtti	Letala/ Laitila	Längelmäki
Lappi (Turku-Pori)	Lieto/ Lundo	Marttila
Lapvärtti/ Lappfjärd	Liminka	Masku
Merikarvia/	Mäntsälä	Solf/ Sulva
Sastmola	Mäntyharju	Sulva/ Solf
Merimasku	Naantali	Tohmajärvi
Metsämaa/ Loimaa	Nivala	Vimpeli/ Vindala
Mietoinen	Pirttikylä/ Pörtom	Vindala/ Vimpeli
Mouhijärvi	Pörtom/ Pirttikylä	Virrat
Muhos	Sastmola/	Yli-kannus
Multia	Merikarvia	
Mynämäki/ Karjala	Sauva/ Karuna	
/ Kannus		

If you're looking for an expert team of genealogists specializing in the US, Canada, Finland, Denmark, Sweden, Norway, and England, I highly recommend Family Sleuths, PO Box 526163 Salt Lake City, Utah 84152-6163.

The above information found in the Family History Library, Salt Lake City, also is explained in much further detail with excellent resources, such as a link to the Kennecott Utah Copper Corporation Employment Records: 1909-1920 in Bingham Canyon, Utah containing a complete listing of all Finns and Scandinavians on the Family Sleuths genealogy Web site at: http://www.familysleuths. com.

The link at: http://www.migrationinstitute.fi/db/articles/art.php?artid=9 - Journal takes you to the site of the Institute of Migration. There you can see the list of surnames from the Family History Library, Salt Lake City, and also buy the book, *The Journal of Pastor Johan Wilhelm Eloheimo from the Evangelical Lutheran Parishes from Calumet, Michigan and Ironwood, Michigan.*

You can order the various Finnish genealogy books at the Family Sleuths Web site. The site also contains an excellent bibliography of books you can order on Finnish genealogy research and also a link to a Journal of Baptisms, Confirmations, Marriages and Deaths: 1891-1910 in the States of Michigan, Wisconsin, Wyoming and Idaho and Others. I highly recommend their research, Web links with articles on genealogy research, and bibliography if you're interested in Finnish genealogy. They have research material explained and books available on subjects ranging from collected employment cards of Finns to parish addresses.

Resources on Finnish Genealogy

Finnish, Scandinavian and U.S. Research
http://www.feefhs.org/FI/FRG-FS.HTML

Family Sleuths
http://www.familysleuths.com

Finnish Genealogy Group
http://www.feefhs.org/MISC/frgfinmn.html

Institute of Migration
http://www.migrationinstitute.fi/db/articles/art.php?artid=9

Finno-Ugric Peoples

In a press release dated April 27, 2005, posted at the Information Center of Finno-Ugric Peoples at: http://www.suri.ee/press/eng/050427.html, members of the European Parliament passed an action plan to improve the situation of Finno-Ugric minorities in Russia. According to the media release: "On 26th of April, members of the Finno-Ugric Forum at the European Parliament approved an action plan to help Finno-Ugric minorities of Russia to improve their situation.

"Pointing at the goals set by the World Congress of Finno-Ugric Peoples, the action plan provides for measures to improve the linguistic and cultural situation of these peoples, bringing it into accord with international standards. The Finno-Ugric Forum urges the official bodies of European Union to enter a dialogue with the Russian authorities on the issues of linguistic and cultural rights of Finno-Ugric minorities. It also stipulates for cultural and youth exchanges and co-operation on the grass-root level.

"The Forum decided to send its delegation to the next meeting of the Consultative Committee of the Finno-Ugric Peoples scheduled for this November in Syktyvkar, the capital city of the Komi Republic (Russia). Members of the European Parliament also agreed to draw a resolution on the continuing violation of human rights in the Republic of Mari El and in the territories of Finno-Ugric peoples of Russia in general. The Finno-Ugric Forum includes 44 delegates of the European Parliament, mostly from Finland, Hungary and Estonia."

For more information, you can read the appendix: English text of the Action Plan approved by the Finno-Ugric Forum of the European Parliament (passed 26.04.2005 in Brussels) at the center's Web site at: http://www.suri.ee/press/eng/050427ap.html. Additional information is at: http://www.suri.ee

Back Door Genealogy

Due to changing borders, a popular back-door method of finding Baltic genealogy records is to contact *English-speaking* real estate agents and lawyers or students' associations. The real estate agents sell online Latvian, Lithuanian, Estonian, Finnish, Swedish, German, or Polish houses to Americans and also search property, tax, and court records.

There also are student associations at various universities that have numerous bilingual students from Baltic countries with academic contacts such as librarians and government archive researchers. Also contact the International Lawyers' Association, Finland at: http://www.forum-legal.com/ilaf/ if you want to search court records.

Contact the Association of Finnish Culture and Identity at: http://www.suomalaisuudenliitto.fi/sl-english.htm. There's a Baltic and Finnish Student Association at Indiana University. Click on http://webdb.iu.edu/InternationalServices/scripts/ois/record.cfm?id=673 for the updated email address. Baltic students speak English and can screen and put you in touch with real estate agents, lawyers, archivists, librarians, and genealogists in the various countries.

Tracing Baltic Genealogy in Some of the 70 Baltic Sea Cities

Let's look at tracing family history online for some of the other nations bordering the Baltic Sea. A few centuries ago, 70 Baltic Sea cities formed the most dominating trading bloc in the world resulting in genealogy 'logs' archived in Swedish or Finnish or in a common 'records' language—Russian or German.

If you come from any of the lands bordering the Baltic Sea, start your ancestry search with the microfiche of Latvian, Lithuanian, Estonian, Swedish, Finnish, Polish or German records and sources at the LDS Family History Library Center or any of its branches in the US, Canada, Britain, Australia, and New Zealand. The Family History Library Center online is at: http://www.genhomepage.com/FHC/fhc.html.

At the LDS Family History Library Center, you'll find a microfiche file for each Baltic nation. Other online sites include the East European Genealogical Society at: http://www.eegsociety.org/Index.html or the Federation of East European Family History Societies. Both societies have maps, surname, ethnic, religious, and village databases. Check out their archives, and the Federation's journal. Their Baltic genealogy sites and databases include BLITZ (Baltic-Russian Research from St. Petersburg), Dags' Latvian Home Page, Latvia Jewish Special Interest Group (Latvia SIG), Lietuvos Bajoru Karaliskoji Sajunga (LBKS)—Royal Lithuanian Nobility Society, and the Lithuanian-American Genealogy Society

◆   ◆   ◆

Latvia

Many Latvian genealogy records are in German. The microfiche of Latvian resources at the LDS Family History Library Center contains a section on where to begin your search in Riga, which includes the Central State *History* Archives called the Centralais Valsts, the Central State Archives, the Lutheran Church, the Catholic Church, and the Orthodox Church. In the other Baltic countries, you'd begin by writing to the same type of central state archives and various churches in each of the other countries bordering the Baltic.

Online, for Latvian genealogy research links, try Dags' Latvian Genealogy Page at: http://feefhs.org/BALTIC/LV/frg-dag.html. There are links to Latvian and Baltic genealogy search contacts such as the Roots Location List Data or addresses for searching church records.

If you want to search genealogy in Latvia, try Latvians Online at: http://latviansonline.com/index.php. and at: http://latviansonline.com/search/index.php. Also see Latvian Research at: http://maxpages.com/poland/Latvian_Research. Check out at the site the Latvia Roots Location List Data, Ancestral File, International Genealogical Index (IGI), and Family Registry. These links include names of researchers working on a particular name. Materials are on microfiche.

The Languages of Land Ownership

Genealogy records from around 1905 in Latvia actually separate the German nobility of Latvia and Estonia from the Latvian-speaking Baltic peoples. The 1905 police were mostly Czarist. German nobility owned most of the land in Latvia and Estonia in the 19th and early 20th century. In Latvia, the genealogy records witness the 1905 first socialist revolution in the Russian empire pitting poverty-stricken Baltic peasants against the German land owners.

Many genealogy records felt the impact of the riots that ended with thousands deported to Siberia. If you trace the maps of the wealthy manor houses and a variety of large buildings in Latvia, you'll see the property changing hands from the German nobility to the Latvian peasants around 1905.

You might be interested in researching land grants, tax records, deeds to property, and notary recordings to see whether your ancestors owned one of these manor houses or ended up in Siberia. A Trans-Siberian genealogy site actually exists at the Trans-Siberian Railway Forum (genealogy and railway history) at: http://www.transsib.ru/cgi-bin/UBB/ultimatebb.cgi?ubb=forum&f=4. For Latvian genealogy, contact Latvian Research at: http://maxpages.com/poland/Latvian_Research.

Searching Female Genealogy

The Baltic lands have been putting their matriarchs on genealogical pedestals since ancient times, and genealogy folklore often follows women's maiden names aggrandized through folk songs and nature. Finns and Latvians have female presidents. The Latvian president is Vaira Vīķe-Freiberga, and the Finnish president is Tarja Halonen. Finland is the first European country to grant women the right to vote (1906). Genealogy is a part of the Māra—the material world and the feminine. In Latvia, genealogy incorporates *dievturība*, the folk religion of genealogy based on folk verses.

You'll find folkloric genealogy alive in the Baltic countries. Folkoric genealogy is about tracing your ancestry and surname origins based on the concept of young people taking advice from older people who get their wisdom from nature. The focus of family history research is that genealogy enriches *dievturība*.

Dievturība allows each individual to understand family folklore according to his own needs and abilities. All new information and research in the fields of genealogy, science, history, folklore and religion serve to further develop dievturība.

Vintage Railroad Maps as a Guide to Genealogy

An old Livonian, Finnish, and Estonian proverb about the Baltic Sea peoples states, "*Genetically, they are related, and so are their railroads.*" So look at a vintage railroad map dated to the year that your relatives or clients lived there. To find a *detailed* old map of the Baltic countries, a great place to start is with former editions of Encyclopædia Britannica dated to the year of your ancestor's residence in one of the Baltic countries.

A good starting point with a map also is the Latvian GenWeb site at: http://www.rootsweb.com/~lvawgw/. At this site you'll see a link for a variety of resources.

John Bartholomew & Son, Ltd, Edinburgh, Scotland, published an excellent 9 ¾" by 7 ¼" *Baltic Railroad Map* that includes only three Baltic nations—Estonia, Latvia, and Lithuania. Those countries had been under Soviet rule since World War II. However, they were independent at the time of the map's publication in 1929.

If you want to learn about the cultural components or history of each country bordering the Baltic that once belonged to the Soviet Union, try the The Red Book of the Peoples of the Russian Empire. Click on various groups such as the Latvians (Livonians) at http://www.eki.ee/books/redbook/livonians.shtml or for special groups within Lithuania, such as the Tatars, try the link to the Polish or Lithuanian Tatars at: http://www.eki.ee/books/redbook/lithuanian_tatars.shtml.

In tracing family history, it's important that you find a vintage map like this one showing details of cities, small towns, railroads, steamship routes, and natural features. It's like finding a map of the old neighborhoods, streets, and houses.

A vintage map will show major cities where you can begin your search in the various halls of records in cities such as Riga, Latvia, Tallinn, Estonia, Jelgava, towns along the Dvina River, Kaunas, Rakwere, Port Kunda, Klaipeda, and other cities whose names have changed since the twenties. For example, Kaunas used to be called Kovno, Rakwere had been Vezenbert, and Klaipeda used to be called Memel.

Depending upon the era, Latvian genealogy records could be recorded in German, Russian or Latvian. Dundaga, Latvia, had been written in German, as Dondangen, and Mitau is now called Jelgava.

The eastern Baltic lands, Latvia, Lithuania, and Estonia witnessed a 1910 dialect struggle that ended with the development of standard national languages. As a result, some genealogy records are archived in the Russian language, even in Poland. Germany, Sweden, and Finland have genealogy records archived in the language of each country. Jewish genealogy records in Poland are recorded and archived in Russian.

◆   ◆   ◆

Poland

A mailing list of surnames for anyone researching genealogy in the former historical borders of Poland including Estonia, Latvia, Lithuania, East Prussia and other Eastern European areas is called PolandBorderSurnames-L. To subscribe to this list, click on their surnames link above and type the word subscribe in the message box or email: polandbordersurnames-l-request@rootsweb.com. Archived records may be in Russian or German rather than in Latvian, Estonian, or Lithuanian.

The Polish Genealogical Society of America's site is at: http://www.feefhs.org/POL/frg-pgsa.html. The site contains maps, ethnic and religious databases, a Polish cross-index, and a link to the Federation of East European Family History Societies.

The Polish-Jewish genealogy Web site is at: http://polishjews.org/. More than 3 million Jews lived in Poland in 1939. One of the provinces with a large Jewish population in Poland was Bialystock, and for genealogy research, an excellent travelogue, cultural, and genealogical history book, *Jewish Bialystok*, by Tomasz Wisniewski (see http://www.zchor.org/BIALISTO.HTM) lists surnames from tombstone rubbings and walking guides. Also, general Polish genealogy sources are at Distant Cousin.com at: http://distantcousin.com/Links/Polish.html. Also see the Web site titled New Poland Genealogy at: http://www.newpoland.com/genealogy.htm.

Jewish Communities in Poland Today

View the Web site, Jewish Life in Poland Today at: http://www.diapozytyw.pl/en/site/zycie/po_1989/. The Ronald S. Lauder Foundation runs several cultural centers in Poland. They are located in Warsaw, Krakow, Lodz and Gdansk, and serve as centers for individuals interested in becoming acquainted with Jewish culture and religion.

According to the Web site, Poland today has two Jewish schools funded by the Lauder Foundation in Wroclaw and Warsaw. In Krakow, the first Jewish religious school, the Pardes Lauder Yeshiva, is open. Three publications for the Jewish audience are published: *Dos Yidishe Vort/Slowo zydowskie*, a bilingual, Polish-Jewish magazine published under the auspices of the Jewish Social and Cultural Association; the cultural and literary magazine *Midrasz,* and *Szterndlech*, which is for young children. There's also the Festival of Jewish culture, organized yearly in Kraków. It includes lectures and concerts, as well as courses in Yiddish and dance, and workshops on calligraphy and traditional paper cutouts.

Check out the Immigration and Ships' Passenger Lists Research Guide at: http://home.att.net/~arnielang/ship05.html - search. Also click on the link to the National Archives if your relatives arrived in New York. The National Archives has passenger arrival records for the port of New York dating from 1820 to 1957. When there are no more written records, perhaps you can find a long-lost descendant of cousins or great grandparents by learning to interpret your DNA-driven genealogy report or DNA test for ancestry.

Polish DNA-Driven Genealogy

Learn to interpret the results of your own DNA test and expand your historical research ability to trace your ancestry. "An interesting idea was expressed by a colleague from Canada, Dr. Charles Scriver," explains geneticist, Dr. Batsheva Bonné-Temir. "At a meeting which I organized here in Israel on Genetic Diversity Among Jews in 1990, Dr. Scriver gave a paper on 'What Are Genes Like that Doing in a Place Like This? Human History and Molecular Prosopography.' Dr. Charles Scriver is founder of the DeBelle Laboratory of Biochemical Genetics in Canada.

He also established screening programs in Montreal for thalassaemia and Tay Sachs Disease. He claimed that "a biological trait has two histories, a biological component and a cultural component."

Most biologists would call DNA a biological component and consciousness of a core identity a trait. The conscious trait of the whole person rather than the molecular level DNA would be the cultural component. A cultural trait would be the environmental familiarity of the whole person's relation to his or her family and community.

According to Bonné-Tamir, at the 1990 meeting in Israel on Genetic Diversity Among Jews, Dr. Charles Scriver stated, "When the event clusters and an important cause of it is biological, the cultural history also is likely to be important because it may explain why the persons carrying the gene are in the particular place at the time."

The term, "when the event clusters" refers to an event when genes cluster together in a DNA test because the genes are similar in origin, that is, they have a common ancestral origin in a particular area, a common ancestor.

"When I look at my own papers throughout the years," says Bonné-

Tamir. "I find that I have been quite a pioneer in realizing the significance of combining the history of individuals or of populations with their biological attributes. This is now a leading undertaking in many studies which use, for example, mutations to estimate time to the most recent ancestors and alike."

What lines of inquiry are used in genetics? Dr. Charles R. Scriver wrote a chapter in Batsheva Bonné-Temir's book, titled *What are genes like that doing in a place like this? Human History and Molecular Prosopography*. The book title is: *Genetic Diversity Among Jews: Diseases and Markers at the DNA Level*. Bonné-Tamir, B. and Adam, A.

Oxford University Press. 1992. With permission, an excerpt is reprinted below from page 319:

"When a disease clusters in a particular community, two lines of inquiry follow:

1. Is the clustering caused by shared environmental exposure? Or is it explained by host susceptibility accountable to biological and/or cultural inheritance?

2. If the explanation is biological, how are the determinants inherited? These lines of inquiry imply that a disease has two different histories, one biological, the other cultural. One involves genes (heredity), pathways of development (ontogeny), and constitutional factors; the other, demography, migration and cultural practice.

Neither history is mutually exclusive. Such thinking shifts the focus of inquiry from sick populations and incidence of disease to sick individuals and the cause of their particular disease. The person with the disease becomes the object of concern which is not the same as the disease the person has." (Page. 319).

After hearing from Dr. Scriver by email, I then emailed Stanley M. Diamond. He contacted writer, Barbara Khait, and got permission for me to reprint in this book some of what she wrote about Diamond's project. It's the chapter, "***Genetics Study Identifies At-risk Relatives***" from *Celebrating the Family* published by Ancestry.com Publishing.

Check out the Web site at: http://shops.ancestry.com/product.asp?productid=2625&shopid=128.

Here's the reprinted article. Persons interested may go to the Web site for more information. I found out about Stanley M. Diamond from Dr. Scriver, since he mentioned Stanley M. Diamond's project in the book chapter Scriver wrote for Batsheva Bonné-Temir's book, *Genetic Diversity Among Jews: Diseases and Markers at the DNA Level*. Barbara Khait's chapter follows.

◆   ◆   ◆

"In 1977, Stanley Diamond of Montreal learned he carried the betathalassemia genetic trait. Though common among people of Mediterranean, Middle Eastern, Southeast Asian and African descent, the trait is rare among descendants of eastern European Jews like Stan. His doctor made a full study of the family and identified Stanley's father as the source.

"Stan was spurred to action by a letter his brother received in 1991 from a previously unknown first cousin. Stan asked the cousin, "Do you carry the beta-thalassemia trait?" Though the answer was no, Stan began his journey to find out what other members of his family might be unsuspecting carriers.

"Later that year, Stan found a relative from his paternal grandmother's family, the Widelitz family. Again he asked, "Is there any incidence of anemia in your family?"His newfound cousin answered, "Oh, you mean beta-thalassemia? It's all over the family!"

"There was no question now that the trait could now be traced to Stan's grandmother, Masha Widelitz Diamond and that Masha's older brother Aaron also had to have been a carrier. Stan's next question: who passed the trait onto Masha and Aaron? Was it their mother, Sura Nowes, or their father, Jankiel Widelec?

"At the 1992 annual summer seminar on Jewish genealogy in New York City, Stan conferred with Or. Robert Desnick, who suggested that Stan's first step should be to determine whether the trait was related to a known mutation or a gene unique to his family.He advised Stan to seek out another Montrealer, Dr. Charles Scriver of McGill University—Montreal Children's Hospital. With the help of a grant, Dr. Scriver undertook the necessary DNA screening with the goal of determining the beta-thalassemia mutation.

"During this time, Stan began to research his family's history in earnest and identified their nineteenth century home town of Ostrow Mazowiecka in Poland. With the help of birth, marriage, and death records for the Jewish population of Ostrow Mazowiecka filmed by The Church of Jesus Christ of Latter-day Saints (LOS), Stan was able to construct his family tree.

"Late in 1993, Dr. Scriver faxed the news that the mutation had been identified and that it was, in fact, a novel mutation. Independently, Dr. Ariella Oppenheim at Jerusalem's Hebrew University-Hadassah Hospital mad e a similar discovery about a woman who had recently emigrated from the former Soviet Union.

""The likelihood that we were witnessing a DNA region 'identical by descent' in the two families was impressive. We had apparently discovered a familial relationship between Stanley and the woman in Jerusalem, previously unknown to either family," says Dr. Scriver.

"It wasn't very long ago when children born with thalassemia major seldom made it past the age of ten. Recent advances have increased life span but, to stay alive, these children must undergo blood transfusions every two to four weeks. And every night, they must receive painful transfusions of a special drug for up to twelve hours.

"The repeated blood transfusions lead to a buildup of iron in the body that can damage the heart, liver, and other organs. That's why, when the disease is misdiagnosed as mild chronic anemia, the prescription of additional iron is even more harmful. Right now, no cure exists for the disease, though medical experts say experimental bone-marrow transplants and gene-therapy procedures may one day lead to one.

"Stan's primary concern is that carriers of thalassemia trait may marry, often unaware that their mild chronic anemia may be something else. To aid in his search for carriers of his family's gene mutation of the beta-thalassemia trait, he founded and coordinates an initiative known as **Jewish Records Indexing-Poland**, an award-winning **Internet-based index of Jewish vital records in Poland**, with more than one million references. This database is helping Jewish families, particularly those at increased risk for hereditary conditions and diseases, trace their medical histories, as well as geneticists."

Says Dr. Robert Burk, professor of epidemiology at the Albert Einstein College of Medicine at Yeshiva University, and principal investigator for the Cancer Longevity, Ancestry and Lifestyle (CLAL) study in the Jewish population (currently focusing on prostate cancer), "Through the establishment of a searchable database from **Poland**, careful analysis of the relationship between individuals will be possible at both the familial and the molecular level.

"This will afford us the opportunity to learn not only more about the Creator's great work, but will also allow (us) researchers new opportunities to dissect the cause of many diseases in large established pedigrees."

Several other medical institutions, including Yale University's Cancer Genetics Program, the Epidemiology-Genetics Program at the Johns Hopkins School of Medicine, and Mount Sinai Hospital's School of Medicine have recognized Diamond's work as an outstanding application of knowing one's family history and as a guide to others who may be trying to trace their medical histories, particularly those at increased risk for hereditary conditions and diseases.

In February 1998, in a breakthrough effort, Stanley discovered another member of his family who carried the trait. He found the descendants of Jankiel's niece and nephew—first cousins who married—David Lustig and his wife, Fanny Bengelsdorf. This was no ordinary find—he located the graves by using a map of the Ostrow Mazowiecka section of Chicago's Waldheim Cemetery and contacted the person listed as the one paying for perpetual care, David and Fanny's grandson, Alex.

"It turned out Alex, too, had been diagnosed as a beta-thalassemia carrier by his personal physician fifteen years earlier. The discovery that David and Fanny's descendants were carriers of the beta-thalassemia trait convinced Stan, Dr. Scriver, and Dr.Oppenheim that Hersz Widelec, born in 1785,must be the source of the family's novel mutation.

"'This groundbreaking work helps geneticists all over the world understand the trait and its effects on one family,' says Dr. Oppenheim. "A most important contribution of Stanley Diamond's work is increasing the awareness among his relatives and others to the possibility that they carry a genetic trait which with proper measures, can be prevented in future generations. In addition, the work has demonstrated the power of modern genetics in identifying distant relatives, and helps to clarify how genetic diseases are being spread throughout the world."

For more information about thalassemia, contact Cooley's Anemia Foundation (129-09 26th Avenue. Flushing,New York, 11354; by phone 800-522-7222; or online at www.cooleysanemia.org). For more about Stanley Diamond's research. visit his Web site (www.diamondgen.org). Thalassemia is not only carried by people living today in Mediterranean lands. **The first Polish (not Jewish) carrier of Beta-Thal** was discovered in the last few years in Bialystok, Poland. Stanley Diamond met with the Director of the Hematology Institute in Warsaw in November 2002, and the Director of the Hematology Institute in Warsaw indicated that they now have identified 52 carriers. Check out these Web sites listed below if the subject intrigues you.

> **"Genealogy with an extra reason"…Beta-Thalassemia Research Project.**
> http://www.diamondgen.org

> **JTA genetic disorder and Polish Jewish history**
> http://www.jta.org/page_view_story.
> asp?intarticleid=11608&intcategoryid=5

> **IAJGS Lifetime Achievement Award**
> http://www.jewishgen.org/ajgs/awards.html

Jewish Records Indexing—Poland
http://www.jri-poland.org

For more Polish genealogy links, try the Polish Genealogy Links site at: http://www.geocities.com/SiliconValley/Haven/1538/Polishpg.html. The Polish Genealogical Society of America's (PGSA) Web site is at: http://www.pgsa.org/. As of May 2, 2005 there were 878,700surnames in PGSA's databases. If you're searching Polish genealogy, attend some of the Polish genealogical conferences.

Digital Library of Wielkopolska Web site with 3971 publications at the time this book went to press is at: http://www.wbc.poznan.pl/ gives you access to the oldest Polish writing relicts. The Web site is in English. According to the site, "You also can read scientific scripts and monographies and see exhibitions with unique resources from various Wielkopolska libraries." Also at the upper right hand corner of the site, click on the flag of language you want—English or Polish.

Also try The Association of Professional Genealogists at: http://www.apgen.org/directory/index.php to find someone who specializes in your particular town or surname research. American military sources links are at the Military Links and Record Sources Web site at: http://www.pgsa.org/MilitaryRec.htm.

The article, Genealogy and Poland—a Guide, is at: http://www.polishroots.com/genpoland/index.htm.

The excellent *Guide* at the Web site notes that, "Millions of people all around the world trace their roots to the territory of present-day Poland. Their ancestors might have been of Polish, German, Jewish, Ruthenian or other ethnic backgrounds and they might have belonged to the Roman Catholic, Greek Catholic, Lutheran, Orthodox, Calvinist or Mennonite Churches, or professed Judaism."

What's great about this site is that has a link to Polish directories at: and answers frequently asked questions with links such as the following questions and links to the answers: For example, the site called: *How to Start my Search for Ancestors* is at http://www.polishroots.org/genpoland/start.htm. It contains information you need for the compilation of data. The next question on How to locate my ancestors' place of origin site is at: http://www.polishroots.org/genpoland/where.htm, and contains the names of localities in Poland and the history of administrative divisions. Many cities in Western Poland retained their German names until 1945.

The link titled, *"My ancestors were Germans (Jews, Russians etc.) Why should I look for them in Poland?"* The site is at: http://www.polishroots.org/genpoland/

polhistory.htm and contains a map of central Europe in 1772 and a 200 year brief history.

The Web site's article explains that during the second half of the 18th century the Kingdom of Poland included all of what we now call Lithuania, Belarus and half of contemporary Ukraine. Nearly half of the contemporary area of Poland then belonged to Prussia (Germany). Historic Prussia on an old map is found in Eastern Germany.

The boundary changes section on what 19th century provinces now belong to Poland is at: http://www.polishroots.org/genpoland/changes.htm.

See the link on What kind of records are available in Poland for my ancestors? Where can I find them?, Investigative research site is at: http://www. polishroots.org/genpoland/records.htm. Note that you can find records of births, deaths, and marriages in parishes.

The site notes that, the Civil Codex of Napoleon Bonaparte required religious clergy of all religions to make duplicates of their registers and to deliver them to the local authorities (the district courts). All of the countries formerly governing the present territory of Poland had to deliver the registers. According to the Web site, "After the fall of Napoleon this practice continued." The Civil Registration Offices (*Standesämter*) in Prussia, established on Oct 1, 1874, controlled the registers. Therefore, registrations of births, marriages and deaths for all religions after 1874 were filed in the Civil Registration offices.

Also, check out the link answering the frequently-asked question of How to obtain a birth/marriage/death certificate from Poland. at: http://www. polishroots.org/genpoland/certif.htm. The link shows you how to deal with archivists, officials, and pastors. If you're looking for meanings of names, click on the site titled, What does my surname mean? It's at http://www.polishroots.org/ genpoland/surnames.htm. You'll find helpful hints on etymology.

Estonia

Numerous English language links for genealogy research, history, language, culture, and message boards of Estonia are at the Estonian Research site at: http:// maxpages.com/poland/Estonian_Research. Estonian genealogy links also are at the Estonian Genealogy Page at: http://www.genealoogia.ee/English/links.html. Estonian family trees online are at: http://www.genealoogia.ee/English/ links.html - eestivosa. For information on World War II casualties in Estonia, try the Museum at: muuseum@okupatsioon.ee which is called the Okupatsioonide Muuseum which will also include a virtual museum online.

Also search online at the Kistler-Ritso Foundation at: http://www.ngonet.ee/
db/ngo?rec=00758. The Foundation's task is to document the catastrophes of the
last fifty years and to find detailed proof about the past based on facts and analysis. The Kistler-Ritso Web site states that, "We are interested in the life of Estonians, and also of Russians, Germans, Jews, Swedes and other minorities under
the totalitarian regime of the second half of the XX century."

Articles about Estonian genealogy in the Estonian language are posted online
at: http://folklore.ee/rl/folkte/pere/pere6.htm. You might want to invest in Web-
translating software from Estonian (or any other language of the Baltic areas) to
English. Or to read information in English about Estonian genealogy, see the
Estonian Family Registry offices online at: http://www.genealoogia.ee/English/
fro.html.

The materials in their archives are births, marriages and deaths of the corre-
sponding county since July 1, 1926 and personal registers for the years 1926-
1940 (1949) for persons who lived in those years in Estonia. After 1940 (in some
places 1949) the registers were not used and the births, marriages and deaths for
Estonia need to be researched separately.

Research can't be done, according to this Web site, in the central Family Registry Office where there are family registers and metrics since 1830s until 1926.
Instead, check Estonian local registry offices. The mailing addresses of the local
registry offices are listed at: http://www.genealoogia.ee/English/fro.html.

Also check out Estonian Genealogy Links in English at: http://www.
genealoogia.ee/English/links.html - artiklid for Estonian genealogy links.

A unique way to link to old genealogy, tax, and property records other than
church-archived marriage records in Estonia is by searching "Baltic Real Estate."
Try the English-speaking agents of Sunshine Estates—International Real Estate
at: http://www.sunshineestates.net/reg_sum/tallinn.html to inquire about real
estate in Tallinn, Estonia. Or if you read Estonian, click on the Estonian Real
Estate Center at: http://www.kinnisvarakeskus.ee/.

Foreigners in Estonia can freely buy and sell residential real estate with no
restrictions, and completion can take less than a month. For genealogy searches,
your purpose in talking to an English-speaking real estate agent located in the
Baltic country would be to make knowledgeable contacts who can find and translate hidden maps, titles, tax, notary, zoning records and other data such as old
institutional, military, dental, medical, school, marriage, divorce, birth, death,
business, census, street directories, and residential property sale certificates or
names of former property owners.

To make contact with genealogists, curators, archivists, librarians, or government records administrators who may not speak English is through a liaison from
foreign student associations in the US, such as the various Latvian, Lithuanian,
Polish, Estonian, Swedish, German, or Finnish student societies at universities
that draw large numbers of students from Baltic countries. The Estonian Association of Teachers of English at: http://www.ngonet.ee/db/ngo?rec=00339 may be
able to help you find a bilingual translator of your genealogy records.

Sweden

Swedish resources are at: http://www.tc.umn.edu/~pmg/swedish.html. See the
Master Index to Swedish Genealogical Data (by surname) at: http://
www3.dcs.hull.ac.uk/genealogy/swedish/. An excellent source also is the book
titled, R.W.Swanson, '*The Swedish Surname in America*', ibid., 3 (1927-1928),
468-477.

Find information about original records in public archives at SVAR (Swedish
National Archives). The Web site is at: http://www.svar.ra.se/. Click on the
English language icon. You'll find databases and indexes. Search for Swedish
archive documents, scanned or on microfiche and book titles with books covering
the Swedish census of 1890, parish records, and genealogy books.

Swedish genealogy publications and archives are highly organized, in multimedia, and available in English and Swedish. You'll also find books on family
patterns in 19th, the Saami, and genealogy publications. The book descriptions
and lists I check out were in English.

The Federation of Swedish Genealogical Societies Web site is at: http://
www.genealogi.se/roots/. This is the English version. There's a Swedish language
site at: http://www.genealogi.se/. Check out the Swedish Soldier's Register at:
http://www.genealogi.se/roots/. This site is in English and recounts some history
of how men were assembled and recruited for the military.

See also the Sweden Genealogy Forum at: http://genforum.genealogy.com/
sweden/ (from Genealogy.com). A Review of Swedish Immigration to America
site is at: http://www.americanwest.com/swedemigr/pages/emigra.htm. Swedes
started to come in 1638, just eighteen years after the landing of the *Mayflower*.
According to the Web site, the "tidal wave of Swedish immigration began in the
mid-1840s." The site also mentions the 17th century history of Swedish immigrants to the US and notes that, "Swedes were not religious dissenters but rather
an organized group of colonizers.

"They had been sent out by the government in Stockholm in order to establish a colony under the Swedish crown in Delaware. The era of New Sweden ended in 1655, when the colony was lost to the Dutch."

Interestingly the Web site reports that the "original settlers remained and kept up their language and culture for a long time." Also noted is that "Many of the descendants of the Delaware Swedes became distinguished fighters for freedom in the war against England in 1776." The site mentions John Morton, "who gave the decisive vote for independence at the Continental Congress in Philadelphia."

An excellent list of links with numerous articles on Swedish genealogy and history is at the Swedish Resources Web site at: http://www.tc.umn.edu/~pmg/swedish.html. Also check out the English language link to the Immigrant Institute in Sweden at: http://www.immi.se/portale.htm. The site states that, "The Immigrant institute is a non-governmental organization which aim is to be a research and documentation centre about immigrants, refugees and racism, with an archive, a library and a museum."

For genealogy information on the Jewish community of Sweden, contact the Jewish Genealogical Society of Sweden. Click on http://www.ijk-s.se/genealogi/index_en.html. The history of Jewish immigration to Sweden link is at: http://www.ijk-s.se/genealogi/index_en.html.

All Jews who were Swedish citizens were allowed to reside anywhere in Sweden. Jews began immigrating to Sweden in the 18th century. By 1850 Jews began to immigrate to Sweden from Mecklenberg, Germany and a few other towns. At the same time, Jews also arrived from Russia and Poland. At first Jews settled in Stockholm, Göteborg (Gothenburg), Norrköping and Karlskrona. Later they moved also to newly-founded Jewish settlements in Malmö, Lund, Kristianstad, Landskrona, Helsingborg, Sölvesborg, Kalmar, Oskarshamn, Växjö, Halmstad, Visby, Karlstad, Sundsvall, Härnösand, and Östersund.

According to the site, "Jewish Immigration to Sweden" at: http://www.ijk-s.se/genealogi/index_en.html, a historical note states that "During the final years of World War II and just afterward, many thousands of Jewish refugees arrived in Sweden, some of whom stayed. During the war more than 7000 Danish Jews and about 925 Norwegian Jews found asylum in Sweden."

In the decade following the war, Jews arrived from Hungary, Czechoslovakia, Poland, and other former Soviet republics. It's estimated that 17,000 Jews live in Sweden currently. That's less than 0.2 percent of the total population. Because of many intermarriages, the number of Swedes with Jewish genealogical roots is much higher. For more information, click on the Web site of the Scandinavia Special Interest Group (SIG) of the Jewish Genealogy site called JewishGen, Inc.

at: http://www.ijk-s.se/genealogi/index_en.html. The site links cover the Jewish communities and/or Jewish genealogy and some history in Sweden, Finland, Norway, Denmark, former Danish colonies, Danish Virgin Island, the Faroe Islands, Guinea, Tranquebar, Iceland, and Greenland.

◆   ◆   ◆

Lithuania

The Lithuanian Global Genealogical Society is at: http://www. lithuaniangenealogy.org/databases/. There are vital records for most states and Lithuanian Parishes of the Roman Catholic Diocese in America at: http:// www.lithuaniangenealogy.org/databases/churches/lt_churches-us.html. The Lithuania Genealogy Forum of Genealogy.com is at: http://genforum.genealogy. com/lithuania/.

Also check out the Lithuanian Research site at: http://www.maxpages.com/ poland/Lithuanian_Research. You can contact Chicago's Balzekas Museum of Lithuanian Culture, Immigration History & Genealogy Department, 6500 South Pulaski Road, Chicago, IL 60629. The Global Resources for Lithuania Web site is at: http://www.angelfire.com/ut/Luthuanian/index.html. The Lithuanian Global Genealogical Society at: http://www.lithuaniangenealogy. org/organizations/index.html - poland lists the address of the **Poland-Lithuanian Community, as the following:** Chairperson: Juozas Sigitas Paranseviėius, ul.Mickiewicza 23, 16-515 Punsk,woj.Suwalki, Poland.

The Web site discussion forum called *'About'* has a Lithuanian Genealogy site of article and resources at: http://genealogy.about.com/od/lithuania/. The site reports that, "The largest Lithuanian resource center outside Lithuania, the Chicago museum offers searches of major Lithuanian-American genealogy sources, as well as an on-staff genealogist of Lithuanian ancestry. Home to the Lithuanian Americal Genealogy Society."

Check out the archives of the museum. To find ancestors in Lithuania, there's a site from 'About' called How to Find Relatives in Lithuania at: http:// genealogy.about.com/gi/dynamic/offsite.htm?   zi=1/XJ&sdn=genealogy&zu= http://www.lfcc.lt/howfind.html. Some addresses recommended for inquiry include the following:

1.   **Lithuanian National Historical Archive:**
     Lietuvos valstybinis istorijos archyvas
     Gerosios Vilties g. 10

2015 Vilnius, Lithuania

Registry department of Lithuanian National Historical Archive:
Lietuvos valstybinis istorijos archyvas, Metriku skyrius
K.Kalinausko g. 21, 2000 Vilnius, LITHUANIA

2. Write a **letter of inquiry** to:
    Bureau of Addresses
    Adresu Biuras
    Vivulskio g. 4a, 2009 Vilnius, LITHUANIA

Phone numbers are included on the Web site. I've left them out in this book because phone numbers could change by the time the book went to press. So check first by writing. Contact each institution at the level of local administration, that is the municipality of each district in Lithuania that you want to search, and direct your questions to the archives department.

There's a link to Lithuanian organizations collected from a variety of countries. The site is at: http://genealogy.about.com/gi/dynamic/offsite.htm? zi=1/ XJ&sdn=genealogy&zu=http://www.lfcc.lt/howfind.html. Click on the Lithuanian Folk Center at: http://genealogy.about.com/gi/dynamic/offsite.htm? zi=1/ XJ&sdn=genealogy&zu=http://www.lfcc.lt/howfind.html. Or check out the mirrored link at the Lithuanian Global Genealogical Society at: http:// genealogy.about.com/gi/dynamic/offsite.htm? zi=1/XJ&sdn=genealogy&zu=http://www.lfcc.lt/howfind.html.

◆   ◆   ◆

Genealogy Research Archives

Estonia

Central Family Registry Office
Pikk 61
15065 Tallinn
Ph (0) 612 5164
Executive Svetlana Toots, *svetlana.toots@mail.ee*
Main specialist Piret Põldmäe
Specialist Mare Verma, *mare.verma@mail.ee*

Tallinn City family registry office
Pärnu mnt 67
10135 Tallinn
(0) 646 3364, *prksa@tallinnlv.ee*
Reception Mon-Fri 9-17

Latvia

Latvian Archives

> Central State History Archives
> Centralais Valsts vestures arhivs
> Slokas iela 16
> Riga, LV 226007
>
> Central State Archives
> Centralais Valsts vestures arhivs
> Bezdeligu iela 1
> Riga, LV 226007
>
> Central State Cine-Phono-Photo Document Archives
> Centralais Valsts Kino-Foto-Fono-Dokumentu arhivs
> Skuna iela 11
> Riga, LV 226007
>
> Lutheran Church
> Latvijas ev. lut. baznicas konsitorija
> Lacplesa iela 4-4
> Riga, LV 226010
>
> Catholic Church
> Katolu baznicas metropolijas Kurija
> M. Pils iela 2a
> Riga, LV 226047
>
> Orthodox Church
> Krievu pareizticiga baznicas parijas parvalde
> M. Pils iela 2a
> Riga, LV 226047

Published Latvian, Lithuanian, and Polish Genealogy & Related Information

Latvijas Ideja Amerika by Osvalds Akmentins. Boston, Massachusetts, USA c 1969.

Lielas Liesmas Atblazma by Margers Stepermanis. Riga 1971.

Jewish Baltic & E. European Communities: Shtetl Finder: Jewish Communities in the 19th and Early 20th Centuries in the Pale of Settlement of Russia and Poland, and in Lithuania, Latvia, Galicia, and Bukovina with Names of Residents: Heritage Books, Bowie, Maryland, USA 1989.

Latvian language Web sites:

http://www.sil.org/ethnologue/families/Indo-European.html

The Latvian alphabet

Uldis Balodis' t Web page on the Latvian language is at:
http://www.goodnet.com/~vanags/valoda.html.

Latvia, Dundaga—Church Records on Microfiche and Microfilm

Seuberlich, Erich.
Kurland: Auszug aus dem Kirchenbuch : Dondangen, 1710-1870.—|EUROPE |
Salt Lake City : Gefilmt durch The Genealogical Society of |FILM AREA |
Utah, 1992.—auf 1 Mikrofilmrolle ; 35 mm.

Mikrofilm aufgenommen von Manuskripten in der Zentralstelle für Genealogie, Leipzig. Extracts of parish registers (marriages, deaths) from the Protestant community of Dondangen, Courland, Russia; now Dundaga, Latvia. Text in German.

Heiraten 1711-1836
-------------------------------1858061
Taufen 1710-1839
item 5.
Konfirmanden 1718-1838
Tote 1712-1844

Kommunikanten 1751-1839
Vereidigungen 1819-1870

◆   ◆   ◆

Scandinavia

Denmark

You'll find excellent computerized genealogy resources for Denmark. For starters, try the Web site at: http://www.geocities.com/aitkenms/denmark.html, and click on the link titled Genealogy Resources on the Internet at: http://www-personal.umich.edu/~cgaunt/dk.html. You'll find more resources for Danish-American genealogy sources at Portals to the World, Resources Selected by the Library of Congress, titled Genealogy: Denmark at: http://www.loc.gov/rr/international/corc.oclc.org/WebZ/XPathfinderQuery7244.html.

For emigration records, click on Danelink.com (linking Danes everywhere) at: http://www.danelink.com/locations/intgenealogy.html.

Danish Emigration Archives site is in English and is at: http://www.emiarch.dk/home.php3. Click on the link to bring up the *Dansk Demografisk Database* and enter the name you wish to research. The Danish Archives (in Danish) site comes up first. So you need to click on the English flag icon at the top right hand corner to bring up the Web site in English. The English language site is at: http://ddd.sa.dk/ddd_en.htm. The Danish language site is at: http://ddd.sa.dk/. Also click on the addresses button. For further information, write to the: **The Danish Emigration Archives,** Arkivstræde 1, P.O. BOX 1731, 9100 Aalborg, Denmark.

Norway

The Velkommen to Norway Genealogy site is at: http://www.rootsweb.com/~wgnorway/index2.htm. There are links to everything from genealogy resources to links to searching the white or yellow pages of the phone books of Norway at the link at: http://www.gulesider.no/gsi/whiteSearchFront.do?spraak=3 (White pages) or the Yellow Pages at: http://www.gulesider.no/gsi/index.do?spraak=3

The Web site (in English) for maps showing boundaries for parishes is at: http://digitalarkivet.uib.no/norkart/index-eng.htm. The links for Norwegian sources online are well-organized. You can find almost all your resources com-

piled as links on one site. The Digital Archives database (*Arkivverket Digitalarkivet*) for census and parish information is in English. Click on the *Arkivverket Digitalarkivet* at: http://digitalarkivet.uib.
no/cgi-win/WebFront.exe?slag=vis&tekst=meldingar&spraak=e.

What's great about this Norwegian genealogy research site is that almost everything you want to begin your search is at this site's many links. Try the Norwegian farm names site (in English) called *Oluf Rhygh* at: http://www.
dokpro.uio.no/rygh_ng/rygh_form.html. Search for farm names as they were used during the years past.

Norwegian genealogy research may have already been done with results published results in a book. In Norway such a book is called a 'bygdebok'. (In this context 'bygd' means 'parish'). Check out the Bydgebok site (in English) at: http://www.nndata.no/home/jborgos/bygdeen.htm. Also look at land records information on finding resources on the Norwegian Land Records site at: http://www.rootsweb.com/~wgnorway/NorLinks8.htm. It includes census, church books, emigrants, farms information, and land information in Norwegian, a tax and land records link, and more sites and links in English.

◆   ◆   ◆

Iceland

The site for Emigration from Iceland to North America is at: http://www.
simnet.is/halfdanh/vestur.htm. Settlers generally went to Alberta, Manitoba, Saskatchewan, in Canada, and in the USA to Minnesota, North Dakota, Utah, Washington, and Wisconsin. The site also published as newsletter. Genealogy.com's Iceland Forum is at: http://genforum.genealogy.com/iceland/. Genealogy in Iceland has excellent documentation with some surnames recorded in Icelandic sources dating from 1560.

Iceland Genealogy Links are at: http://iceland.vefur.is/Education/Genealogy/.
Also click on the Iceland surnames site (Virtually Virtual Iceland) at: http://
www.simnet.is/gardarj/family.htm. More genealogy links for Iceland is at the Genealogy site at: http://www.samkoma.com/cgi/links.pl.cgi?061. Also try the Emigration from Iceland to North America map site at: http://www.isholf.is/
halfdanh/islmap.htm. According to the site, "As each Icelander's name is an individual property, the names do not change in marriage." Women keep their names.

For example, according to the Web site sample names explanation, Sveinbjörg Sigurðardóttir is a woman. Her name ends in 'dóttir.' That means and sounds like the word 'daughter.' She is married to Þórður Hannesson. Note that their daughter, Halldóra

Þórðardóttir has taken as her surname the first name of her father, which is Þórður and adds the word dóttir to the ending. That becomes her surname that she will carry throughout her life and will not change when she marries.

A man takes his father's first name and adds 'sson' to the ending. For example, Haraldur Sveinsson has a son named Jóhann Már Haraldsson. Note that the son has taken as his surname his father's first name, Haraldur and shortened it to Harald and then added 'sson.' He's Harald's son.

Also, according to the Icelandic surnames Web site, when Jóhann Már Haraldsson marries Halldóra Þórðardóttir, their son could be named Gestur Þór Jóhannsson, and their daughter could be named Bára Sif Jóhannsdóttir. Note their son's middle name is taken from the wife's father's first name. Their daughter's last name, Jóhannsdóttir is taken from her father's surname with the 'dóttir' ending added to Jóhanns, whereas her brother's surname is Jóhannsson (that is, 'Jóhanns' with 'son' added.) Because Icelandic lettering is different, if an Icelander moves to the USA or Canada, (or any English-speaking country), English typefonts may change spelling, but frequently not pronunciation.

4

Genealogy in the Balkans, Eastern Europe & the Middle East

Have any of your ancestors ever lived under the former Ottoman Empire? The Ottoman Empire lasted from 1300 until 1922. In 1924 Kemal Ataturk abolished the Muslim caliphate and founded the Republic of Turkey. So regardless of the language spoken by your ancestors—Slavic, Arabic, Greek, Judezmo, Uralic, Yiddish, Romanian, or Turkish, the Ottoman Empire controlled and kept careful census records in Turkish using Arabic script in the following countries of Europe and the Middle East known today, but not necessarily before 1924 as the following names:

Hungary, Yugoslavia, Croatia, Bosnia, Albania, Macedonia, Greece, Romania, Moldova, Bulgaria, southern Ukraine, Turkey, Georgia, Armenia, Iraq, Kuwait, Cyprus, Syria, Lebanon, Israel/Palestine, Jordan, Eastern and Western Saudi Arabia, Oman, Bahrain, eastern Yemen, Egypt, northern Libya, Tunisia, and northern Algeria.

In addition, more recent records in Arabic or in the language of the country emphasized are kept in the national archives and in the courts dealing with property-related issues, assets left behind, divorce decrees, and other legal documents. Often when a population is forced out, the individual country, such as present-day Egypt, may then determine that assets, property, and religious items taken away or left behind such as Judaica, Hellenica, and Armenica are declared antiquities of that country that cannot be removed.

You can approach genealogy by running a teen genealogy camp for foreign travel. If you get enough tourists, you can go free and emphasize genealogy research. Another approach is to collect memorabilia from your ethnic group such as Hellenica, Judaica, Armenica, Arabica, and other objects. Every object you collect in genealogy as far as records or actual objects opens a door. As you step over the threshold, you can see time and place in the context of that culture.

◆   ◆   ◆

Middle Eastern & East European

Genealogy opens portals to the artistic, cultural, religious, social, historical, and economic environment in which a particular item was designed and brought forth, from people to their icons. Genealogy is cultural geography as well as a history and ethnography of human genes.

Look at ethnic objects along with the census or other genealogy records. There are so many locations to cover the settlement of your peoples, the human race. Genealogy allows you to view a juxtaposition of demography with memorabilia and ethnic or religious items. Learn how to research your own group and show others about the life of the people you choose to study, their history and design.

That's why running a teen (or other age group) genealogy camp is fun, especially in researching the former Ottoman Empire—or any other location that you want to emphasize, perhaps your own ethnic history.

How do you start? The Family History Library (Salt Lake City, UT) has a catalog that can give you rewarding and rich research ideas. So if it's the former Ottoman Empire you want to emphasize, or how the world of antiquity blends into your relatively modern genealogy, first check the Family History Library catalog (Salt Lake City, UT) for books, microfilms, civil registration, localities and jurisdictions.

Then search the Ottoman Census and Population Registers by country named in Turkish the Nüfus Defter. Check the online library catalog at Bogaziçi University (a.k.a. the University of the Bosphorus). See http://www.geog.port.ac.uk/hist-bound/country_rep/ottoman.htm. Also check out the flyer: http://www.hanover.edu/haq_center/Bogazici-Flyer.html

Records are found in the Ottoman Census archives in Turkey pertaining to tax collection during the Ottoman rule. Moslems weren't taxed. Before 1881, each census focused on tabulating male names to find Moslem men to conscript into the military service and non-Moslem men to pay personal tax. Search records according to the religion and ethnic group. Start your search with the list of countries under the Ottomans and pick your ancestor's homeland.

Egypt was under the former Ottoman Empire. Therefore, if you are a Jew from Egypt (regardless of whether your family members are Ashkenazim,

Sepharadim, or Mizrahi), check out The Historical Society Of Jews From Egypt. Their Web site is at: http://hsje.org/. This site is designed to gather, and provide historical and current information on the Jews From Egypt, one of the most ancient established societies in the world."

According to their Web site, "We will attempt to cover the period from Joseph Saadia el Fayoumi (Saadia Gaon) to the present day." The Web site notes that, "This organization shall be known as Historical Society of Jews from Egypt, and not of Egypt or of Egyptian Jews, but from Egypt for the purpose will be to include all our co-religionists whose lineage have sojourned in the Jewish Communities of Egypt."

Contact them if you had relatives who lived in the Jewish communities of Egypt. Some Romanian and Greek Jews also lived in the Jewish communities of Egypt and some Ashkenazim also. According to their Web site, "The aims of this society are to preserve, maintain, coordinate the implementation, and to convey our rich heritage to our children and grand children's, using all educational means at our disposal to bring into being the necessary foundations."

Referring to Romania and in particular, Bessarabia, some Romanian Jews migrated to Palestine in the Ottoman era. This migration included Ashkenazim and Sephardim. Numerous Sephardim and Mizrahi had migrated to Palestine in earlier times and a smaller number of Ashkenazim. Your genealogy source here could be to consult a Jewish genealogy journal such as Avotaynu at: http://www.avotaynu.com.

Research the Jews of Egypt Web site at: http://www.us-israel.org/jsource/anti-semitism/egjews.html, which notes: "In 1979, the Egyptian Jewish community became the first in the Arab world to establish official contact with Israel. Israel now has an embassy in Cairo and a consulate general in Alexandria. At present, the few remaining Jews are free to practice Judaism without any restrictions or harassment. Shaar Hashamayim is the only functioning synagogue in Cairo. Of the many synagogues in Alexandria only the Eliahu Hanabi is open for worship.[4]." The source of this information on their Web site is listed as Jewish Communities of the World.

According to researcher, Kahlile Mehr, "For searching the Ottoman period in most countries under the former Ottoman Empire, the researcher would have to read Turkish in Arabic script. The Family History library was able to film some Christian church records in Israel during the 1980s. But for most of the populace, the commonly known genealogical sources of the West simply do not exist. The best known source is the Nufus registers."

All the articles and information on Bulgaria, Macedonia, and Croatia written by former staff writer for the Family History Library, Salt Lake City, UT, Khalile Mehr, are copyrighted by The Family History Library.

"The Family History Library filmed the Nufus registers in the Israeli State Archives for Israel, parts of Jordan and Egypt. A description of these can be found in the catalog at www.familysearch.org.

"If you're searching various ethnic groups in Bessarabia, it was not part of Romania except during the period between World War I and II. It was historically part of the Ottoman and then the Russian Empire. Today, it is Moldova."

There was a time in the late 18th century and early 19th century when Bessarabia fell out of the Ottoman Empire and became under the rule of the Russians. At that time a large immigration of German Christians and German Jews as well as Jews from Poland, Ukraine, Belarus, and surrounding areas flocked to Bessarabia. So you have a community of Protestant Germans in Bessarabia along with German and Polish Jews. The immigration took place as soon as Bessarabia fell into Russian hands and out of Ottoman hands for that period of time.

You can trace names that show up in Poland such as Herkowicz to Romanian, where the spelling changes to Herkowitz and later to the Romanian spelling, Herkovici, in some cases. Countries change names. Bessarabia, once a place with its own name rather than a province in a country, then becomes an area within a country, and finally today, falling in the borders of Moldova and Romania.

5

Translating Names

Don't skip generations. Each generation is a vital link in countries where thousands have the same name. Check out the Middle EastGenWeb Project at: http://www.rootsweb.com/~mdeastgw/index.html.

Some religious names are used by Moslems and Christians. Christian European names are translated into Arabic in Arabic-speaking countries. For example, in Lebanon, Peter becomes Boutros and George becomes Girgis or Abdul Messikh, meaning servant of the Messiah (Christ). Shammout (strong), Deeb (wolf), or Dib (bear). Nissim (miracles) is used by Jewish Levantines, and Adam is used by Jewish, Christian, and Moslem families.

Women had the choice of taking their husband's surnames or keeping their maiden names. Neutral names, used by Moslems, Jews, and Christians such as Ibrahim (Abraham) or Yusef (Joseph) came from the Old Testament. In Lebanon, Christians often used neutral names such as Tewfik (fortunate).

Arabic-speaking and Turkic-speaking countries didn't use surnames until after the end of the Ottoman Empire. Then in Lebanon and Syria many Christians took as their surnames European or Biblical first male names such as the Arabic versions of George, Jacob, Thomas, and Peter which were in Arabic: Girgis, Yacoub, Toumas, and Boutros. Others took popular surnames describing their occupations such as Haddad meaning 'smith.'

After 1928 in Turkey, but not in any of the other Middle Eastern nations, a modified Latin alphabet replaced Arabic script. Four years later (1932) the Turkish Linguistic Society simplified the language to unify the people. Surnames were required in 1934 and, old titles indicating professions and classes were dropped. (See "Turkey" Web site at: http://www.kusadasitravel.com/turkey.html.)

In Middle Eastern countries under the former Ottoman Empire, such as Lebanon/Syria, each child was given a first name but most people in the Middle East had no surname until 1932. Also the father's given name was given as a middle name such as Yusef Girgis, meaning Yusef (Joseph), son of George. It came in handy in the days before surnames were required. Now it's used as a middle name.

Many Syrian and Lebanese families, particularly Christians, after 1932 took similar names such as Peter Jacobs or George Thomas. The name 'Thomas' in Lebanon is spelled in translation as either Touma or Toumas. Many Assyrian males in Northern Iraq took the popular name Sargon, an ancient king.

When surnames in Lebanon became a requirement, you have very popular names such as Peter George Khoury in America being Boutros Girgis Khouri in Lebanon or Syria when translated into Arabic. In the Levant, daughters have a first name and their father's given name meaning "daughter of Yusef" "'bint' Yusef" where bint and binti means 'daughter.' Outside the home, females would be called with the proper respect "daughter of Yusef or "Bint Yusef." Inside the home to immediate family, a female would be known by her first name, which could be Ayah. She would be registered as Ayah Yusef. She'd be known by a first name, Ayah and a surname, Yusef. Translated into English at Ellis Island, it could have become Aya Joseph.

When surnames became a requirement, many included professions or place names, especially Halaby (from Aleppo) or Antaky (from Antioch). The largest Lebanese community in America is in Dearborn, Michigan.

In Lebanon, most names were Christian prior to 1870, and the Christian names could also be European, especially Greek names like Petros (Peter) which later becomes Boutros in Arabic. If you're searching Assyrians, check out the Assyrian Nation Communities Web site at: http://www.assyriannation.com/communities/index.php.

6

Researching Assyrian Presbyterian Genealogy Records

According to the Public Services and Outreach division of the Presbyterian Historical Society, while the Presbyterian Church sent missionaries to the Middle East, materials at the Presbyterian Historical Society document their activities there and do not contain any information about individuals from the Middle East who immigrated to the United States. To get an idea of the types of materials at the Presbyterian Historical Society useful for genealogists, review the following sections of their website at: http://www.history.pcusa.org/famhist/ or http://www.history.pcusa.org/collect/.

This second page also provides links to their on-line finding aids, http://www.history.pcusa.org/finding/index.html, and catalog, CALVIN, http://www.history.pcusa.org/dbtw-wpd/WebOPACmenu.htm.

Search each to see what they might have for your area of interest.

Records of individual congregations are the main resource for family history research at the society. There are no centralized denominational registers of church memberships, baptisms, or marriages; nor is there a comprehensive index to the thousands of family names included in the records in our holdings.

To start a search, it is essential to know both the location (city and state) and the full and correct name of the congregation associated with the individual you are researching. They do not have lists of churches by township, city, or county, or street name cross indexes.

Research genealogy records of members of the Assyrian Presbyterian Church in the US or in Iraq and Iran. Search Assyrian colonies in various US cities for genealogy records related to the Presbyterian Church.

If you are searching Assyrian records, and your family belonged to the Presbyterian Church, check out the Presbyterian Church Historical Society at: http://history.pcusa.org/finding/phs 379.xml - scopecontent where you can find book titles and/or records such as the Assyrian and National Church History, volumes 1 and 2. Look up Isaac B. Moorhatch (1880–) Papers, 1938, Finding Aid to Record Group 379, © Presbyterian Historical Society , Philadelphia, PA 19147.

From the early 20th century, many Assyrians immigrating to the US joined the Presbyterian church. This is due to the missionaries in Persia and Iraq in the early 20th century. For example, In 1910 Isaac Moorhatch established the Assyrian Presbyterian Church of Gary, Indiana.

In 1923 he arrived in Philadelphia, where the Assyrian colony asked him to serve as their pastor. After ordination, he took charge of the Persian/Assyrian Presbyterian Mission. He served this mission until retirement in 1950.

So your first step is to find out where the Assyrian colonies were in the US. Was one of your relatives a missionary in a country then under the former Ottoman Empire?

Isaac Moorhatch was born in Urumia, Persia, the son of Presbyterian missionaries. He grew up in Iran and attended the Presbyterian college in Urumia. In 1897 he began working as an evangelical and educational missionary for the Board of Foreign Missions (PCUSA).

So search the Presbyterian colleges in various Middle Eastern countries when they were under the Ottoman Empire. In 1909 Moorhatch arrived in the United States with the intention of entering a Presbyterian seminary and returning to work among the Persian Moslems after graduation. In the end he enrolled in the Baptist Theological Seminary in Kansas City, KS in 1912.

According to the Web site of the Presbyterian Church History records at: http://history.pcusa.org/finding/phs 379.xml - scopecontent, "In 1910 Moorhatch established the Assyrian Presbyterian Church of Gary, IN. In 1923 he arrived in Philadelphia, where the Assyrian colony asked him to serve as their pastor. After ordination, he took charge of the Persian/Assyrian Presbyterian Mission. He served this mission until retirement in 1950."

If you research the collection of Presbyterian Church History records, you can read Moorhatch's two-volume manuscript work titled: Assyrian and National Church History: History of Iran: Rise of Islam. The work is written in Aramaic. Each volume includes a table of contents. So if you come from an Assyrian family or any other ethnic group that is able to read Aramaic, such as numerous Jews and a few groups in Syria, you can read or even translate the Aramaic to English.

If you're searching the collection of Presbyterian Church history, records less than 50 years old are restricted. Contact the archivist. The collection was processed in 1993. Your reference point would be: Finding Aid to Record Group 379, Box 1 Folder 1. Assyrian and National Church History, volumes 1 and 2. Folder 2-3.

After 1870, in Lebanon and Syria names in Christian families became Arabic rather than European due to increasing pressure by the Ottoman Empire on Christians to use Arabic instead of Greek names. After the demise of the Ottoman Empire at the close of World War I, Hellenistic names such as Kostaki (Constantine) became popular in Beirut.

The distinctly Christian Lebanese surnames Khoury (priest) or Kourban sprang up again when Lebanon became a French protectorate. Neutral, Greek, and Old Testament names also return. You see many French first names in Christian families between 1914 and 1950.

After the 1950s, Christian and French first names dwindle, and Arabic names appear. If your ancestors were Moslem, instead of a surname prior to 1932, you were known as "son of" (Ibn) as in Ibn Omar, for a male, and for a married woman with children called, "mother of" (om) as in Om Kolthum, (mother of Kolthum).

You'd be called mother of your first born son, (Om___Name of first born son) (Om Ahmed). If you had no sons, you'd be called mother of your first born daughter (Om Rania) (Om___Name of first born daughter). Single women often were called "daughter of" as in Bint Ahmed (daughter of Ahmed).

Arabic women's first names were plentiful, popular, and used at mainly at home. Examples include Samara, Zobaida, Rayana, Rania, Anissa, Dayala, Azma, Aya, or Salwa. Children had first names.

If your ancestors were Armenian living in the Levant you might have the name Ter or Der before a surname designating descent from an Armenian Apostolic priest followed by a name ending in ian or yan meaning "son of" such as Manvelian or a place name such as Halebian (from Aleppo) when translated into English. If you're Armenian searching Turkish census records, the pre-1920 border of Armenian habitation usually was south of Lake Van, near Mush (in Armenia), and Bairt and Dersim (in Turkey). Each religion had a different status under the former Ottoman Empire—Moslems first class and conscripted into the military; all other religions, not conscripted, but taxed.

Narrow the Categories

Categorize the religion—not only Catholic, but Melkite Catholic or Maronite Catholic. Antiochian Syrian Orthodox or Roman Catholic? Byzantine Catholic (Byzantic) or Greek Orthodox? Lebanese immigrant to Cairo, Egypt and Coptic Orthodox? Moslem? Jewish? Druze? Armenian Apostolic? Sephardim? Ashkenazim? Protestant? Greek Orthodox? Greek Catholic? Bulgarian or Romanian Orthodox? Serbian? Croatian?

Color-code cards or files noting the date, religion, ethnic group, and town. When did the immigrant arrive in the US from a Middle Eastern country? Was it before or after the end of the former Ottoman Empire? For example, Antioch, now in Turkey used to be in Syria before World War II. And before 1918, Syria and Lebanon was one province under the Ottoman Empire. So use old and new maps to see what country to emphasize at which dates.

National Archives in the Country of Origin

Maps of old neighborhoods show locations of houses. Start with the national archives in the country of origin. For Syria that would be the Syrian National Archives in Damascus, Aleppo, Homs, or Hama where court records are archived for the years 1517 to 1919. If the relatives lived before the end of the Ottoman Empire or before World War I, also search the census records of the former Ottoman Empire in Turkey rather than the archives in the country of origin that may not have existed before the end of the Ottoman Empire.

Records stand alone rather than in groups of catalogs. Check separate Jewish genealogy sources and synagogue documents for the Jewish records of Mizrahi and Sephardim, such as marriage ketubim, bar mitzvah records, births, deaths, rabbinical documents such as a 'Get' for a divorce or a pedigree called a Yiccus.

If you're checking Sephardic (Jewish) records of the former Ottoman Empire, there's an excellent article on Jewish genealogy published in Los Muestros magazine, a publication of Sephardic and Middle Eastern Jewish genealogy titled Resources for Sephardic Genealogy at: http://www.sefarad.org/publication/lm/010/cardoza.html. Also see the magazine, Los Muestros at: http://www.sefarad.org/publication/lm/010/som10.html for archived Sephardic genealogy articles.

Another excellent publication of Jewish genealogy, Avotaynu maintains a Web site at: http://www.avotaynu.com/. If you're looking for Jewish records in the Middle East, also check the Sephardic associations, for example, Sephardim.com at http://www.sephardim.com/. Look for memorabilia, diaries, house keys, and maps of neighborhoods.

For Sephardic genealogy in the former Ottoman Empire, contact the Foundation for the Advancement of Sephardic Studies and Culture Web site at: http://www.sephardicstudies.org/cal2.html to learn how to interpret calendars and how to read birth certificates. You'll learn how to decipher the handwritten entries using Arabic script. Regardless of the religion of the individual, this site shows you how to read the certificates written with certain types of scripts.

The site also shows the dialects spoken in the various areas of the Ottoman Empire. Also there is information on how to read the Arabic script but Turkish language writing on gravestones, especially in Turkish cemeteries. The site shows you how to read the alphabet encountered in genealogical research in the former Ottoman Empire. Emphasis is on interpreting Sephardic birth certificates.

◆   ◆   ◆

How to Translate and Locate without Surnames

What's in the census? Ottoman census records for the period 1831-1872 were compilations of male names and addresses for fiscal and military purposes. Instead of population counts, the Ottoman records contain the name of the head of household, male family members, ages, occupation, and property.

You won't find surnames in old records. Most Middle Eastern countries didn't require surnames until after the fall of the Ottoman Empire. If you're searching Middle Eastern genealogy before 1924, begin by familiarizing yourself with the record keeping and social history of the Ottoman Empire.

Turkish language written in Arabic script is the key to searching genealogy records in European and Middle Eastern areas formerly ruled by the Ottomans. You'll need an Arabic-English dictionary or instruction guide that at least gives you the basic Arabic script alphabet.

You'll also need the same type of phrase book with alphabet translation for modern Turkish written using Latin letters. You can put the both together to figure out phrases.

Find in your town a graduate student or teacher from abroad who reads Arabic script and modern Turkish. Hire the student or teacher to copy the records you want when overseas. Barter services. Or contact the Middle East history and area studies, archaeology, or languages departments of numerous colleges.

Who teaches courses in both Turkish and Arabic? Contact private language schools such as Language School International, Inc. at: http://www. languageschoolsguide.com/listingsp3.cfm/listing/4092.

What Religious Group Will You Search?

Social history is the key to genealogy. Records that existed under the Ottoman Empire listed names of the head of household and parents, residence, dates and places of birth and baptism, marriage, death and burial. Records also have entries for ages for marriage and death.

Baptisms included names of the godparents. Deaths sometimes included the cause of death. For Christians, entries sometimes identified residence for those not of the parish. Check the state archives in the country of your ancestors and also in Turkey. Then check the court, notary, and property records.

Contact the parish churches to look at parish registers and synagogues to look at the Jewish registers. If you're checking Bulgaria, Macedonia, or Greece, numerous pre-1872 registers are located in Greece. "The Bulgarian Orthodox Church was subordinate to the Patriarchate in Greece before 1872," notes researcher, Khalile Mehr. Find out whether a country had its state church subordinate to another country's church with records archived in a different language.

Check Business, School Alumni, Medical, Military, Marriage, and Property Records

Research wills and marriage records in order to track down property records. Search medical and dental records, hospitals, orphanages, prisons, asylums, midwives' records, marriage certificates, business licenses, work permits, migration papers, passports, military pensions, notaries, sales records of homes or businesses, or any other court, military, or official transaction that might have occurred.

Other sites: For the Balkans, look at the Center for Democracy and Reconciliation in Southeast Europe's Web site at: http://www.cdsee.org/teaching_packs_belgrade_bio.html.

Search the 'Annual' Census and the Population Registers

Check recorded births and deaths in the first Ottoman census of 1831. Each census focused on tabulating male names to find Moslem men to conscript into the military service known as "The Army." Before 1881, the annual census registered only the male population. Search the names of committee members.

Committees were set up each year to register the males in order to keep tabs on migrations in and out of each district. When the census wasn't taken, the Population Register of Moslem males kept careful records of migrations.

Find out in which local district or 'kaza' your ancestor lived. Ottomans called their annual census the sicil-i nüfus after 1881 or the nüfus between 1831-1850. You can research the Ottoman Census and Population Registers named in Turkish the Nüfus Defter. Ottoman population demographics and statistics adjusted to satisfy tax desires, since the non-Moslem population was taxed but not conscripted into military service.

The annual census didn't cover every year. Check the Ottoman census for the years1881-1883, and 1903-1906. Family historians can search each census as well as separate registers to view supplemental registration of births, marriages, divorces, and deaths.

After 1881, the census takers counted all individuals (not only Moslem males) in the census and in the population registers. Sometimes people who thought all genealogy records were destroyed in fires in their native country are surprised to learn that census records may be archived far away in Turkey. If you need text or a Web site translated into numerous languages, check out the Systran Web site at: http://www.systranbox.com/systran/box. You can translate free an entire Web site or 150 words of text.

7

Armenian Genealogy

Check out these resources on the Web: The Armenian Research List is an on-line posting of Armenian genealogy and family history questions and answers at: http://feefhs.org/am/frg-amgs.html. Go to the Armenia Genealogy Forum. Check out this small group of dedicated Armenian-Americans that are actively engaged in seeking out Armenian records for preservation through microfilming and in assisting the formation of the first Armenian Family History Center (in-country) at Yeravan. If you want to research resources about Jews in medieval Armenia, check out the Web site at: http://www.khazaria.com/armenia/armenian-jews.html.

Then go to the Armenian Research List at: http://feefhs.org/am/amrl.html. The Armenian Research List is an on-line posting of Armenian genealogy and family history questions and answers. If you have Armenian ancestry, you are encouraged to submit your own summary genealogy and your questions. Go to the Armenian surnames as well as given male and female names at: http://feefhs.org/am/frg-amgs.html.

Search the Armenian Apostolic Church Parish Records. Then click on the online Armenia Genealogy Forum at: http://genforum.genealogy.com/armenia/. You can also search Armenian genealogy resources at http://www. distantcousin.com. Check out genforum.genealogy.com/Armenia/ and also http://www.distantcousin.com/Links/Ethnic/Armenia/.

An Armenian genealogy Web site also is at: http:// www.geocities.com/Paris/ Palais/2230/index2.html. Search Armenian genealogy at: genealogy. freewebsitehosting.com/ links/armeniangenealogy. And links to Armenian gene-alogy resources Web sites are at: www.rootsweb.com/~armwgw/links.html. Then go to the Genealogy Register: Armenia at: http://genealogyregister.com/Asia/Armenia/. You'll find there these wonderful links to resources for searching Armenian genealogy such as the following: Family trees, the Armenia Genealogy Forum. It's a list of postings where Armenians having lost their relatives during the deportations and the genocide search members of their families and their descendants. The site features also a chat room.

The Armenia Research List contains postings by individuals who search information about lost family members during the genocide. There is also an archive. Click on Armeniagenweb at: http://www.rootsweb.com/~armwgw/. It has links to Armenian mailing lists and surname pages. You'll also find at the Armenian Genealogical Society. an Armenian research list and lists of Armenian names and surnames.

For passenger lists of ships transporting immigrations, check out the Armenian Genealogical Web Page . It also has a bibliography, and presents the book of a genealogist, cemetery data, maps, genocide survivor stories, information about Armenian legionnaires during World War I.

The Distant Cousins: Armenian Genealogy Resources Features an Armenian surname search engine, a list of web resources and mailing lists, links for Armenian family historians including books and personal homepages. You can also read the Family Questionnaire. It's provided by the Armenian Historical Association of Rhode Island. The questionnaire is intended for determining the contribution of Armenians to the history of Rhode Island.

You need various personal and family data to answer the questionnaire. There's also a link to a genealogist specializing in Armenian research. All these informational links are at the Genealogy Register at: http://genealogyregister. com/Asia/Armenia/. There are surname lists and a home page.

Check it out. I highly rate and recommend this Web site for Armenian genealogy resources research. Click on the link to the Armenia Genealogy Forum at: http://genealogyregister.com/Asia/Armenia/. It has a list of postings where relatives may search for the descendants of lost and deported family members' names. If you're Armenian, also check out the Turkish Armenian Reconciliation Commission (TARC) at: http://www.asbarez.com/TARC/Tarc.html.

◆   ◆   ◆

Web Resources and Books on Former Ottoman Empire Genealogy Web Sites

Albanian Research List: http://feefhs.org/al/alrl.html

Armenian Genealogical Society: http://feefhs.org/am/frg-amgs.html

Egyptian Genealogy: http://www.daddezio.com/egypgen.html

Egyptian Genealogy—Kindred Trails (tm): http://www.kindredtrails.com/egypt.html

Egyptian Royal Genealogy: http://www.geocities.com/christopherjbennett/

Historical Society of Jews from Egypt: http://www.hsje.org/homepage.htm

Iranian: Persian Watch Center: Iranian-American AntiDiscrimination Council http://www.antidiscrimination.org/

The Iranian: http://www.iranian.com/Features/2002/December/LA2/index.html

Iran: Payvand's Iran News: http://www.payvand.com/news/00/aug/1054.html

Also see: Iranian American Jewish Federation and also the Council of Iranian American Jewish Organizations: P.O.BOX 3074, Beverly Hills, CA. 90212. See news article at Payvand's Iran News at: http://www.payvand.com/news/00/feb/1014.html

Excellent Genealogy and Related Books on Iran: Also see: http://payvand.com/books/

Another Sea, Another Shore: Stories of Iranian Migration
by Shouleh Vatanabadi, et all (2003)

Funny in Farsi: A Memoir of Growing Up Iranian in America
by Firoozeh Dumas (2003)

Wedding Song: Memoirs of an Iranian Jewish Woman
by Farideh Goldin (2003)

Exiled Memories: Stories of the Iranian Diaspora
by Zohreh Sullivan (2001)

Journey from the Land of No : A Girlhood Caught in Revolutionary Iran
by Roya Hakakian (2004)

Inside Iran: Women's Lives
by Jane Mary Howard (2002)

The National Iranian American Council: www.niacouncil.org

Jewish Genealogy: http://www.jewishgen.org/infofiles/

Lebanon Genealogy: http://genforum.genealogy.com/lebanon

http://www.mit.edu:8001/activities/lebanon/map.html

Lebanese Descendants of the Bourjaily Family (Abou R'Jaily):
http://www.abourjeily.com/Family/index.htm

Descendants of Atallah Abou Rjeily, born about 1712

Lebanese Club of New York City:

http://nyc.lebaneseclub.org/

http://www.rootsweb.com/~lbnwgw/lebclubnyc/index.htm

Lebanese Genealogy: http://www.rootsweb.com/~lbnwgw/

Middle East Genealogy: http://www.rootsweb.com/~mdeastgw/index.html

Middle East Genealogy by country: http://www.rootsweb.com/~mdeastgw/
index.html - country

Polish Genealogical Society of America: http://feefhs.org/pol/frg-pgsa.html

Sephardim.com: http://www.sephardim.com/

Syrian and Lebanese Genealogy: http://www.genealogytoday.com/family/
syrian/

Syria Genealogy: http://www.rootsweb.com/~syrwgw/

Syrian/Lebanese/Jewish/Farhi Genealogy Site (Flowers of the Orient):

http://www.farhi.org

Turkish Genealogy Discussion Group: http://www.turkey.com/forums/forumdisplay.php3?forumid=18

Turkish Telephone Directories Information: Türk Telekomünikasyon (Telecommunication) http://ttrehber.gov.tr/rehber_webtech/index.asp

Croatia Genealogy Cross Index: http://feefhs.org/cro/indexcro.html

Eastern Europe: http://www.cyndislist.com/easteuro.htm

Eastern European Genealogical Society, Inc.: http://feefhs.org/ca/frg-eegs.html

Eastern Europe Index: http://feefhs.org/ethnic.html

India Royalty: http://freepages.genealogy.rootsweb.com/~royalty/india/persons.html

Romanian American Heritage Center: http://feefhs.org/ro/frg-rahc.html

Slavs, South: Cultural Society: http://feefhs.org/frg-csss.html

Ukrainian Genealogical and Historical Society of Canada: http://feefhs.org/ca/frgughsc.html

Rom (Gypsies): http://www.cyndislist.com/peoples.htm - Gypsies

See: McGowan, Bruce William, 1933- Defter-i mufassal-i liva-i Sirem : an Ottoman revenue survey dating from the reign of Selim II./ Bruce William McGowan.

Ann Arbor, Mich.: University Microfilms, 1967.

See: Bogaziçi University Library Web sites:

http://seyhan.library.boun.edu.tr/search/wN{232}ufus+Defter/wN{232}ufus+Defter/1,29,29,B/frameset&FF=wN{232}ufus+Defter&9,9,

or http://seyhan.library.boun.edu.tr/search/dTaxation+—+Turkey./dtaxation+turkey/-5,-1,0,B/exact&FF=dtaxation+turkey&1,57,

◆   ◆   ◆

Jurisdictions and Localities in Bulgaria:

Michev N. and P. Koledarov. *Rechnik na selishchata i selishchnite imena v Bulgariia, 1878-1987* (Dictionary of villages and village names in Bulgaria, 1878-1987), Sofia: Nauka i izkustvo, 1989 (FHL book 949.77 E5m).

8

Greek Genealogy

Greek Genealogy Web sites offer links to information on videos, publications, and rich oral history. Everybody becomes Greek for a day at Greek music and food festivals. At one Greek genealogy Web site at: http://www.daddezio.com/catalog/grkndx20.html, you'll learn that name days instead of birthdays are celebrated in Greece according to "fairly rigid conventions."

The Internet has numerous Greek genealogy Web sites, some helping to reunite numerous adoptees with their original families through genealogy research. To start your Greek genealogy search, I highly recommend the book titled, A History of the Greeks in the Americas 1453-1938. You can find it online at Amazon.com at the Web site: http://www.amazon.com/exec/obidos/ASIN/1882792157/. You'll find an excellent publication on Greek genealogy titled: Greek Genealogy Publications by Lica H. Catsakis at the Web site: http://www.feefhs.org/misc/pub-lhc.html.

Also I highly recommend these books on Greek genealogy:

The Greeks in America
http://www.amazon.com/exec/obidos/ASIN/0822510103/

The Family in Greek History
http://www.amazon.com/exec/obidos/ASIN/0674292707/

Check out these Greek genealogy Web sites:

goGreece.com: Genealogy
http://gogreece.com/society_culture/genealogy.html

Hellenes-Diaspora Greek Genealogy
http://www.geocities.com/SouthBeach/Cove/4537/Main1.html

- Begin your genealogy search with maps of your ancestor's town, city, and neighborhood. For example, you'll find an excellent source with Greek Genealogy Research, 2nd Edition (1993), 82 pages, with assistance from Dan Schlyter, and Greek Gazetteer, Volume 1 (1997), 120 pages, by Lica Catsakis.

It's easier to find information on searching Greek genealogy than in some of the other countries of Eastern Europe and the Middle East that formerly were under the Ottoman Empire, except where fire destroyed records as it did in parts of Crete. At the Web site titled "Greece.com Society and Culture" at http://gogreece.com/society_culture/genealogy.html, you'll find "an extensive collection of links to web sites relevant to genealogical research, as well as, mailing lists, and articles relevant to Greek culture."

What's great about this Web site is that contains a description and list of the Greek genealogy sites. Also try the message board at: GreekFamilies.com at: http://www.greekfamilies.com/pages/138257/index.htm. Look at the Hellenic Genealogy Web site at: http://www.geocities.com/SouthBeach/Cove/4537/. Also, you'll find excellent Web sites on Greek (Hellenic) genealogy at Dimitri's Surname Database at: http://www.dimitri.8m.com/surnames.html.

You can search many Greek surnames there and their ancestral origins. For example, the Greek surname, Fotiadis comes from Thessalonikis in Macedonia. So to look up the origins, note that the variant spellings of Photiadis and Fotiadis are variations of the same name and search in both the "F" and the "P" files. On this surname database, it's listed under "F."

If you're ancestors are Greek, chances are you've kept in contact with other Greek family members, unless you're an adoptee or come from a family that has intermarried several generations back. Then here's your chance to get in touch again. Go to the Greek Roots Center at: http://www.butterbox.gr/. Roots Research Center is a non-profit, voluntary, non governmental organization, helping adults adoptees with Greek roots to discover their origins.

The Roots Research Center has information on orphanages in Greece. Write to them at: Roots Research Center, P.O Box 71514, Vyron, 16210, Athens,Greece. They cooperate with all Founding houses of Greece, Red Cross reunion section, International Social Service Greek section, Hellenes Diasporas and every other willing Organization and offer "an independent mediation service where prospective adoptive parts, birth relatives can be helped to make cooperative arrangements about contact."

There are many Greek children who were adopted by families in many different countries, including the USA. Some of them don't have written records or adoption files. If you want to meet your birth family or find out more about your Greek roots, you should know that some Greek families who want to find descendants of adopted children can't find missing members because they can't afford to pay for research in other nations. If this is your genealogy research project, feel free to contact the Roots Research Center at: 56 PANEPISTIMIOU STR 104 31, in Athens, or at their Confidential Address, P.O Box 71514, 16210 Gr.

9

Macedonian Genealogy of the Ottoman Empire Era

All the information on Macedonia, Croatia, Bulgaria, is copyrighted by the Family History Library, Salt Lake City, UT, and the information was sent to me by its author, former staff writer for the Family History Library, Mr. Kahlile Mehr. From this material, the information on Bulgaria, Macedonia, and Croatia has been summarized. For further information, consult the Family History Library as they have excellent sources of information on genealogy in these Balkan countries. Acknowledgement and thanks to Mr. Mehr and the Family History Library. Hungarian material was sent to me by its author, Anthony Trendl, Community Editor, the Hungarian Bookstore.

For Macedonia, Croatia, and Bulgaria begin your genealogy records search with parish registers. Then proceed to civil registration and the censuses. Since most of the Christian population of Macedonia is Macedonian Orthodox, which is similar to Serbian Orthodox, if you're searching parish registers from 1800 to the present, you can probably find records from 1800 forwards in time in the parish registers. You'll find the parish registers in the national, historical, and community archives as well as in various churches.

If you're looking for civil registration, there wasn't any until 1946. For dates before 1913, look to the Ottoman population registers, because after 1913 Macedonia was then part of Serbia. Write to the Ministry of Internal Affairs to look through civil registration materials. The Ministry of Internal Affairs is not the state archives.

Your next step would be to turn to the censuses. They were under the Ottoman population registers before 1913. When the Ottoman Empire fell, Macedonia became part of Serbia. Therefore, 1921 became the year of the first national census at the time that Macedonia then became an area within Yugoslavia.

Next you'll want to turn to the Ottoman population registers. You can find the census returns/population registers from 1829 or 1831. When you skip to 1881-1889, you'll find that by that time the records have been meticulously swept within a single system. You'll view the census returns at the district level (kaza).

At first only Moslem males were registered, but the information portrays a vivid picture as described because not only are the birth dates recorded or the migrations in and out, but also eye color and complexion down to the freckles. You'll note that what was recorded included whether they moved, date of death, and military service dates.

When you get to the 1881 census and later tabulations of population, you'll see that the goal was to establish a demography or population figures for political and social history. Not only Moslem males, but all people were then counted in both the census and the population registers after that date.

The registers listed all family members; sex; birth date; residence; age; religion; craft or occupation; marital status, marriage date; health; military status. It's a good way to find out the religion or occupation of family members.

Your third step would be to turn to records in the Family History Library collection. According to the Library, "Virtually no manuscript materials have been filmed by the Family History Library." If your family comes from one of the countries under the former Ottoman Empire, it would be great if you can donate manuscript materials to be filmed. Ask them first if they are accepting materials and in what form.

Research Procedures

The catalog of the Family History Library may have records listed by the name of the district or the town. According to the Family History Library, look for jurisdictions and localities in Slovenia by consulting a book of place names in the former Yugoslavia. The Family History Library in Salt Lake City refers researchers to the book titled: *Imenik mesta u Jugoslaviji* (Places names in Yugoslavia). Beograd: Novinska Ustanova Sluñbeni List SFRJ, 1973. (949.7 E5u; film 874,462 item 2)

Have you researched records at the national level? If so, look for records from a specific town or area. The films are not housed in the Family History Library. Order films prior to arriving in Salt Lake City by calling or writing: Family History Library, Attn: Library Attendants, 35 N. West Temple Street, Salt Lake City, UT 84150-3400, telephone: 801-240-2331.

War, earthquakes, and fire have destroyed lots of Macedonian archives and records. You have to tend with the destruction of documents from the Balkan wars as well as World War I and II. What if you had to search the ancient library at Alexandria? Yet all is not lost. Between 1918 and 1941, you can search the state archive in Beograd for genealogy records in what was called Macedonia when your relatives lived there.

World War II devastated the archives of Skopje. The Archive of Macedonia was established in 1951. It has a website at http://www.arhiv.gov.mk/Ang1.htm. You'll have to allow for the 1963 earthquake that demolished the facility, but a new building rose in 1969. What you can search there are nine regional archives located in Bitola, Kumanovo, Ohrid, Prilep, Skopje, Strumica, Tetovo, Titov Veles, and Stip. What genealogy records that remain at the Archive of Macedonia includes mostly material from after 1969. Therefore, it's wise to check with them to see whether anything exists from a former period.

If you're researching religion, in 1870 the newly established Bulgarian exarchate received the support of Macedonians, mainly because of its Slavic character. In 1958, the Macedonian Orthodox Church was reestablished in Ohrid. So Macedonia broke free of the Ottoman Empire during the Balkan wars of 1912-1913. Searching records could include tracking relatives to Greece, Bulgaria, or Serbia as Macedonia was divided between Serbia and Greece with a tiny part going to Bulgaria.

Find out whether your relatives lived in Aegean Macedonia (Greece), Vardar Macedonia (Serbia), or Pirin Macedonia (Bulgaria). After 1991, land-locked Macedonia became a small, independent nation. Records could be difficult to find, but also may be hidden in church parishes and family keepsakes. Some records along with religious items were sewn inside of clothing, quilt, and drapery hems. So check out your relatives' oral histories and traditions.

10

Croatia Genealogy Research

First look at the Family History Library's microfilm collection on Croatia. They have about 2,600 rolls of microfilm that were sent in from Croatia since filming began there in 1985. Filming has occurred at the central state archive and regional archives of Osijek, Varañdin, Zadar, Split, Dubrovnik, Rijeka, and Pazin.

If you're looking at parish registers, they start in the 1700s and are archived until the present. Roman Catholic parishes kept registers earlier than Orthodox parishes which were required to keep them only after 1777.

According to the Family History Library, "Civil transcripts of registers were mandated during the 19th century. A tabular format was adopted after 1848. In 1946, civil registration replaced parish registration of vital events.

As of 1945 most registers were turned over to civil authorities and deposited in the local city hall. Older registers have been and continue to be transferred to the district historical archives or the Croatia State Archive."

To find the registers, contact the Civil Registry offices. If you need post World War Two material from the Civil Registers—after 1946, they are there. However, civil registration before May 1946 contains the names and data on Moslems only. After 1946, civil authorities in Croatia and the rest of Yugoslavia began universal registration.

Next, look at the censuses that start in the year 1785 and continue until the present. During the Ottoman Empire, the census followed the usual name-taking for taxation or conscription and to provide a demography of the people in Croatia.

If you want military records of ancestors, the first military census began in 1785. By 1804-5, you have the civil census. Regular censuses were conducted in 1857, 1869, and every ten years, 1880-1910. Go to the archives of each district or city to find a name lists if it is available.

The Family History Library in Salt Lake City recommends for searching gene-alogy records of Croatia the book titled: *Imenik mesta u Jugoslaviji* (Places names in Yugoslavia). Beograd: Novinska Ustanova Sluñbeni List SFRJ, 1973. (949.7 E5u; film 874,462 item 2)

This book will help you to identify the jurisdictions and localities. If you can't read the place names in Yugoslavia, then check out the Family History Library Catalog to see if any records are listed under the name of the town or the district.

Your next step would be to search records on a national level. Look for specific towns or villages and cities. The films are not housed in the Family History Library. Order films prior to arriving in Salt Lake City by calling or writing: Family History Library, Attn: Library Attendants, 35 N. West Temple Street, Salt Lake City, UT 84150-3400, telephone: 801-240-2331.

If you've exhausted the Croatian social associations in the US, then turn to the Croatia State Archive, Hrvatski Dravni Arhiv, Maruliev Trg. 21, 10000 Zagreb, telephone: 385-01-4801-930, fax 385-01-4829-000, email hda@arhiv.hr, web http://zagreb.arhiv.hr.

Instead of actually going to the country in person, email first to set up appointments where you'll go if you actually make a trip over there. Old books were transferred to the archives in 1957—that means books more than 1000 years old. Check out the town halls because they have registers dating before World War II.

After the war, the churches kept registers. There was a census in 1957. If you're looking for old records before 1857, then go to archives at the church reg-isters as well as the state archives. A lot of registers remain in parishes.

Look for transcripts in the Archbishopric Archive. According to the Family History Library, "Pedigrees are scattered in the collection. Though censuses were conducted in 1857, 1869, 1880, 1890, and 1900, there are no census records in the archive."

The charge 88 kuna/hour for research.There are twelve district historical archives and contact information is available on the web site. Check out the Zagreb Historical Archive. Historijski arhiv Zagreb, Opatika 29, 10000 Zagreb, telephone: 385-01-4551-375, fax 385-01-4851-374, povijesni-arhiv-zg@zg.tel.hr, open 9:00-14:00 daily. The Family History Library notes that "A good genealogy website is found at: http://www.croatia-in-english.com/gen/index.html."

There are numerous Croatian social halls and associations in the USA and other countries because more than a quarter of all Croatians lived outside of Croatia by 1970. Check these social and fraternal or family associations for genealogy connections and books, published or unpublished, written by individuals for their own families.

Croats are mainly Roman Catholic, and speak Croation, and Serbs are mostly Orthodox and speak Serbian. The language of the records is either Latin, Croatian, Hungarian, or Italian. Besides Roman script, there is also Glagolitic script.

11

Bulgaria Genealogy

Check out the Bulgaria Genealogy forum at: http://genforum.genealogy.com/ bulgaria/. If you're Jewish, also check out the Sephardi Connection Discussion Forums People Finder at the Sephardi Connection. Their Web site is at: http:// sephardiconnect.com/webx/webx.cgi?sephard-13@%5E185@.ee6c850.

If you're Christian, look at the Orthodox and Catholic records which date back to around 1850. A few Catholic books go back to slightly before 1797. These genealogy records have the names of the head of household and parents, residence, dates and places of birth and baptism, marriage, death and burial; as well as ages in entries for marriage and death.

According to the Family History Library in Salt Lake City, baptisms include names of the godparents. Deaths sometimes include the cause of death.

Entries sometimes identify residence for those not of the parish. Some parish registers have been sent to the state archives or the national museum. Visit the parish churches to look at parish registers.

Some pre-1872 registers are in Greece. Before 1872 the Bulgarian Orthodox Church was subordinate to the Patriarchate in Greece. If you're looking for civil registration, the records begin around 1893 when the process of civil registration began.

According to the Family History Library, "Birth, marriage, and death records have the exact date of the event, including time of day for births; name of the principal and parents' names; occupation and religious preference of parents; name of informant for births and witnesses for marriages; residence for parents of new born, of the groom and bride for marriages, and of the deceased for deaths; age at death, cause of death, and burial place in death records."

Go to the district archives in each of the 26 districts of Bulgaria to find specific records for particular areas. To record all the vital information in the same building, in 1920 family registers came into practice.

To find these family registers before 1920, look to the national census. It began in 1880. The first national census took place right after Bulgaria's liberation from Ottoman rule.

Because 19th century name lists are not available, you'd have to turn to the Ottoman census records for the period 1831-1872. Only these records were enumerations of males for tax, fiscal, and military purposes. They contain the name of the head of household, male family members, ages, occupation, and property.

To start with the Family History Library, go to their small book collection and microfilms of civil registration, 1893-1906, for the Bulgarian districts of Sofia and Pazardzhik. You're going to have to list the local areas or jurisdictions to narrow down your search. To find these jurisdictions, you need the book by Michev N. and P. Koledarov. *Rechnik na selishchata i selishchnite imena v Bulgariia, 1878-1987* (Dictionary of villages and village names in Bulgaria, 1878-1987), Sofia: Nauka i izkustvo, 1989 (FHL book 949.77 E5m).

Once you have the name of the district and town, go to the Family History Library Catalog (Salt Lake City). There may be records listing under the name of the district in Bulgaria. If you can't find anything, then check national level records of a specific town rather than the district.

You can see some of these towns on films. The films are not housed in the Family History Library. Order films prior to arriving in Salt Lake City by calling or writing: Family History Library, Attn: Library Attendants, 35 N. West Temple Street, Salt Lake City, UT 84150-3400, telephone: 801-240-2331.

To narrow down the districts, there are only twenty six. In each of the districts, there is an archive. In that archive you have church records and civil registration records. Then narrow down still more as you go to the churches and monasteries.

You won't find vital records in the National Historical Archive in Sofia, according to the Family History Library research. A guide exists to the holdings of this archive: *Putevoditel na Tsentralniia Durzhaven Istoricheski Arkhiv*, Sofia: Nauka i izkustvo, 1970 (FHL book 949.77 A5p).

To research deeper, turn to the Ottoman census records at the Oriental Department of the Cyril and Methodius National Library, Sofia. What if you don't read Bulgarian? If you get to the records at the Cyril and Methodius National Library, find a translator or translation manual and then go onto the next nation in nearby Istanbul.

Once in Istanbul, look at the archives of the Ottoman Empire. You've now reached the core of the former Ottoman Empire. It seems everything lands up in Istanbul, or does it? That depends on what else is in the various churches or synagogues depending upon your ethnic identity or religion. Check out the genealogy site on the Web at: http://www.rootsweb.com/~bgrwgw/index.html - NEW.

When searching Bulgaria, understand it was the first state to join the Ottoman Empire and the last to be liberated. Bulgaria was under the former Ottoman Empire from 1396-1878, only to be liberated by the Russian army. Another country was added to Bulgaria called Eastern Rumelia, in the southeast.

More territory was added by 1913 during the Balkan wars. A lot of records were hidden because Bulgaria allied with Germany in both World Wars. So if you're of ethnic groups whose records were hidden, such as Sephardic Jews, you need to go to synagogues and Sephardic organizations to find links and leads to where the records can be found. In 1990 Bulgaria became an independent country.

Records are kept in different places for different ethnic groups. You have besides Bulgaries, the Rom people (Gypsies), Turks, Macedonians, Armenians, Russians and Sephardic Jews. If you need to learn Bulgarian before searching records, the Slavic language is written in Cyrillic script.

When you search records, the languages will change with the ethnicity of the people being recorded. Records are found not only in Bulgarian, the main language, but also in Turkish, Greek, and Old Church Slavonic as well as the Sephardic records of synagogues and Jewish schools in Hebrew and Judezmo/ Ladino. Acknowledgement and credit for this information on Bulgaria, Croatia, and Macedonia is given to the Family History Library, Salt Lake City, UT.

12

Hungary Genealogy Records

Start your search of genealogy records for Hungry when it was under the former Ottoman Empire by going to the Hungarian Bookstore site on the Web at: http://www.hungarianbookstore.com/. They have links to many Hungarian sites and publications. Join various Hungarian associations.

These include the American Hungarian Foundation, the American Hungarian Library and Historical Society, and the various Hungarian Genealogy Societies in your locality. Contact the Carpatho-Rusyn Society. Gather your maps.

You can also contact the Hungarian Genealogy of Greater Cleveland and the Cleveland Hungarian Heritage Museum, if you're visiting Ohio. Then look at the Hungarian Phone Book if you can read Hungarian. Search for familiar surnames. Look in the Budapest City Archives, the National Archives of Hungary, the HungaryGenWeb, and the Map pages of Eötvös University, Department of Cartography. If you go to the Hungarian Bookstore Web site at: http://www.hungarianbookstore.com/, you'll find links to various genealogy Web sites and even a Hungarian language radio station.

It's a good start to join a Hungarian or Hungarian-American group and also to subscribe to a magazine from your ancestor's town. Check out the Web site on East European genealogy at: http://www.feefhs.org. Or if you can write in Hungarian, consider joining soc.culture.magyar, a Google newsgroup online. It's at: http://groups.google.com/groups?hl=en&lr=&ie=UTF-8&oe=UTF-8&group=soc.culture.magyar.

According to email from Anthony Trendl, community editor, The Hungarian Bookstore, I asked the following question:

Where would be the best place to start to search Hungarian genealogy if one only speaks English? Mr. Trendl's answer by email is the following:

Anne,

That's a big question. :)

My caveat is I'm not a professional genealogist. We're still getting into this ourselves. My dad's side is Hungarian (I'm American), and my fiancée is from Hungary. I only speak English, and have the same handicap as those in your book…

The wars and such have chopped up the country, and in some cases, destroyed records. Don't be discouraged. There is still hope.

Some of what it takes to research Hungarian genealogy is logical, and useful in any genealogical project. Here's what's off the top of my head.

- The most obvious start is to talk to everyone in your family. This isn't always easy, since most have never been interviewed and aren't used to thinking what you, the reporter might want to know. Bring a tape recorder. Follow-up with new questions.

- Watch History Detectives on PBS. These sharp sleuths have little to do with genealogy, but they do research in the same kind of creative manner that you will find helpful.

- Be organized in your research. Label things, scan things, and start connecting the dots. As your work grows, so will your files. Good organization can keep a researcher from going batty later on.

- Make copies of everyone in your family's baptismal, wedding, and death records.

- Do some reading on the communities from where you think you came from. There are plenty of good resources for history out there.

- Remember communism revised some of the history books to suit their views. Look at the book's copyright date. Suspect anything before 1989.

- Remember religion in Hungary is largely cultural. Don't presume that just because someone claims to be Catholic, for example, that they've ever been actually involved in the parish serving that area. Also, some Jews converted rather than be killed.

- As country lines have change, recognize sometimes city names have changed as well. In doing some reading…even starting with the local library's travel guides, you'll start to get a feel for an area. Some are more English-speaking than others.

- Remember the Holocaust hit Hungarians hard. It wasn't just Jews, but those suspected of being Jewish, and those who simply were Hungarian.

- Go to Hungary. Research your tail off, save all of it on a CD, and come on over to Hungary to do more. Plan ahead, and have an itinerary and meetings planned. If it is a social trip, just be sure to be disciplined. Hungary is beautiful, and it is easy to get sidetracked.

- When you go to Hungary, bring your camera and have unlimited film. Ask permission when inside places.

- Take pictures of your relatives.

- Churches can be a great asset. Baptisms, weddings, all that sort of thing often are recorded. Even though you may not read Hungarian, learning a few key words to understand headings can help.

- Buy a dictionary that covers both languages. Get a real one, not one of those travel ones. You want to learn the word for "baptism' not 'bathroom' :)

- Find a Hungarian friend willing to help.

- Consider hiring a translation service. We used one here in Chicago to translate medical records while we prepared papers for INS.

- When surfing the web, you can still use Hungarian sites. Many have English versions. Look for the little Britiish flag.

- Google has a Hungarian version. That's no small thing, since it can help you isolate your research.

- Surnames change. Not only do people drop accents from their name, but occasionally, the spelling changes. In America, you might find Kovach, but in Hungary, it is likely spelled Kovacs. Same pronunciation, different spelling.

- Join a genealogy club. Eastern Europe is more than just Hungary, but there are lots from Eastern and Central Europe roots that have already tread the path you are starting on. Don't be shy. Ask questions.

- Remember to do special searches on female relatives to find out their maiden names from hidden sources such as widows' military pension applications, medical records, tax and inheritance or probate records, notary records, baptisms, ships' passenger records, new country entry files, cemetery stone rubbings, ethnic associations, charity contribution records, social services, censuses, charity receiving files, and religious affiliation or school records. Hungarian ethnic and genealogy Web sites often have genealogy sections that include lots of links to official city sites in Hungary, like for Pecs and Szeged. You'll also see a number of useful books, software applications and magazines, all available for purchase. Also look at the following Web sites: http://www.hungarianbookstore.com/genealogy.htm (Genealogy links—including online discussion boards, plus a short essay)

http://www.hungarianbookstore.com/language.htm (Dictionaries, tips, and some online dictionary links readers can use for free)

http://www.hungarianbookstore.com/news.htm (Magazines, newspapers...very useful for the researcher looking to know the culture. Many are in English).

http://www.hungarianbookstore.com/groups.htm (Listing of Hungarian social clubs in the USA, including online discussion boards. Very useful for researchers trying to learn about the ins and outs of the country. They can also be a great resource to find professional assistance.)

I'm interested in reading your book when is ready. I also review on Amazon, and am ranked among their top reviewers. The link below will take you to my area on Amazon. Contact me again to get a current address if you'd like to send a review copy. I review nonHungarian-related books as well, so don't be surprised to see my thoughts on the latest bestseller next to a book on Hungarian poetry. :)

About HungarianBooks editor@hungarianbookstore.com

I hope this helps you Anne. Feel free to quote me as you like, and reference our site when you do.

Anthony Trendl

community editor
editor@hungarianbookstore.com

The Hungarian Bookstore
http://www.hungarianbookstore.com

The Hungarian Bookstore connects Hungarians with their culture by providing a directory of churches, restaurants and grocery stores. We sell books, DVDs, CDs, music, videos, magazines, newspapers and more.

13

Searching Several Areas Formerly Under the Ottoman Empire

If your relatives lived under the former Ottoman Empire in the following areas: Hungary, Yugoslavia, Croatia, Bosnia, Albania, Macedonia, Greece, Romania, Moldova, Bulgaria, southern Ukraine, Turkey, Georgia, Armenia, Iraq, Kuwait, Cyprus, Syria, Lebanon, Israel/Palestine, Jordan, Eastern and Western Saudi Arabia, Oman, Bahrain, eastern Yemen, Egypt, northern Libya, Tunisia, and northern Algeria, the first step to take after gathering your own family or client's materials such as birth, marriage, and death certificates, military service, or maps of old addresses and towns is to join associations and subscribe to magazines about that area of the world.

Whether your relatives or clients had ancestors who came from Albania, Romania, Moldova, Cyprus, Syria, Egypt, Yemen, Libya, Tunisia, Northern Algeria or any of the European countries under the Ottoman Empire before 1914, you gather your materials and start your search in pretty much the same way.

You look at church parishes, synagogues, mosques, religious schools, public schools, marriage licenses, death certificates, birth certificates, passports, ship passenger registries, dates entered the US or Canada or any other country, and you contact people in ethnic associations. Online you search for magazines published in the town or near the city of your ancestor's or client's birth.

You look at material in the Family History Library if it's there, or you go to the various genealogy groups for Eastern European or Middle Eastern genealogy and ancestry research. If you belong to a particular ethnic or religious group you go to records kept by your ethnic or religious group.

Jewish genealogy records would be kept in different places than Christian records in most of the countries under the Ottoman Empire, but not always and not in every country. Check out individual town registers as they may not have classified always by religion. Some countries had population registers for all males or heads of households and for all family members.

Other countries recorded the migrations in and out of the country, and still other countries kept a record of what the person looked like, military service, and property ownership for tax collection purposes or notary recordings. Research notaries and court records as well as wills and recorded marriages.

Some people migrated from one country that was under the Ottoman Empire to a country that wasn't. Have you researched back-migration records, when they exist, from Romania to Poland or Ukraine? If you're Sephardic, a good source is Sephardim.com at: http://www.sephardim.com/. Search their engine for surnames.

The Sephardic names search engine lists names going back to the 14th century and beyond by alphabet letter. For example, the name Leven, a Sephardic name in the 14th century, shows up later as an Ashkenazi name (Levin/Levine/Lewin) in Poland (and what is now Belarus) in the 18th century and also showing a migration to Bessarabia, Romania, in the late 18th century coming from Poland.

Another excellent site is Sephardic Genealogy Forum at: http://www.orthohelp.com/geneal/sources2.HTM. At that Web site you might want to check out the passenger lists of Spaniards and/or Sephardim sailing to the Americas between 1500 and 1800. The archive of passengers is still in Seville. You'll find the records in the Archivo General de Indias.

The list of passengers from each ship sailing to America up to1800, the records state each passenger name and place of birth, name of parents and their brithplaces, the job and destination of the passenger after arrival in the Americas. If you write to the archives in Seville, include the following: passenger name and the approximate date of the trip to America. Address your inquiry addressed to: Archivo General de Indias, Avda. Constitucion s/n, SEVILLA–SPAIN. Phone: +34-95-4500530. Fax: +34-95-4219485. Consult also the Sephardic Forum: http://www.jewishgen.org/sefardsig/SefardForum.htm

For information on other Jewish migrations to Palestine/Israel, write to: Batya Unterschatz, Director, Jewish Agency Bureau of Missing Relative, P.O.Box 92, Jerusalem 91000. Also see: Avotaynu, Publishers of Works on Jewish Genealogy (Journal and Books) at: http://www.avotaynu.com/

◆   ◆   ◆

Books to Research recommended by the Web site at Sephardim.com:

Assis: Jews in the Crown of Aragon (Part II 1328-1493); Regesta of the Cartas Reales in Archivo de la Corona de Aragon. Ginzei am olam:Central Arch Hist of Jewish People, Jerusalem.

Beinart: Conversos on Trial. The Inquisition in Ciudad Real. Magnes Press, Hebrew University,Jerus. 1981.

Raphael: Expulsion 1492 Chronicles. Carmi House Press.

Tello: Judios de Toledo—2 Vols. Instituto B Arias Montano. Consejo Sup de inverstigacions Científicas.

14

Teaching or Taking Your Genealogy and/or Personal History Course: Finding Those Female Ancestors

5–6 Week Course in Writing and Publishing Personal Histories, Genealogy, Family Histories, Folklore, Memoirs, and Corporate Success Stories/Case Histories Gift Books

How to Write, Publish, and Promote Memoirs, Events, Business Success Stories, or Documentary-Style Gift Books and Keepsake Life Story Highlights

5–6 Week Course

Creating Salable Gift Books Based on Celebrations and Commemorations

Start with Vignettes

Have you searched enough military widows' pensions or notaries' applications to finally see that female ancestor's maiden name? Maybe now it's time to research, write, record, edit, and publish audio memoirs gift books and/or paper personal or corporate histories books, keepsake albums, videos, or time capsules. Put direct experience in a small package and launch it worldwide. In how many formats would you enjoy presenting personal history?

Write your ancestor's (or your own) life story in short vignettes of 1,500 to 1,800 words. Write eulogies and anecdotes or vignettes of life stories and personal histories for mini-biographies and autobiographies. Then condense or contract the life stories or personal histories into PowerPoint presentations and similar slide shows on disks using lots of photos and one-page of life story.

Finally, collect lots of vignettes and flesh-out the vignettes, linking them together into first-person diary-style novels and books, plays, skits, or other larger works. Write memoirs or eulogies for people or ghostwrite biographies and autobiographies for others.

If ghostwriting is too invisible, write biographies and vocational biographies, success stories and case histories, and customize for niche interest groups. Your main goal with personal history and life stories is to take the direct experience itself and package each story as a vignette.

The vignette can be read in ten minutes. So fill magazine space with a direct experience vignette. Magazine space needs only 1,500 words. When you link many vignettes together, each forms a book chapter or can be adapted to a play or script.

By turning vignettes into smaller packages, they are easier to launch to the media. When collected and linked together, they form a chain of vignettes offering nourishment, direction, purpose, and information used by people who need to make choices. Here's how to write those inspiration-driven, persistence-driven life stories and what to do with them. Use universal experience with which we all can identify.

Included are a full-length diary-format first person novel and a three-act play, including a monologue for performances. There's a demand for direct life experiences written or produced as vignettes and presented in small packages.

Save those vignettes electronically. Later, they can be placed together as chapters in a book or adapted as a play or script, turned into magazine feature, specialty, or news columns, or offered separately as easy-to-read packages.

◆   ◆   ◆

Use General Statements, Proverbs, Slogans, or Mottos, and 'Brand' the Event

Here's how to write, edit, dramatize, package, promote, present, publish & launch gift books as personal histories, autobiographies, biographies, vignettes, and eulogies: launching the inspiration-driven or design-driven life story and detailing your purpose.

Use personal or biographical experiences as examples when you write your essay. Begin by using specific examples taken from your personal experience, personal history, or biographical resources.

Start with a general statement, motto, slogan or proverb to connect the public to your client or the client's attitude, purpose, achievements, or service. Then relate the general to your specific personal experience. You don't have to only write about your client or yourself. You can write about someone else as long as you have accurate historical facts about that person, and you state your credible resources. 'Brand' your client's event as a stage of life celebration. With a business success story, 'brand' the type of event, such as a grand opening with the most important reason or purpose of the event—a good product.

Here's an example of two opening sentences that state the general and then give the specific personal experience. "Mom's a space garbage woman. She repairs satellites." Let's analyze all the different parts of an informed argument essay. By analyzing the result in depth instead of only skimming for breadth, you will be able to write concretely from different points of view.

You'll learn how to construct a memoirs or commemoration gift book from bare bones—from its concept. You start with a concept. Then you add at least three specific examples to your concept until it develops into a mold. A mold is a form, skeleton or foundation. Think of concept as conception. Think of mold as form or skeleton. Think of awning as the outer skin that covers the whole essay and animates it into lively writing.

You don't want your memoirs or other gift book to be flat writing. You want writing that is animated, alive, and able to move, motivate, or inspire readers. Finally, you cover the mold with an awning.

The mold is your pit, skeleton or foundation. Your mold contains your insight, foresight, and hindsight. It has the pitfalls to avoid and the highlights. You need to put flesh on its bones.

Then you need to cover your mold with an awning. You need to include or protect that concept and mold or form by including it under this awning of a larger topic or category. The awning holds everything together. It's your category under which all your related topics fall. That's what the technique of organizing your essay or personal history is all about.

In other words, concept equals form plus details. Story equals form plus details. That's the math formula for writing an essay if you'd like to put it into a logical equation of critical thinking. C = Fo + De. That's what you need to remember about writing an essay: your concept is composed of your form (mold, foundation, or skeleton) and details. A concept isn't an idea. It's the application of your idea.

A concept is what your story is about. Your concept is imbedded in your story. A story can mean your personal history or any other story or anecdote in your essay, or any highlight of your life or specific life experience. A concept also can be a turning point such as rites of passage or take place at any stage of life.

When writing the informed argument, you will be able to give examples backed up with resources. That's what makes an essay great—knowing what examples to put into the essay at which specific points in time.

Gone will be general, vague, or sweeping statements. Therefore, I'd like each of you on this learning team to start planning your essay by analyzing and discussing the parts that chronologically go into the essay. That's how you organize essays in a linear fashion.

Take an essay apart just as you would take a clock or computer apart, and put it back together. Now all the parts fit and work. Taking apart an essay helps you understand how to plan and write your own essay-writing assignments or personal history as a time capsule.

Here's how to take apart a memoir or life story or a business success case history. Some of your gift books will commemorate an event such as a bar/bat mitzvah, confirmation, sweet sixteen party, graduation, wedding, baby shower, anniversary or retirement. Your business clients may want to commemorate a grand opening or narrate a business history. To analyze a memoir in depth, you break the significant events into its six parts: statement-of-position, description, argumentation, exposition, supplementation and evaluation just as you would take apart a persuasive essay. Use the same format as if you'd write a persuasive essay destined to convince. This is your foundation or umbrella. On top of this framework, you'd add the creative elements that make the life story or business success narration able to hold the attention of the reader. Remember that this is a coffee-table type gift book.

If you need to find out what the parts of a persuasive life story are, they are similar to the six parts of a persuasive essay. You can organize the parts of a life story as you would organize the six parts of an essay as explained in the book titled, *The Informed Argument*. (**ISBN:** 0155414593). Use the same technique when writing life stories, skits, plays, persuasive essays, and gift books based on significant events of lives or business histories. This technique works because readers look to be convinced by experiences backed up by facts. It works for persuasive essays, and it works as well for life story experiences. Action verbs also help you organize your gift book topics or chapters by achievements done and results obtained or problems solved. For more ideas, you also can look at some action verbs in another book titled, *801 Action Verbs for Communicators. (***ISBN:* 0-595-31911-4).

Argumentation is part of a memoirs gift book if handled with courtesy and details that can be fact-checked or verified, if at all possible. Include resources and photos or video clips or audio interviews on a disk placed in an envelope at the back of the book if at all possible. Or use interviews in text in print paperback books. Before you even get to the expressive part of argumentation, you have to state your position and describe it by using specific examples. Then you get to the informed argument in the middle of your essay.

After you've finished arguing logically using critical thinking and your resources, you use exposition. Then you use supplementation, and finally evaluation. To practice writing personal history essays in text or on video, define and analyze the words 'exposition' and 'supplementation.' Use exposition and supplementation in at least one sentence each as an example of how you would use it in your essay. Don't stick to only what is familiar.

My dictionary defines 'exposition' as "a careful setting out of the facts or ideas involved in something." The principal themes are presented first in a 'music' exposition. Apply it now to an essay. Present your principal themes first in your personal history. Supplementation means adding to your work to improve or complete it.

The goal of an essay is to analyze your informed argument in depth. That's why there are six parts to an essay. Knowing what those six parts are as well as showing examples gives you the experience you need to plan and organize your essay. The result is that once you have organized your plan in writing, the essay almost writes itself.

Use proverbs, quotations, (with credits) and flesh out the proverbs or quotes with details of life stories and events. Keep an old proverb or quotation in front of you when you write. A memoirs book is about wanting others to know that your client cares.

One goal of a memoirs book is to let the reader know that the client cares more about the readers than the readers would care what the client knows. It's a great saying to remind others why the client is creating a book. Everyone has a life story of great value.

How do you present the outcome of significant events, family or business history, or commemorations as a gift book? How do you publish the book? You start with your time and money budget and only then begin to break your organizing, writing, editing, and publishing into weekly tasks. The first week is for interviewing and gathering significant facts, events, and turning points.

A gift book may be presented also as a skit, play, or monologue and/or as a narrative book of highlights. For business histories and success stories, the narrative also can be turned into a 28 ½ minute infomercial script with two or more people interviewing the client.

The business success story infomercial, like the life story interview, needs a list of questions to present in advance that would take a specific time to answer such as a half-hour to an hour. Business infomercials usually are limited to 28 ½ minutes. Attention span for viewing is short. So write in seven to 10-minute chunks of reading or viewing time that allows time out for breaks.

◆   ◆   ◆

"The Mind that Alters, Alters All"

—**William Blake**

Course Overviews: Weeks 1 through 5–6

Week 1

1. Put Direct Experience In A Small Package And Launch It Worldwide. Make Time Capsules.

2. Write, Record, & Publish Purpose-Driven Personal History Dramatize, Package, Promote, Present, & Launch Your Purpose.

3. Edit, Dramatize, Package, Promote, Present, Publish, Record, Produce, & Launch Time Capsules of Personal Histories, Autobiographies, Biographies,

Vignettes, and Eulogies: Launching the Inspiration-Driven or Design-Driven Life Story and Detailing Your Purpose.

Week 2

Use Simplicity and Commitment in Personal History Writing, Time Capsules, and Videos. Here's useful insight to those who may someday write fiction, or their life stories, true experiences, or other people's life stories as vignettes or books created by linking a dozen or more vignettes together into a publishable book. Your aim is to produce time capsules or keepsake albums and other family history-related books, videos, audio projects, memory and/or prayer boxes, or memorabilia as heirlooms.

Look for insight, foresight, and hindsight. Mentoring is about pointing out what pitfalls to avoid. Instead of a formula, aim for simplicity, commitment, and persistence. Use simplicity in your writings.

Week 3
How to Motivate People to Interview One Another for Personal History Productions

People are "less camera shy" when two from the same peer group or class pair up and interview each other on video camcorder or on audio tape from a list of questions rehearsed. People also can write the questions they want to be asked and also write out and familiarize themselves with the answers alone and/or with their interviewers from their own peer group.

Some people have their favorite proverbs, or a logo that represents their outlook on life. Others have their own 'crusade' or mission. And some have a slogan that says what they are about in a few words…example, "seeking the joy of life," or "service with a smile."

A play can come from someone's slogan, for example. A slogan, logo, proverb, or motto can form the foundation for a questionnaire on what they want to say in an oral history or personal history video or audio tape on in a multimedia presentation of their life story highlights.

Week 4

1. **How to Gather Personal Histories**

2. Use the following sequence when gathering oral histories:

3. Develop one central issue and divide that issue into a few important questions that highlight or focus on that one central issue.

4. Write out a plan just like a business plan for your oral history project. You may have to use that plan later to ask for a grant for funding, if required. Make a list of all your products that will result from the oral history when it's done.

5. Write out a plan for publicity or public relations and media relations. How are you going to get the message to the public or special audiences?

6. Develop a budget. This is important if you want a grant or to see how much you'll have to spend on creating an oral history project.

7. List the cost of video taping and editing, packaging, publicity, and help with audio or special effects and stock shot photos of required.

8. What kind of equipment will you need? List that and the time slots you give to each part of the project. How much time is available? What are your deadlines?

9. What's your plan for a research? How are you going to approach the people to get the interviews? What questions will you ask?

10. Do the interviews. Arrive prepared with a list of questions. It's okay to ask the people the kind of questions they would like to be asked. Know what dates the interviews will cover in terms of time. Are you covering the economic depression of the thirties? World Wars? Fifties? Sixties? Pick the time parameters.

11. Edit the interviews so you get the highlights of experiences and events, the important parts. Make sure what's important to you also is important to the person you interviewed.

12. Have the person you've interviewed approve of the selected highlights, experiences, or turning points to make sure what you select is the same as what the person wants included and emphasized in the memoirs gift book. Make any adjustments.

13. Process audio as well as video, and make sure you have written transcripts of anything on audio and/or video in case the technology changes or the tapes go bad.

14. Save the tapes to compact disks, DVDs, a computer hard disk and several other ways to preserve your oral history time capsule. Donate any tapes or CDs to appropriate archives, museums, relatives of the interviewee, and one or more oral history libraries. They are usually found at universities that have an oral history department and library such as UC Berkeley and others.

15. Check the Web for oral history libraries at universities in various states and abroad.

16. Evaluate what you have edited. Make sure the central issue and central questions have been covered in the interview. Find out whether newspapers or magazines want summarized transcripts of the audio and/or video with photos.

17. Contact libraries, archives, university oral history departments and relevant associations and various ethnic genealogy societies that focus on the subject matter of your central topic.

18. Keep organizing what you have until you have long and short versions of your oral history for various archives and publications. Contact magazines and newspapers to see whether editors would assign reporters to do a story on the oral history project.

19. Create a scrapbook with photos and summarized oral histories. Write a synopsis of each oral history on a central topic or issue. Have speakers give public presentations of what you have for each person interviewed and/or for the entire project using highlights of several interviews with the media for publicity. Be sure your project is archived properly and stored in a place devoted to oral history archives and available to researchers and authors.

20. **Recorded and Transcribed Oral History Techniques (Video and/or Audio)**

21. Begin with easy to answer questions that don't require you explore and probe deeply in your first question. Focus on one central issue when asking questions. Don't use abstract questions. A plain question would be "What's your purpose?" An abstract question with connotations would be "What's your crusade?" Use questions with denotations instead of connotations. Keep questions short and plain—easy to understand. Examples would be, "What did you want to accomplish? How did you solve those problems? How did you find closure?" Ask the familiar "what, when, who, where, how, and why."

22. First research written or visual resources before you begin to seek an oral history of a central issue, experience, or event.

23. Who is your intended audience?

24. What kind of population niche or sample will you target?

25. What means will you select to choose who you will interview? What group of people will be central to your interview?

26. Write down how you'll explain your project. Have a script ready so you don't digress or forget what to say on your feet.

27. Consult oral history professionals if you need more information. Make sure what you write in your script will be clear to understand by your intended audience.

28. Have all the equipment you need ready and keep a list of what you'll use and the cost. Work up your budget.

29. Choose what kind of recording device is best—video, audio, multimedia, photos, and text transcript. Make sure your video is broadcast quality. I use a Sony Digital eight (high eight) camera.

30. Make sure from cable TV stations or news stations that what type of video and audio you choose ahead of time is broadcast quality.

31. Make sure you have an external microphone and also a second microphone as a second person also tapes the interview in case the quality of your camera breaks down. You can also keep a tape recorder going to capture the audio in case your battery dies.

32. Make sure your battery is fully charged right before the interview. Many batteries die down after a day or two of nonuse.

33. Test all equipment before the interview and before you leave your office or home. I've had batteries go down unexpectedly and happy there was another person ready with another video camera waiting and also an audio tape version going.

34. Make sure the equipment works if it's raining, hot, cold, or other weather variations. Test it before the interview. Practice interviewing someone on your equipment several times to get the hang of it before you show up at the interview.

35. Make up your mind how long the interview will go before a break and use tape of that length, so you have one tape for each segment of the interview. Make several copies of your interview questions.

36. Be sure the interviewee has a copy of the questions long before the interview so the person can practice answering the questions and think of what to say or even take notes. Keep checking your list of what you need to do.

37. Let the interviewee make up his own questions if he wants. Perhaps your questions miss the point. Present your questions first. Then let him embellish the questions or change them as he wants to fit the central issue with his own experiences.

38. Call the person two days and then one day before the interview to make sure the individual will be there on time and understands how to travel to the location. Or if you are going to the person's home, make sure you understand how to get there.

39. Allow yourself one extra hour in case of traffic jams.

40. Choose a quiet place. Turn off cell phones and any ringing noises. Make sure you are away from barking dogs, street noise, and other distractions.

41. Before you interview make sure the person knows he or she is going to be video and audio-taped.

42. If you don't want anyone swearing, make that clear it's for public archives and perhaps broadcast to families.

43. Your interview questions should follow the journalist's information-seeking format of asking, who, what, where, where, how, and why. Oral history is a branch of journalistic research.

44. Let the person talk and don't interrupt. You be the listener and think of oral history as aural history from your perspective.

45. Make sure only one person speaks without being interrupted before someone else takes his turn to speak.

46. Understand silent pauses are for thinking of what to say.

47. Ask one question and let the person gather his thoughts.

48. Finish all your research on one question before jumping to the next question. Keep it organized by not jumping back to the first question after the second is done. Stay in a linear format.

49. Follow up what you can about any one question, finish with it, and move on to the next question without circling back. Focus on listening instead of asking rapid fire questions as they would confuse the speaker.

50. Ask questions that allow the speaker to begin to give a story, anecdote, life experience, or opinion along with facts. Don't ask questions that can be answered only be yes or no. This is not a courtroom. Let the speaker elaborate with facts and feelings or thoughts.

51. Late in the interview, start to ask questions that explore and probe for deeper answers.

52. Wrap up with how the person solved the problem, achieved results, reached a conclusion, or developed an attitude, or found the answer. Keep the wrap-up on a light, uplifting note.

53. Don't leave the individual hanging in emotion after any intensity of. Respect the feelings and opinions of the person. He or she may see the situation from a different point of view than someone else. So respect the person's right to feel as he does. Respect his need to recollect his own experiences.

54. Interview for only one hour at a time. If you have only one chance, interview for an hour. Take a few minutes break. Then interview for the second hour. Don't interview more than two hours at any one meeting.

55. Use prompts such as paintings, photos, music, video, diaries, vintage clothing, crafts, antiques, or memorabilia when appropriate. Carry the photos in labeled files or envelopes to show at appropriate times in order to prime the memory of the interviewee. For example, you may show a childhood photo and ask "What was it like in that orphanage where these pictures were taken?" Or travel photos might suggest a trip to America as a child, or whatever the photo suggests. For example, "Do you remember when this ice cream parlor inside the ABC movie house stood at the corner of X and Y Street? Did you go there as a teenager? What was your funniest memory of this movie theater or the ice cream store inside back in the fifties?"

56. As soon as the interview is over, label all the tapes and put the numbers in order.

57. A signed release form is required before you can broadcast anything. So have the interviewee sign a release form before the interview.

58. Make sure the interviewee gets a copy of the tape and a transcript of what he or she said on tape. If the person insists on making corrections, send the paper transcript of the tape for correction to the interviewee. Edit the tape as best you can or have it edited professionally.

59. Make sure you comply with all the corrections the interviewee wants changed. He or she may have given inaccurate facts that need to be corrected on the paper transcript.

60. Have the tape edited with the corrections, even if you have to make a tape at the end of the interviewee putting in the corrections that couldn't be edited out or changed.

61. As a last resort, have the interviewee redo the part of the tape that needs correction and have it edited in the tape at the correct place marked on the tape. Keep the paper transcript accurate and up to date, signed with a release form by the interviewee.

62. Oral historians write a journal of field notes about each interview. Make sure these get saved and archived so they can be read with the transcript.

63. Have the field notes go into a computer where someone can read them along with the transcript of the oral history tape or CD.

64. Thank the interviewee in writing for taking the time to do an interview for broadcast and transcript.

65. Put a label on everything you do from the interview to the field notes. Make a file and sub file folders and have everything stored in a computer, in archived storage, and in paper transcript.

66. Make copies and digital copies of all photos and put into the records in a computer. Return originals to owners.

67. Make sure you keep your fingerprints off the photos by wearing white cotton gloves. Use cardboard when sending the photos back and pack securely. Also photocopy the photos and scan the photos into your computer. Treat photos as antique art history in preservation.

68. Make copies for yourself of all photos, tapes, and transcripts. Use your duplicates, and store the original as the master tape in a place that won't be used often, such as a time capsule or safe, or return to a library or museum where the original belongs.

69. Return all original photos to the owners. An oral history archive library or museum also is suitable for original tapes. Use copies only to work from, copy, or distribute.

70. Index your tapes and transcripts. To use oral history library and museum terminology, recordings and transcripts are given "accession numbers."

71. Phone a librarian in an oral history library of a university for directions on how to assign accession numbers to your tapes and transcripts if the materi-

als are going to be stored at that particular library. Store copies in separate places in case of loss or damage.

72. If you don't know where the materials will be stored, use generic accession numbers to label your tapes and transcripts. Always keep copies available for yourself in case you have to duplicate the tapes to send to an institution, museum, or library, or to a broadcast company.

73. Make synopses available to public broadcasting radio and TV stations.

74. Check your facts.

75. Are you missing anything you want to include?

76. Is there some place you want to send these tapes and transcripts such as an ethnic museum, radio show, or TV satellite station specializing in the topics on the tapes, such as public TV stations? Would it be suitable for a world music station? A documentary station?

77. If you need more interviews, arrange them if possible.

78. Give the interviewee a copy of the finished product with the corrections. Make sure the interviewee signs a release form that he or she is satisfied with the corrections and is releasing the tape to you and your project.

79. Store the tapes and transcripts in a library or museum or at a university or other public place where it will be maintained and preserved for many generations and restored when necessary.

80. You can also send copies to a film repository or film library that takes video tapes, an archive for radio or audio tapes for radio broadcast or cable TV.

81. Copies may be sent to various archives for storage that lasts for many generations. Always ask whether there are facilities for restoring the tape. A museum would most likely have these provisions as would a large library that has an oral history library project or section.

82. Make sure the master copy is well protected and set up for long-term storage in a place where it will be protected and preserved.

83. If the oral history is about events in history, various network news TV stations might be interested. Film stock companies may be interested in copies of old photos.

84. Find out from the subject matter what type of archives, repository, or storage museums and libraries would be interested in receiving copies of the oral history tapes and transcripts.

85. Print media libraries would be interested in the hard paper copy transcripts and photos as would various ethnic associations and historical preservation societies. Find out whether the materials will go to microfiche, film, or be digitized and put on CDs and DVDs, or on the World Wide Web. If you want to create a time capsule for the Web, you can ask the interviewee whether he or she wants the materials or selected materials to be put online or on CD as multimedia or other. Then you would get a signed release from the interviewee authorizing you to put the materials or excerpts online.

86. Also find out in whose name the materials are copyrighted. Obtain at least one-time print and electronic rights to the material to publish as a gift book for your client. Get it all in writing, signed by those who have given you any interviews, and from those who own the latest publishing rights, even if you have to call upon a local intellectual property rights attorney.

Week 5–6 (Summary)

1. Document Recovery
2. How to Open a DNA-Driven Genealogy Reporting and Production Service

1. Overview: Document Recovery

How do you rescue and recover memories from mold using conservation techniques? You transport horizontally and store vertically. Store documents and photos in plastic holders, between sheets of waxed paper, or interleave with acid-free paper. Books are stored spine down. Archive DVDs and CDs in plastic holders and store in plastic crates. To conserve time capsules, according to the American Institute for Conservation of Historic and Artistic Works (AIC), in Washington, DC, neutralize that acid-wracked paper.

2. Overview: DNA-Driven Genealogy Reporting Service

A memoirs gift book may include a report on DNA-driven genealogy test results. Include an interpretation on how to understand and 'read' the test, findings, or other information about genetic anthropology and its possibilities concerning genealogy. This information may be included in a memoirs gift book slanted to genealogy information when records of surnames can no longer be found.

If you decide to open an online, home-based DNA-driven genealogy reporting and production service, reports and time capsules could include the possible geographic location where the DNA sequences originated. Customers usually want to see the name of an actual town, even though towns didn't exist 10,000 years ago when the sequences might have arisen.

The whole genome is not tested, only the few ancestral markers, usually 500 base pairs of genes. Testing DNA for ancestry does not have anything to do with testing genes for health risks because only certain genes are tested—genes related to ancestry. And all the testing is done at a laboratory, not at your online business.

If you're interested in a career in genetics counseling and wish to pursue a graduate degree in genetics counseling, that's another career route. For information, contact The American Board of Genetic Counseling. Sometimes social workers with some coursework in biology take a graduate degree in genetic counseling since it combines counseling skills with training in genetics and in interpreting genetics tests for your clients.

◆   ◆   ◆

"The best way to become acquainted with a subject is to write a book about it."

—Benjamin Disraeli (1804–1881)

Benjamin Disraeli, novelist, debater, and prime minister in England A nearly three-page listing of Disraeli's quotations appear in *The Oxford Dictionary of Quotations.*

15

50 Strategies on How to Write Genealogy, Memoirs, and Life Story Gift Books and Time Capsules

Start with a Vignette…Link the Vignettes…Dramatize…and Novelize.

1. Contact anyone's family members to gain permission to write their family member's memorials.

2. Write memoirs of various clerical or other religious or social leaders.

3. Write two to four dozen memorials for houses of worship. Put these memorials in a larger book of memoirs for various organizations, religious groups, houses of worship, or professional associations.

4. Find a model for your biographies.

5. These could be based on a book of vocational biographies or centered on any other aspect of life such as religious or community service as well as vocations.

6. Read the various awards biographies written and presented for well-known people.

7. Focus on the accomplishments that stand out of these people or of you if you're writing an autobiography.

8. Use oral eulogies as your foundation. You'll find many oral eulogies that were used in memorial services.

9. Consult professionals who conduct memorial services to look at their eulogies written for a variety of people and presented at memorial services.

10. Stick to the length of a eulogy. You'll find the average eulogy runs about 1,500 to 1,800 words. That' is what's known as magazine article average length. Most magazines ask for feature articles of about 1,500 words. So your eulogies should run that same length.

11. When read aloud, they make up the eulogy part of a memorial service. At 250 to 300 words double-spaced per page, it comes to about five-to-seven pages and is read aloud in about seven to 10 minutes.

12. Take each 1,500-1,800 word eulogy and focus on the highlights, significant events, and turning points. Cut the eulogy down to one page of printed magazine-style format.

13. Keep the eulogy typeset so that it all fits on one page of printed material in 12 point font.

14. You can package one-page eulogies for memorial services or include a small photo on the page if space permits.

15. Cut the eulogy down to 50-70 words, average 60 words for an oral presentation using PowerPoint software for a computer-based slide show complete with photos.

16. Put the PowerPoint show on a CD or DVD. Use the shorter eulogy focusing on significant points in the person's life. The purpose of a PowerPoint eulogy is to show the person lived a purposeful life—a design-driven, goal-driven life with purpose and concrete meaning in relation to others.

17. Write biographies, memoirs, and autobiographies by focusing on the highlights of someone's life or your own life story. Turn personal histories into life stories that you can launch in the media. You need to make a life story salable. It is already valuable.

18. Read autobiographies in print. Compare the autobiographies written by ghostwriters to those written by the authors of autobiographies who write about their own experiences.

19. Read biographies and compare them to autobiographies written by ghost writers and those written as diary novels in first person or as genre novels in first person. Biographies are written in third person.

20. If you write a biography in third person keep objective. If you write an autobiography in first person you can be subjective or objective if you bring in other characters and present all sides of the story equally.

21. If you're writing a biography, whose memories are you using? If you write an autobiography, you can rely on your own memory. Writing in the third person means research verifying facts and fact-checking your resources for credibility. How reliable is the information?

22. Use oral history transcriptions, personal history, videos, audio tapes, and interviews for a biography. You can use the same for an autobiography by checking for all sides of the story with people involved in the life story—either biography or autobiography.

23. With personal histories and oral histories, be sure to obtain letters of permission and to note what is authorized. Celebrities in the public eye are written about with unauthorized or authorized biographies. However, people in private life who are not celebrities may not want their name or photo in anyone's book. Make sure everything you have is in writing in regard to permissions and what information is permitted to be put into your book or article, especially working with people who are not celebrities and those who are.

24. When interviewing, get written approval of what was said on tape. Let the person see the questions beforehand to be able to have time to recall an answer with accuracy regarding facts and dates or times of various events. Give peoples' memories a chance to recall memories before the interview.

25. Write autobiographies in the first person in genre or diary format. You can also dramatize the autobiography in a play or skit first and then flesh it out into novel format. Another alternative is to focus only on the highlights, events, and turning points in various stages of life.

26. Ghost-written autobiographies usually are written in the first person. A ghost-writer may have a byline such as "*as told to*" or "*with*____(name of ghostwriter)."

27. Condense experience in small chunks or paragraphs. Use the time-capsule approach. Use vignettes. Focus on how people solved problems or obtained results or reached a goal. Find out whether the person wants you to mention a life purpose. Emphasize how the person overcame challenges or obstacles.

28. In an autobiography, instead of dumping your pain on others because it may be therapeutic for you, try to be objective and focus on what you learned from your choices and decisions and how what you learned transformed your life. Be inspirational and nurturing to the reader. Tell how you learned, what you learned, how you rose above your problems, and how you transcended the trouble. Focus on commitment and your relationship to others and what your purpose is in writing the autobiography.

29. Stay objective. Focus on turning points, highlights, and significant events and their relationship to how you learned from your mistakes or choices and rose above the trouble. Decide what your life purpose is and what points you want to emphasize. If you want to hide facts, decide why and what good it will do the reader. Stay away from angry writing and focus instead on depth and analysis.

30. Don't use humor if it puts someone down, including you. Don't put someone down to pick yourself up.

31. Make sure your writing doesn't sound like self-worship or ego soothing. Don't be modest, but don't shock readers either.

32. Before you write your salable autobiography, find out where the market is and who will buy it. If there is no market, use print-on-demand publishing and select a title most likely to be commercial or help market your book. At least you can give copies to friends and family members. Or self-publish with a printer. Another way to go is to self-publish using print-on-demand software yourself. Then distribute via advertising or the Internet and your Web site.

33. You'd be surprised at how many people would be interested in your life story if it were packaged, designed, and promoted. So launch your life story in the

media before you publish. Write your life story as a novel or play or both. Every life story has value. I believe all life stories are salable. The hard part is finding the correct niche market for your experiences. So focus on what you are and what you did so people with similar interests, hobbies, or occupations may learn from you. Market to people who are in the same situation as you are.

34. Divide your biography into the 12 stages of life. Then pare down those 12 significant events or turning points and rites of passage into four quarters—age birth to 25 (young adult), age 26-50 (mature adult), age 51-75 (creative adult) and age 76-100 (golden years of self fulfillment).

35. Start with a vignette focusing on each of the most important events and turning points of your life. Do the same in a biography, only writing in third person. For your own life story, write in first person.

36. What's important for the reader to know about your life in relation to social history and the dates in time? For example, what did you do during the various wars?

37. Keep a journal or diary, and record events as they happen. Focus on how you relate to social history. Write in your diary each day. Use the Web and create a diary or Web *blog*.

38. If you keep a daily journal, and make sure it is saved on a computer disk or similar electronic diary, you can put the whole journal together and create a book or play online or have a digital recording of your life. It's your time capsule in virtual reality.

39. A daily journal will keep memories fresh in your mind when you cut down to significant events for a book. You want to recall significant events in detail with resources.

40. If you're young, keep a daily journal on a computer disk and keep transferring it from one technology to the next as technology evolves. Keep a spare saved and up on the Web so you can download it anytime. Use some of the free Web site space available to people online.

41. If you write a book when you're older, at least you'll have all the youthful memories in detail where you can transfer the notes from one computer to

another or upload from your disk to a browser for publication with a print-on-demand publisher.

42. Keep writing short vignettes. Include all the details as soon as possible after the event occurs. When you are ready to write a book, you'll be able to look back rationally and from a much more objective and mature perspective on the details. Then you can decide what to put into a salable life story that's about to be published.

43. Don't listen to people who tell you that if you are not famous, your life story is only fit for your own family because no one else will buy it. Fiddle-de-sticks!

44. There are events that happened to you or experiences in your line of work, travel, parenting, research, or lifestyle that people want to read because you have experiences to share.

45. Find a niche market of people with similar interests and market your life story to them.

46. Try out the waters first with a short vignette in magazines. If the magazines buy your vignette, your slice of life story, then you can write a book. Can you imagine if all the travelers and archaeologists, parenting experts and teachers didn't value their life story to the point that they thought it was fit only for relatives (who may be the only ones not interested in reading it because they already know your life story). In fact, your relatives may be angry at you for spilling the details to the public.

47. Instead, focus on that part of your life where you made a choice or decision with which everyone can identify. Inspire and motivate readers. If your experience is universal, we can all identify with it. We all go through the same stages of life.

48. So let us know how you overcame your obstacles, solved problems, and rose above the keen competition.

49. Or if you didn't, let us know how you learned to live with and enjoy your life. Readers want nourishment. If your life isn't about making a difference in the world, then write about how you handled what we all go through.

50. We want to read about the joy of life, and your design-driven life full of purpose, meaning, and inspiration. We want to read about the universal in you with which we can identify. Most of all readers want information in a life story or personal history from which we can make our own choices. Keep your life story as a novel to 12 to 24 short chapters. Write in short, readable chunks.

16

Simplicity

Week Two:

Use Simplicity and Commitment in Personal History Writing or Time Capsules

Here's useful insight to those who may someday write fiction, or their life stories, true experiences, or other people's life stories as vignettes or books created by linking a dozen or more vignettes together into a publishable book. Look for insight, foresight, and hindsight. Mentoring is about pointing out what pitfalls to avoid. Instead of a formula, aim for simplicity, commitment, and persistence. Use simplicity in your writings.

Simplicity means whatever you write gives you all the answers you were looking for in exotic places, but found it close by. This is the formula for selling anything you write, should you desire to send your writing to publishers. You find simplicity in universal proverbs. Then you expand the proverbs to slice-of-life vignettes. Finally, you link those short vignettes.

Suddenly you have a book-length work of writing that can be divided into short vignettes again to be serialized. With most people's attention span set on seven-minutes per vignette, each vignette can emphasize simplicity, commitment, and universal values. Your conclusion would be to focus on answers that can be found close by. If you're ever looking for 'formulas' in writing any type of literature, this is it: Simplicity shows how you found the answers you were looking for in exotic places but found close by. In your readings you can see the patterns and universals such as commitment that are valued in the story.

You can choose what the writer emphasizes as important. In your own writing, look around for your favorite proverbs and see how you can expand them in your writing to work with your own stories. Enjoy and find wisdom in creative expression. Write about how people interpret family history or diaries as creative writing, or how do DNA-testing companies interpret ancestry-related DNA tests to the general public.

What Makes a Personal History or Life Story Highlight Salable as a Play or Skit?

Q. What makes a life story saleable?

Buzz appeal…High velocity personal memoir…A life story is salable when it has universal appeal and identity. An example is a single parent making great sacrifices to put bread on the table and raise a decent family in hard times.

Many people identify with the universal theme of a life story. Buzz appeal draws in the deep interest of the press to publicize and lend credibility to a life story, to put a spin on it in the media, and to sell it to the public because all readers may be able to see themselves in your life story.

Q. To whom do you sell your life story to?

You sell your life story to publishers specializing in life stories. If you look under biographies in a book such as Writer's Guide to Book Editors, Publishers, and Literary Agents, 1999-2000, by Jeff Herman, Prima Publishing, you'll see several pages of publishers of life story, biography, and memoirs or autobiography.

A few include The Anonymous Press, Andrews McMeel Publishing, Applause Theatre Book Publishers, Barricade Books, Inc., Baskerville Publishers, and many more listed in that directory. Also take a look at Writers Market, Writers Digest Books, checkout Memoirs in the index. Publishers include Feminist Press, Hachai, Hollis, Narwhal, Northeastern University Press, Puppy House, Westminster, John Knox,and others.

Check categories such as creative nonfiction, biography, ethnic, historical, multicultural and other categories for lists of publishers in your genre. Don't overlook writing your life story as a play, monologue, or script or for the audio book market.

Q. How do you present your life story in order to turn it into a saleable book, article, play, or other type of literature so that other people will want to read it?

You write a high-velocity powerful personal memoir or autonomedia which emphasizes cultural criticism and theory. Or you write a factual expose, keep a journal on the current cultural pulse, or write a diary about what it feels like to be single and dating in your age group—thirty something, sixty-something, or whatever you choose. You become an investigative biographer. You write a riveting love story, or how to use love to heal. Perhaps you write about breaking through old barriers to create new publishing frontiers.

Q. How do you write a commercial biography?

Make sure someone wants to buy it before you write the whole thing. The details will be forthcoming in the course as it begins. Then contact the press, reporters in the media with credibility who write for a national daily newspaper or reputable magazine. Also contact radio and cable TV stations to do interviews on a selected event in your life story or biography. Pick a niche market where the particular audience has a special interest in that experience.

Q. What's the difference between authorized and unauthorized?

Authorized means you have permission and approval from the person about whom you're writing. Unauthorized means you gather information from relatives and friends or others who have researched verifiable facts about the person, but the person about whom you're writing has not given you permission to write his or her biography.

Q. Who gets assigned to write biographies of celebrities or other famous people?

Usually newspaper columnists who cover the beat or subject area, or you're a known writer who contacts an agent specializing in writing or ghostwriting celebrity biographies. You can enter this profession from a variety of doors and wear many hats.

Personal historians, librarians, teachers, reporters, documentarians, videographers, novelists, politicians, researchers, scientists, entertainment personnel, and biographers as well as experts in psychology, law enforcement, or military service can research and write biographies of famous people. Many well-known freelance writers are hired by the agents of celebrities to write or ghost-write biographies and autobiographies.

Writing Your Ending First Gives You Closure And Clues How To Solve The Problems In Your Life Story. Teaching Life Story Writing On The Internet

When you write a salable life story, it's easier to write your ending first. Eventually, with experience working with a variety of life stories, you can start quality circles or classes in life story writing (writing your salable memoirs, autobiography, biography, corporate history, family history, your diary as a commercial novel or play or true confession, true story, or true crime book or story or script).

Also, you can teach life story writing, interviewing, or videobiography on the Internet for yourself or for an existing school or program. It's relaxing and comforting to sit at home in perfect quiet and type a lecture into a screen browser such as the courses that can be offered through www.blackboard.com and other programs. Or teach online using a live chat screen. Customize your course to the needs of your students.

You may need certification or a graduate degree to teach for a university online, but there's also adult education classes given in nontraditional settings such as churches, libraries, and museums.

Online, you can offer independent classes and go into business for yourself as a personal historian. Another way is to offer time capsules, keepsake albums, gift baskets, greeting cards, life stories on video, DVD, or transcribed from oral history. Work with libraries, museums, or your own independent classes.

You can work at home or be mobile and travel to other people's homes or senior centers and assisted living recreation rooms, community centers, or schools and theaters to work with life stories. Some companies have put life-story recording kiosks in public places such as train stations or airports.

Check out the StoryCorps Web site at http://www.storycorps.net/. Find your own mission or purpose and create your own business recording the life stories of a variety of people in video, sound, text, or multimedia formats. It's all part of the time-capsule generation that emphasizes your life story has value and needs to be preserved as part of history.

The revelation is that your life story isn't only for your family and friends anymore. As part of history, the world can now experience the one universal that connects us—life, and within a life story—insight, foresight, and hindsight.

Diaries of senior citizens are in demand. To sell them, you need buzz appeal, visibility in the press for writing simple stories of how you struggled to put bread on the table and raised a family alone, or what you've learned from your mistakes or experiences, how you solved problems, gave yourself more choices, grew, and came to understand why you were transformed. People are looking for universal experiences to help them make decisions.

Start by finding a newspaper reporter from a publication that is well-respected by the public, and have that person write about your life story experience or what you do with other peoples' life stories as a personal historian. That's the first step to introducing a 'salable' life story.

The technique differs from writing a life story like a first-person diary novel for only your family and/or friends. With a 'salable' life story, you write about the universal experiences that connect all of us. If readers or viewers can identify with what you have to say, your words open doors for them to make decisions and choices by digesting your information.

The Proliferation of Playwriting Courses Online Targets Writing Your Genealogy or Life Story

The sheer number of classes on the Internet is like an explosion of education. You can now earn a masters degree in the techniques of teaching online from universities such as the California State University at Hayward in their continuing education department. What I see happening is that according to display ads in a variety of magazines of interest to writers, a proliferation of writing courses online has broken out.

How do you develop buzz appeal, pre-sell your book, create press coverage of their writing, all before you send it to a publisher or agent? A few years ago diaries were "in" just like several years before that the books about angels were "in style." What will be next?

Back in the year 2000, what enthralled readers included simple stories on how single parents put bread on the table, reared a family, and learned from their mistakes. What will be big in the future in publishing will be simple tales of what you learned. Details would include how you (or your client) came to understand, and what you'll share with readers. The theme of a memoirs gift book is about what your client learned from past mistakes. The book would be about what significant events and facts helped your client to grow and become a better person making the world a gentler place.

Those life stories in demand by the public that go beyond coffee-table gift books for relatives and friends also include values, virtues, and ethics in simple stories that help people heal. Universal stories with which we all can identify and use to solve problems and make decisions are salable.

Confirm with your client if you're ghostwriting a book for sale to the public for a flat fee, or whether you're doing work for hire for a flat fee with all publishing rights on a book that you can sell to the public. Or are you signing a contract to write, edit, and publish a few copies of a private book that you can't sell publicly, but the client can buy copies from you and sell himself to relatives, friends, or business employees. Discern whether the book actually is an infomercial presented as a case history success story to promote a business or product.

Gift books destined for the self help and inspirational markets or the "mind-body-spirit" markets that are based on people's life stories, generally show readers how to have more choices. These gift books of information and photos show people how one person found alternative solutions, possibilities, and explored avenues of information with which to solve problems and make decisions. A lot of those books come from salable diaries and life stories as well as corporate and executive histories.

What sold widely by 2002 emphasized how people escaped domestic violence, by becoming financially self-sufficient. Methods of solving problems included looking creatively at more possibilities and alternatives. By 2003-2004 books focused on creativity enhancement and self-expression.

The year 2003 became a utopia for discussing decisions chosen in various self-help diaries or personal history novels, and journals on creativity enhancement through life stories. You only have to look at the book lists in the publisher's magazines to see what the fad genre is for any one year and interview publishing professionals for the trends and directions for the following year.

Write about the human side of careers worked at for years. What did you retire to? How did you survive historic events, rear your family, or solve problems?

The purpose of personal history writing can be, among other goals, to find closure. Those who can't use a hand-operated mouse and need to use a foot pedal mouse, breath straw, or other devices can still operate computers. Others need assistance software to magnify the screen or audio software such as "Jaws," to hear as they type on keyboards.

The idea is to use personal history and life story writing as a healing instrument to make contact with others, find this closure, relieve stress, to talk to parents long gone, to make decisions on how to grow, find understanding, learn from past mistakes, grow, and become a better person in one's own eyes.

Other students take a personal history, oral history, or life story writing classes to pass on to their grandchildren a script, a novel, a story, or a collage of their life experiences, and still others want corporate histories of how they founded their companies and became role models of success for business students to simulate, how they became successful giants for others to follow and benchmark.

Still other students are visionaries who want their life stories to be used to enhance the creativity of readers. Some of my students want to write their life story as a computer or board game on how they solved their own problems that are universal to all of us. And you have students who want careers as personal historians recording, transcribing, and preserving in a variety of formats the personal histories of individuals, families, corporations, art forms, and institutions.

Some are into conservation of videos, photographs, text material, tape recordings, CDs, DVDs, and other multimedia formats. All are involved in making time capsules for future researchers, historians, scholars, librarians, genealogists, and specialists who research personal and oral history or specialized history, such as music and art or rare books and manuscripts.

Others are collectors. Most want a time capsule of a relative, complete with not only a relative's keepsake albums or video diary, but sometimes even a DNA printout for ancestry.

If you look in many publications of interest to writers, you might see online or correspondence courses offered to writers at American College of Journalism, Burlington College, Columbus University, specialists in distance education, or at Gotham Writers' Workshops at www.writingclasses.com. There's Writers Digest School, and data bases where you can learn about agents at Agent Research & Evaluation, 334 E. 30, NYC, NY 10016 or on the Web at www.agentresearch. com. These are some of the online classes in writing advertised. You'll also see ads for classes in personal story writing in some of these publications.

You can get paid to teach what you love to do so much—share your writing techniques and write. Some writing schools online may put articles up on their trade journal online. And you can always sell articles to paying markets and use the clips with resumes. Thanks to the Internet—even a disabled teacher who isn't able to speak before a class for health reasons or drive to class, can teach and write online.

Personal history writing courses could also aim to show research on how creative writing can heal or have therapeutic qualities in gentle self-expression and quality circles online, and now I've found students who learn how to write a life story as therapy to heal and to find closure, solve problems, and to explore more choices, alternatives, and growth towards a kinder and gentler world.

You can focus strictly on recording, transcribing, and archiving people's or corporation's personal or oral histories and preserving them in a variety of formats as time capsules or target the more creative end of teaching writing personal histories as books, plays, or skits.

In other words, you can be both a personal historian and a writing coach or focus on either career or business—oral and personal historian, or teacher of courses or "quality circles" in writing autobiographies and biographies for commercial markets.

You can start private classes on a mailing list and chat board. A fair price to charge could be about $80 per student for advanced workshops in writing salable material for 4-week courses with a 10-page critique per student. Your aim would be to be an online job coach in a writing or personal history career. Help students find ways to get into print by referring you them to resources. Show how to make writing more commercial. Reveal the techniques of effective story writing in your true story, biography, memoirs, autobiography, diary, journal, novel, story, play, or article.

A lot of biography writing is focused on interviews, whereas writing a diary or monologue focuses on inner reflections and expressions in explaining how you came to understand, learn from your past mistakes or experiences and good choices, and share how you solved problems, grew, and changed or were transformed.

Personal diaries start out with poetic-like descriptions of the senses, with lines such as "Cat shadow plump I arrive, carrying my Siamese kitten like a rifle through Spokane, while the only sensation I feel is my hair stretched like flaxen wires where my new kitten, Patches, hangs on.

A gentle clock, the red beams of light reflected in his blue eyes remind me that my tattered self also must eat. His claws dig into my purse strap like golden flowers curling in unshaven armpits. I inhale his purrs like garlic, warm as the pap mom cat, Rada-Ring flowed into Patches nine weeks ago."

Have an enriching writing experience. I truly believe writing heals in some ways. It's a transformative experience like meditation or having the comforting feeling of watching a waterfall in natural settings or sitting in a garden of hanging green plants. Writing recharges my energy must like petting my kitten, Kokowellen, a Siamese while sitting my orchid garden listening to soothing melodies.

You might want to critique for pay, the pages of other people's writing of personal histories if they want to write for the commercial markets. In that case, critiquing may be done by email and online.

That way they don't send any hard copy to mail back or get lost. You always keep a copy. However, I recommend teaching online a course with the critique, as you'll get far more for your $80 for each ten pages of critiquing as a fair price, plus the tuition of the course as perhaps another $80.

The course provides resources, techniques, and ways to revise your material that helps you gain visibility. It's important to pre-sell your book and gain publicity for your writing before you send it off to a publisher or agent. You'll want to know how not to give too much away, but how to attract positive attention so people will eagerly look forward to hearing more from you.

Keep a separate mailing list for your online students. Make a mailing list. Plays or monologues written from memoirs and diaries or excerpts and highlights of life stories are in right now in the publishing world. It's not a passed fad, yet, like the angel books were a decade ago. If you're writing a diary, you want to write something in your first or second page after the opening that goes like this to be more commercial:

"Eagerness to learn grows on me. I see it reflected in the interviewers who stare at me, their enthusiasm is an approval of my expansive mind. I read so much now, just to look at the pages is to feel nourished. A kind of poetry turns into children's books on DVDs like a stalk that grows no where else is in season.

Creativity, like color, runs off my keyboard into the cooking water of my screen, drenched in pungent brainstorming. Writing online puts me in every farmer's kitchen. My computer has a good scent, and the stories written on its screen are apples bursting on the trees of my fingers. On my Web site, photos hang like lanterns. Teaching online ripens my stories. I analyze what effective storytelling means. Picture the colorful pagodas of the mind in three dimensions with musical wind chimes and gentle palm-latitude breezes.

If you come across writers block, try writing the lyrics to a song as a way to start writing your life story. You don't need to read notes, just fiddle with the words based upon an experience in time. Start by writing the ending first. Perhaps your title on salable diaries could be, "Pretty Little Secret," or "Ending the Silence," or "Results of Promises," or "Guided by a Child's Silence," or "Unraveling a Tale," or "Bravery and Unspeakable Links," or "Unveiled, Unbridled, Unbound." My title was "Insight, Hindsight, Foresight."

17

How to Motivate People to Interview One Another for Personal History Productions

Week Three:

Use slogans or mottos to help people describe what their life story is basically about in theme. Nearly everyone can think of a slogan or motto that describes their life purpose or what they stand for. This slogan breaks the ice to begin answering questions that will form the basis of a life story or memoir.

People are "less camera shy" when two from the same peer group or class pair up and interview each other on video camcorder or on audio tape from a list of questions rehearsed. People also can write the questions they want to be asked and also write out and familiarize themselves with the answers alone and/or with their interviewers from their own peer group.

Some people have their favorite proverbs, or a logo that represents their outlook on life. Others have their own 'crusade' or mission. And some have a slogan that says what they are about in a few words…example, "seeking the joy of life," or "service with a smile."

Gift books destined for coffee tables can be a life story narration with photos on the left side and text on the right side. The reason is that most people's eyes immediately travel to the right side or page of a book for text and to the left side for photos. (The right hemisphere of the brain controls the left eye and is wired for visuals. The left hemisphere of the brain controls the right eye and right side of the body and is wired for verbal tasks such as reading or speaking in words. Left-handed people may work opposite.)

Memoir books or life story plays may come from someone's slogan, for example. A slogan, logo, proverb, or motto can form the foundation for a questionnaire on what they want to say in an oral history or personal history video or audio tape on in a multimedia presentation of their life story highlights.

Here are some ways to interview people for personal history time capsules or how to inspire them to interview one another in a group setting or in front of a video camcorder in private with only interviewer and interviewee present.

And then there are those who want to tape themselves alone in their room or office with a camcorder on a tripod and a remote control device or a tape recorder and photographs. When records stop, there are always the DNA-driven genealogy and ancestry printouts.

Some people enjoy writing their life stories more than they like to speak about it. Or they prefer to read from a script as an audio tape. For those whose voices are impaired or for those who prefer to let a synthetic software voice tell their story, I recommend software such as TextAloud.

This software allows anyone to cut and paste their writing from a disk such as a floppy disk, CD, DVD, or hard drive disk to the TextAloud software and select the type of voice to read their writing. With AT&T Natural Voices, you can select a male or female voice.

There are also voices with accents, such as a British accent male voice, and voice software available in a variety of languages to read writing in other languages. TextAloud is made by Nextup.com at the Web site: http://www.nextup. com/. According to their Web site, "TextAloud MP3 is Text-to-Speech software that uses voice synthesis to create spoken audio from text. You can listen on your PC or save text to MP3 or wave files for listening later." I play the MP3 files on my MP3 player.

I save the files to a CD as MP3 files. In this way I can turn my writing into audio books, pamphlets, or articles, poetry, plays, monologues, skits, or any form of writing read aloud by the synthetic software voice software. I save my audio files as MP3 files so I can play my personal history audio in my MP3 player on in my personal computer. MP3 files are condensed and take up a lot less room in your computer or on a Web site or CD and DVD disk than an audio .wav file.

For people who are creating "celebration of life" oral or personal history audio tapes, it works well especially for those who prefer not to read their own writing aloud to a tape recorder. Although most people would like to hear their relatives' voices on tape in audio and video, some people are not able to read their works aloud to a recorder or camcorder.

The synthetic voices will turn any type of writing saved on a disk as a text file into recorded voice—from short poetry to long-length books. The voices are usually recorded with Total Recorder software and saved as an MP3 file so they can be played on MP3 players or on most computers with CD players.

For those taping persons live in video to make time capsules or other keepsake albums in voice and/or video, it's best to let people think what they are going to say by handing them a list of a few questions. If you're working with a group of older adults, let one of the group members interview another group member by asking each question from a list of several questions.

If you give someone a week's notice to come up with an answer to each question from a list of ten questions and give them two minutes to respond to each question by discussing how it relates to events in their lives or their experiences, you have a twenty minute video tape.

If you allow only a minute for each question from a list of thirty questions, you have a thirty-minute tape. Times may not be exact as people tend to elaborate to flesh out a question. Let the interview and interviewee practice before recording. So it's good to pair up two people. One will ask the interview questions, and the other will answer, talking about turning points and significant events in their lives.

They can be asked whether they have a personal proverb or slogan they live by or a motto or personal logo. Tapes can be anywhere from a half hour to an hour for life stories that can be saved as an MP3 file to a CD. Other files such as a Wave file (.wav) take up too much space on a CD. So they could be condensed into an MP3 file and saved that way. TextAloud and Total Recorder are software programs that save audio files. You can also use Music Match to convert .wav files to MP3 files.

I use TextAloud software and Total Recorder. Also I save the files as MP3 files for an audio CD that will also go up on a Web site. I use Windows Media Player to play the video files and save them as a Windows Media file (WMV file) so they can be easily uploaded to a Web site and still play in Windows Media Player that comes with Windows XP software.

When making time capsules in multimedia, I save on a CD and/or a DVD, and upload the file from my hard disk to a Web site. Copies of the CDs can be given to relatives, the interviewee, museums, libraries, and various schools who may be interested in oral history with a theme.

The themes can be celebrations of life, living time capsules, or fit into any group theme under an umbrella title that holds them together. This can be an era, such as living memories of a particular decade, life experiences in oral history of an area in geography, an ethnic group, or any other heading. Or the tapes can be of individuals or family groups.

Not only life stories, but poetry, plays, novels, stories, and any other form of creative nonfiction or fiction writing can be recorded by synthetic voices as audio story or book collections. Some work well as children's stories and other types of writings as life stories or poetry.

Themes can vary from keepsake albums to time capsules to collections of turning points in history from the life stories of individuals. Also, themes can be recorded as "old time radio" programs or as oral military history from the experiences of veterans and notated to the Veterans History Project at the Library of Congress or other groups and museums. Make sure you have signed *release forms* that also release you from liability should any problems arise from putting someone's life story and name on the Web and/or donating it to a library or other public archive.

A good example of a release form is the one posted at the Veteran's History Project Web site where life stories of veterans are donated to the Library of Congress and accessible to the public for educational or scholarly research. Check out the .PDF release forms for both the interviewer and the interviewee at their Web site. The release form for veterans is at: http://www.loc.gov/folklife/vets/vetform-vetrelease.pdf.

18

Before Video Recording Life Stories of Older Adults: Questions to Ask

Interviewing for Writing Plays and Skits from Life Stories for Junior and Senior High-School Students and/or Mature Adults.

STEP 1: Send someone enthusiastic about personal and oral history to senior community centers, lifelong learning programs at universities, nursing homes, or senior apartment complexes activity rooms. You can reach out to a wide variety of older adults in many settings, including at libraries, church groups, hobby and professional or trade associations, unions, retirement resorts, public transportation centers, malls, museums, art galleries, genealogy clubs, and intergenerational social centers.

STEP 2: Have each personal historian or volunteer bring a tape recorder with tape and a note pad. Bring camcorders for recording video to turn into time capsules and CDs or DVDs with life stories, personal history experiences, memoirs, and events highlighting turning points or special times in people's lives.

STEP 3: Assign each personal historian one or two older persons to interview with the following questions.

1. What were the most significant turning points or events in your life?

2. How did you survive the Wars?

3. What were the highlights, turning points, or significant events that you experienced during the economic downturn of 1929-1939? How did you cope or solve your problems?

4. .What did you do to solve your problems during the significant stages of your life at age 10, 20, 30, 40, 50, 60 and 70-plus? Or pick a year that you want to talk about.

5. What changes in your life do you want to remember and pass on to future generations?

6. What was the highlight of your life?

7. How is it best to live your life after 70?

8. What years do you remember most?

9. What was your favorite stage of life?

10. What would you like people to remember about you and the times you lived through?

STEP 3:
Have the student record the older person's answers. Select the most significant events, experiences, or turning points the person chooses to emphasize. Then write the story of that significant event in ten pages or less.
STEP 4: Ask the older person to supply the younger student photos, art work, audio tapes, or video clips. Usually photos, pressed flowers, or art work will be supplied. Have the student or teacher scan the photos onto a disk and return the original photos or art work or music to the owner.
STEP 5:The personal historian, volunteer, student and/or teacher scans the photos and puts them onto a Web site on the Internet at one of the free communities that give away Web site to the public at no cost…some include http://www.
tripod.com, http://www.fortunecity.com, http://www.angelfire.com, http://www.geocities.com, and others. Most search engines will give a list of communities at offering free Web sites to the public. Microsoft also offers free family Web sites for family photos and newsletters or information. Ask your Internet service provider whether it offers free Web site space to subscribers. The free Web sites are limited in space.
For larger Web site spaces with room for audio and video material and other keepsake memorabilia, purchase a personal Web site from a Web-hosting company. Shop around for affordable Web site space for a multimedia life story time capsule that would include text, video and/or audio clips, music, art, photos, and any other effects.

1. Create a Web site with text from the older person's significant life events

2. Add photos.

3. Add sound or .wav files with the voice of the older person speaking in small clips or sound bites.

4. Intersperse text and photos or art work with sound, if available.
    Add video clips, if available and won't take too much bandwidth.

5. Put Web site on line as TIME CAPSULE of (insert name of person) interviewed and edited by, insert name of student who interviewed older person.

STEP 6: Label each Web site Time Capsule and collect them in a history archives on the lives of older adults at the turn of the millennium. Make sure the older person and all relatives and friends are emailed the Web site link. You have now created a time capsule for future generations.

This can be used as a classroom exercise in elementary and high schools to teach the following:

1. Making friends with older adults.

2. Learning to write on intergenerational topics.

3. Bringing community together of all generations.

4. Learning about foster grandparents.

5. History lessons from those who lived through history.

6. Learning about diversity and how people of diverse origins lived through the 20th century.

7. Preserving the significant events in the lives of people as time capsules for future generations to know what it was like to live between 1900 and 2000 at any age.

8. Learning to write skits and plays from the life stories of older adults taken down by young students.

9. Teaching older adults skills in creative writing at senior centers.

10. Learning what grandma did during World War 2 or the stock market crash of 1929 followed by the economic downturn of 1930-1938.

What to Ask People about Their Lives before You Write a Play or Skit

Step 1
When you interview, ask for facts and concrete details. Look for statistics, and research whether statistics are deceptive in your case.
Step 2
To write a plan, write one sentence for each topic that moves the story or piece forward. Then summarize for each topic in a paragraph. Use dialogue at least in every third paragraph.
Step 3
Look for the following facts or headings to organize your plan for a biography or life story.

1. PROVERB. Ask the people you interview what proverb represents their life stories. Look at a book of proverbs, but develop an original proverb not copyrighted or cliché. Proverbs can be found in libraries or even on tee shirts and bumper stickers. Create your own as you work with your client.

2. PURPOSE, MOTTO, OR SLOGAN. Ask the people you interview or a biography, for what purpose is or was their journey? Is or was it equality in the workplace or something personal and different such as dealing with change—downsizing, working after retirement, or anything else? If your client had to create/invent a slogan or aspiration that fit that person, what would it be? One slogan might be something like the seventies ad for cigarettes, "We've come a long way, baby," to signify ambition achieved. Look for an original slogan, not a copyrighted slogan or a cliché.

3. IMPRINT. Ask what makes an imprint or impact on people's lives and what impact the people you're interviewing want to make on others?

4. STATISTICS: How deceptive are they? How can you use them to focus on reality?

5. How have the people that you're interviewing influenced changes in the way people or corporations function? How does your client share meaning (communicate) with others?

6. What is your client's goal in life? To what is the person aspiring?

7. What kind of communication skills does the person have and how are these skills received? Are the communication skills male or female, thinking or feeling, yin or yang, soft or steeled, and are people around these people negative or positive about those communication skills?

8. What new styles is the person using? What kind of motivational methods, structure, or leadership? Is the person a follower or leader? How does the person match his or her personality to the character of a corporation or interest?

9. How does the person handle change?

10. How is the person reinforced?

Once you have titles and summarized paragraphs for each segment of your story, you can more easily flesh out the story by adding dialogue and description to your factual information. Look for differences in style between the people you interview? How does the person want to be remembered?

Is the person a risk taker or cautious for survival? Does the person identify with her job or the people involved in the process of doing the work most creatively or originally?

Does creative expression take precedence over processes of getting work out to the right place at the right time? Does the person want his ashes to spell the words "re-invent yourself" where the sea meets the shore? This is a popular concept appearing in various media.

19

Search the Records in the Family History Library of Salt Lake City, Utah

Make use of the database online at the Family History Library of Salt Lake City, Utah. Or visit the branches in many locations. The Family History Library (FHL) is known worldwide as the focal point of family history records preservation.

The FHL collection contains more than 2.2 million rolls of microfilmed genealogical records, 742,000 microfiche, 300,000 books, and 4,500 periodicals that represent data collected from over 105 countries. You don't have to be a member of any particular church or faith to use the library or to go online and search the records.

Family history records owe a lot to the invention of writing. And then there is oral history, but someone needs to transcribe oral history to record and archive them for the future.

Interestingly, isn't it a coincidence that writing is 6,000 years old and DNA that existed 6,000 years ago first reached such crowded conditions in the very cities that had first used writing extensively to measure accounting and trade had very little recourse but to move on to new areas where there were far less people and less use of writing?

A lot of major turning points occurred 6,000 years ago—the switch to a grain-based diet from a meat and root diet, the use of bread and fermented grain beverages, making of oil from plants, and the rise of religions based on building "god houses" in the centers of town in areas known as the "cereal belt" around the world.

Six thousand years ago in India we have the start of the Sanskrit writings, the cultivation of grain. In China, we have the recording of acupuncture points for medicine built on energy meridians that also show up in the blue tattoos of the

Ice Man fossil "Otsi" in the Alps—along the same meridians as the Chinese acupuncture points.

At 6,000 years ago the Indo European languages spread out across Europe. Mass migrations expanded by the Danube leaving pottery along the trade routes that correspond to the clines and gradients of gene frequency coming out of the cereal belts.

Then something happened. There was an agricultural frontier cutting off the agriculturists from the hunters. Isn't it a coincidence that the agricultural frontiers or barriers also are genetic barriers at least to some degree?

Oral History

Here's how to systematically collect, record, and preserve living peoples' testimonies about their own experiences. After you record in audio and/or video the highlights of anyone's experiences, try to verify your findings. See whether you can check any facts in order to find out whether the person being recorded is making up the story or whether it really did happen.

This is going to be difficult unless you have witnesses or other historical records. Once you have verified your findings to the best of your ability, note whether the findings have been verified. Then analyze what you found. Put the oral history recordings in an accurate historical context.

Mark the recordings with the dates and places. Watch where you store your findings so scholars in the future will be able to access the transcript or recording and convert the recording to another, newer technology. For instance, if you have a transcript on paper, have it saved digitally on a disk and somewhere else on tape and perhaps a written transcript on acid-free good paper in case technology moves ahead before the transcript or recording is converted to the new technology.

For example, if you only put your recording on a phonograph record, within a generation or two, there may not be any phonographs around to play the record. The same goes for CDs, DVDs and audio or video tapes.

So make sure you have a readable paper copy to be transcribed or scanned into the new technology as well as the recordings on disk and tape. For example, if you record someone's experiences in a live interview with your video camera, use a cable to save the video in the hard disk of a computer and then burn the file to a CD or DVD.

Keep a copy of audio tape and a copy of regular video tape—all in a safe place such as a time capsule, and make a copy for various archives in libraries and university oral history preservation centers. Be sure scholars in the future can find a way to enjoy the experiences in your time capsule, scrapbook, or other storage device for oral histories.

Use your DNA testing results to add more information to a historical record. As an interviewer with a video camera and/or audio tape recorder, your task is to record as a historical record what the person who you are interviewing recollects.

The events move from the person being interviewed to you, the interviewer, and then into various historical records. In this way you can combine results of DNA testing with actual memories of events. If it's possible, also take notes or have someone take notes in case the tape doesn't pick up sounds clearly.

I had the experience of having a video camera battery go out in spite of all precautions when I was interviewing someone, and only the audio worked. So keep a backup battery on hand whether you use a tape recorder or a video camera. If at all possible, have a partner bring a spare camera and newly recharged battery. A fully charged battery left overnight has a good chance of going out when you need it.

20

Writing Skits for Personal History

Emphasize the commitment to family and faith. To create readers' and media attention to an oral history, it should have some redemptive value to a universal audience. That's the most important point. Make your oral history simple and earthy. Write about real people who have values, morals, and a faith in something greater than themselves that is equally valuable to readers or viewers.

Publishers who buy an oral history written as a book on its buzz value are buying simplicity. It is simplicity that sells and nothing else but simplicity. This is true for oral histories, instructional materials, and fiction. It's good storytelling to say it simply.

Simplicity means the oral history or memoirs book or story gives you all the answers you were looking for in your life in exotic places, but found it close by. What's the great proverb that your oral history is telling the world?

Is it to stand on your own two feet and put bread on your own table for your family? That's the moral point, to pull your own weight, and pulling your own weight is a buzz word that sells oral histories and fiction that won't preach, but instead teach and reach through simplicity.

That's the backbone of the oral historian's new media. Buzz means the story is simple to understand. You make the complex easier to grasp. And buzz means you can sell your story or book, script or narrative by focusing on the values of simplicity, morals, faith, and universal values that hold true for everyone.

Doing the best to take care of your family sells and is buzz appeal, hot stuff in the publishing market of today and in the oral history archives. This is true, regardless of genre. Publishers go through fads every two years—angel books, managing techniques books, computer home-based business books, novels about ancient historical characters or tribes, science fiction, children's programming, biography, and oral history transcribed into a book or play.

The genres shift emphasis, but values are consistent in the bestselling books. Perhaps your oral history will be simple enough to become a bestselling book or script. In the new media, simplicity is buzz along with values.

Oral history, like best-selling novels and true stories is built on simplicity, values, morals, and commitment. Include how one person dealt with about trends. Focus your own oral history about life in the lane of your choice. Develop one central issue and divide that issue into a few important questions that highlight or focus on that one central issue.

When you write or speak a personal history either alone or in an interview, you focus on determining the order of your life story. Don't use flashbacks. Focus on the highlights and turning points. Organize what you'll say or write. An autobiography deals in people's relationships. Your autobiography deals as much with what doesn't change—the essentials—as what life changes you and those around you go through.

Your personal history gift book should be more concrete than abstract. You want the majority of people to understand what you mean. Generally, people at first glance understand more concrete details than abstract ideas.

Resources for Paper Conservation of Your Genealogy/Family History Book

American Institute for Conservation
1717 K Street, NW, Suite 200
Washington, DC 20006
http://aic.stanford.edu
info@aic-faic.org

Light Impressions (Archival Supplies)
PO Box 22708
Rochester, NY 14692-2708
http://www.lightimpressionsdirect.com

Bibliography:

WAAC Newsletter
http://palimpsest.stanford.edu/aic'disaster

WAAC Newsletter, Vol. 19, No 2 (May, 1997) articles and charts online by Betty Walsh, Conservator, BC Archives, Canada and the Walsh's information at: http://palimpsest.stanford.edu/waac/wn/wn10/wn10-2/wn10-202.html. The site contains material from the WAAC Newsletter, Volume 10, Number 2, May 1988, pp.2-5.

Curatorial Care of Works of Art on Paper, New York: Intermuseum Conservation Association, 1987.

Library Materials Preservation Manual: Practical Methods for Preserving Books, Pamphlets, and Other Printed Materials, Heidi Kyle. 1984

Archives & Manuscripts: Conservation–A Manual on Physical Care and Management, Mary Lynn Ritzenthaler, Society of American Archivists: Chicago, 1993.

"It's not enough to create magic. You have to create a price for magic, too. You have to create rules."

—Eric A. Burns, Gossamer Commons, 06-15-05

21

Genealogy as Social History

Genealogy records, autobiographies, memoirs, monologues, skits, plays, biographies, personal histories, plays, DNA-driven genealogy reports, and monologues present points of view within the umbrella of social history and geography. When looking at genealogy through the lens of social history, ask whether all sides are given equal emphasis? Will the researchers choose favorite characters?

Life stories, and genealogy records, like cameras, give fragments, points of view, and bits and pieces. Sometimes you only see names and dates. In a video about someone's family history, viewers will see what the videographer or photographer intends to be seen. When interviewing people to obtain slices of life, the interviewee will be trying to put his point of view across and tell the story from his perspective.

Autobiographies, biographies, personal histories, plays, and monologues present a point of view. In a chronological autobiography, you write in the first person, like in a diary. Only the work reads like a good novel. Autobiographies cover most of your life at different ages or stages, such as coming-of-age stories.

Memoirs are slices of life—significant events and turning points or life experiences that are emphasized to show your life's purpose. Are all sides given equal emphasis? Will the audience choose favorite characters?

Genealogy information combined with autobiography or memoirs as time capsules or gift books include both photos and text. The chapters are like narrated camera scenes that give fragments, points of view, and bits and pieces. Plays and skits use dialogue to show life stories against social history and current events of that time.

Will the photographer or videographer be in agreement with the interviewee? Or if you are recording for print transcript, will your point of view agree with the interviewee's perspective and experience if your basic 'premise,' where you two are coming from, are not in agreement? Think this over as you write your list of questions. Do both of you agree on your central issue on which you'll focus for the interview?

How are you going to turn spoken words into text for your paper hard copy transcript? Will you transcribe verbatim, correct the grammar, or quote as you hear the spoken words? Oral historians really need to transcribe the exact spoken word. You can leave out the 'ahs' and 'oms' or loud pauses, as the interviewee thinks what to say next. You don't want to sound like a court reporter, but you do want to have an accurate record transcribed of what was spoken.

You're also not editing for a movie, unless you have permission to turn the oral history into a TV broadcast, where a lot gets cut out of the interview for time constraints. For that, you'd need written permission so words won't be taken out of context and strung together in the editing room to say something different from what the interviewee intended to say.

Someone talking could put in wrong names, forget what they wanted to say, or repeat themselves. They could mumble, ramble, or do almost anything. So you would have to sit down and weed out redundancy when you can or decide on presenting exactly what you've heard as transcript.

When someone reads the transcript in text, they won't have what you had in front of you, and they didn't see and hear the live presentation or the videotape. It's possible to misinterpret gestures or how something is spoken, the mood or tone, when reading a text transcript. Examine all your sources. Use an ice-breaker to get someone talking.

If a woman is talking about female-interest issues, she may feel more comfortable talking to another woman. Find out whether the interviewee is more comfortable speaking to someone of his or her own age. Some older persons feel they can relate better to someone close to their own age than someone in high school, but it varies. Sometimes older people can speak more freely to a teenager.

The interviewee must be able to feel comfortable with the interviewer and know he or she will not be judged. Sometimes it helps if the interviewer is the same ethnic group or there is someone present of the same group or if new to the language, a translator is present.

Read some books on oral history field techniques. Read the National Genealogical Society Quarterly (NGSQ). Also look at The American Genealogist (TAG), The Genealogist, and The New England Historical and Genealogical Register (The Register). If you don't know the maiden name of say, your grandmother's mother, and no relative knows either because it wasn't on her death certificate, try to reconstruct the lives of the males who had ever met the woman whose maiden name is unknown.

Maybe she did business with someone before marriage or went to school or court. Someone may have recorded the person's maiden name before her marriage. Try medical records if any were kept. There was no way to find my mother's grandmother's maiden name until I started searching to see whether she had any brothers in this country. She had to have come as a passenger on a ship around 1880 as she bought a farm. Did her husband come with her?

Was the farm in his name? How many brothers did she have in this country with her maiden surname? If the brothers were not in this country, what countries did they come from and what cities did they live in before they bought the farm in Albany? If I could find out what my great grandmother's maiden name was through any brothers living at the time, I could contact their descendants perhaps and see whether any male or female lines are still in this country or where else on the globe.

Perhaps a list of midwives in the village at the time is recorded in a church or training school for midwives. Fix the person in time and place. Find out whom she might have done business with and whether any records of that business exist. What businesses did she patronize? Look for divorce or court records, change of name records, and other legal documents.

Look at local sources. Did anyone save records from bills of sale for weddings, purchases of homes, furniture, debutante parties, infant supplies, or even medical records? Look at nurses' licenses, midwives' registers, employment contracts, and teachers' contracts, alumni associations for various schools, passports, passenger lists, alien registration cards, naturalization records, immigrant aid societies, city directories, and cross-references.

Try religious and women's clubs, lineage and village societies, girl scouts and similar groups, orphanages, sanatoriums, hospitals, police records. Years ago there was even a Eugenics Record Office. What about the women's prisons? The first one opened in 1839—Mount Pleasant Female Prison, NY.

Try voters' lists. If your relative is from another country, try records in those villages or cities abroad. Who kept the person's diaries? Have you checked the Orphan Train records? Try ethnic and religious societies and genealogy associations for that country. Most ethnic genealogy societies have a special interest group for even the smallest villages in various countries.

You can start one and put up a Web site for people who also come from there in past centuries. Check alimony, divorce, and court records, widow's pensions of veterans, adoptions, orphanages, foster homes, medical records, birth, marriage, and death certificates, social security, immigration, pet license owners' files, prisons, alumni groups from schools, passenger lists, military, and other legal records.

When all historical records are being tied together, you can add the DNA testing to link all those cousins. Check military pensions on microfilms in the National Archives. Research the public records bibliographies, directories, and censuses.

◆   ◆   ◆

Preparing Personal History Time Capsules for a Journey

Be personal in a personal history life story. The more personal you are, the more eternal is your life story. More people will view or read it again and again far into the future. You can emphasize your life's journey and look at the world through your own eyes. To make the structure salable, 'meander' your life as you would travel on a journey. Perhaps you're a winding river meandering around obstacles and competitors. At each stop, you learn your own capabilities and your own place in the world.

The more you meander, the more you take away the urgency from your story that sets up tension in the audience and keeps them on the edge of their seat. Don't let the meandering overpower your sense of urgency. Don't dwell on your reaction. Focus on your action to people and situations. Stay active in your own personal history. In other words, don't repeat how you reacted, but show how you acted.

Before you sit down to write your autobiography, think of yourself in terms of going on a journey inside the privacy of your purse or wallet. May your purse is the only place where you really do have any privacy. Come up for air when you have hit bottom. Bob up to the sunshine, completely changed or at least matured.

If you have really grown, you will not be blinded by the light, in the figurative sense, as the song goes. Instead, the light gives you insight. So now you have vision along with some hindsight. The next step is learning how to promote and market your salable personal history or life story.

A biography reports the selected events of another person's life—usually 12 major events in the six various significant events also known as "turning points" and also known as "transition points" of life that would include the highlights of significant events for each of the six stages of growth: 1) infanthood, 2) childhood, 3) teen years 4) young adulthood 5) middle life 6) maturity.

Selling Life Stories

Launch your salable life story in the major national press and in various newspapers and magazines of niche markets related to the events in your life, such as weekly newspapers catering to a group: senior citizens, your ethnic group, your local area, or your occupation or area of interest. Your personal history time capsule may be saved to disk and also uploaded to the Web. What about looking for movie deals and book publishers?

If you don't have the money to produce your autobiography as a video biography, or even a film or commercial movie, or publish it for far less cost as a print-on-demand published book, you may wish to find a co-production partner to finance the production of your life story as a cinematic film or made-for-TV video.

At the same time you could contact literary agents and publishers, but one front-page article in a national newspaper or daily newspaper can do wonders to move your life story in front of the gaze of publishers and producers. While you're waiting for a reporter to pay attention to the news angle you have selected for your life story, I highly recommend Michael Wiese's book <u>Film and Video Marketing</u> because it lists some co-production partners as the following:

Private Investors/Consortiums

Foreign Governments (blocked funds)

Financiers

Corporations

Theatrical Distributors

International Theatrical Distributors

International Sales Agents

Home Video

International Home Video

Pay TV

Syndicators

Record Companies

Music Publishers

Book Publishers

Toy Companies

Licensing and Merchandising Firms

Sponsors (products, services)

Public Relations Firms

Marketing Companies/Consultants

Film Bookers

You can also contact actors, directors, producers, feature distributors, home video distributors, entertainment lawyers, brokers, accountants, animation houses, production houses, video post production houses, labs, film facilities, and agents with your script and ask the owners whether they'd be interested in bartering budget items, deferring, or investing in your script.

Private investors could also be professional investors, venture capitalists, and even doctors and dentists who may wish to finance a movie if the potential interests them. You can sell points in your film to investors who finance it as a group of investors, each buying a small percentage of the film for an investment fee.

Or you can approach film investment corporations that specialize in investing in and producing films as partners. They are publicized or listed in the entertainment trade magazines going to producers and workers in the entertainment and film or video industry.

You market your script not only to agents and producers, but to feature distributors, film financiers and co-production partners. This is the first step in finding a way to take your autobiography from script to screen. Learn who distributes what before you approach anyone.

If you want to approach video instead of film, you might wish to know that children's video programming is the fastest-growing genre in original programming. Children's titles account for 10%-15% of the overall home video revenues. According to one of Michael Wiese's books written in the nineties, *Home Video: Producing For The Home Market*, "With retail prices falling and alternative retail outlets expanding, children's programming will soon become one of the most profitable segments of the video market." He was right.

What has happened in the new millennium is that children's program is doing wonderfully. Why? Children's video is repeatable. Children watch the same tape 30 to 50 times. Children's video sells for comparatively lower prices than feature films.

Children's video also rents well. Children's tapes sell it toy stores, book stores, children's stores, and in stores like Woolworth's and Child World. Manufacturers sell tapes at Toy Fair and the American Booksellers Association conventions.

For these reasons, you may wish to write your autobiography as a script for children's video or as a children's book. Video is a burgeoning industry.

According to the market research firm, Fairfield Group, in 1985, the prerecorded video business earned $ 3.3 billion in sales and rentals. This nearly equaled the record and theatrical box office revenues for the same year. The world VCR population is about 100 million. Today we have the DVD and the Internet streaming video.

Back in 1985, the U.S. and Japan accounted for half of the VCRs, followed by the United Kingdom, (9 million) West Germany (nearly 7 million), and Canada, Australia, Turkey, and France (about 3 million each). Spain reported 2 million VCRs. By 1991, the number of VCR ownership increased as prices slowly came down.

Today, in the 21st century, the prerecorded video business has quickly moved to DVD disks, downloadable at a price Internet-based movies, and video tapes are on the way to being a memory of the eighties and early nineties. In the next decade, another media format will be in fashion to replace videos on DVDs and streaming Internet video. The idea is to keep transferring the story from one form of technology to another so that videos made today will be able to be viewed by people in the next century.

The European VCR markets grew faster than in the U.S. during the eighties and nineties just as the DVD markets grew in the early 21st century because there were fewer entertainment alternatives—fewer TV stations, restricted viewing hours, fewer pay TV services, and fewer movie theatres.

You should not overlook the foreign producers for your script. Include Canadian cable TV, foreign agents, and foreign feature film and video producers among your contacts. Most university libraries open to the public for research include directories listing foreign producers. Photocopy their addresses and send them a query letter and one-page synopsis of your script. Don't overlook the producers from non-English speaking countries. Your script can be translated or dubbed.

You might attend film market type conventions and conferences. They draw producers from a variety of countries. In 1989 at the former Cinetex Film Market in Las Vegas, producers from Canada, Italy, Israel, Spain, and other foreign countries sat next to script writers. All of them were receptive to receiving scripts.

They handed one another their business cards. You can learn a lot at summer film markets and film festivals about what kind of scripts are in demand.

Keep a list of which film markets will meet. In the U.S. there are 3 to 5 film markets a year and many more film festivals. Seek out the foreign and local producers with track records and see whether they'd be interested in your script if you have a life story in the form of a script, treatment, or story. Perhaps your theme has some relation to a producer's country or ethnic group. Lots of films are made in Asia, in the Middle East (Israel, Egypt and Tunisia), in Latin America, and Europe or Canada.

Seek out the Australian producers also and New Zealand or India. If you have a low-budget film or home video script set in Korea, Philippines, Japan, or Taiwan, or a specialty film such as Karate or something that appeals to the Indian film market, contact those producers and script agents in those countries. Find out the budget limitations that producers have in the different countries.

Social issues documentaries based on your autobiography are another market for home video. Vestron and other home video distributors use hard-hitting documentaries. Collecting documentary video tapes is like collecting copies of National Geographic magazine. You never throw them out. Tapes are also sold by direct mail. Companies producing and distributing documentaries include MCA, MGM/UA, Vestron, Victory, CBS/Fox, Warner, Media, Karl, Monterey, Thorn/EMI, Embassy, and USA, to name a few.

If you write your autobiography or another's biography as a romance, you might wish to write a script for the video romance series market. Romance video has its roots in the paperback novel. However, the biggest publishers of romance novels have little recognition in retail video stores.

How do romance videos or life stories sell in bookstores? Among consumers that are voting, yes, wholesalers and retailers, voting no. Bookstores are voting, yes. The problem is with pricing. To sell romance videos in bookstores, the tapes would have to be sold at less than $29. In video stores, they can be positioned the same as $59 feature films on video.

Production costs to make high quality romance videos are high. Top stars, top writers, hit book titles, exotic locations, music and special effects are required. Huge volumes of tapes must be sold to break even. Then producers have to search for pay TV, broadcast, or foreign partners. The budget for a one-hour video tape of a thin romance story comes to $500,000.

It's far better to make a low-budget feature film. Romance as a genre has never previously appealed to the video retail buyer. In contrast, a romance paperback sells for a few dollars. Now the question remains: Would women buy a romance-genre video DVD priced at $9.95?

Romance novels successfully have been adapted to audio tape for listening at far less than the cost of video. There is a market for audio scripts of short romance novels and novellas. What is becoming popular today are videos and 'movies' downloadable from the Internet that you can watch on your computer screen or save to a DVD since DVD burners became affordable and popular. Try adapting highlights of your romance or life story novel to a play, skit, or monologue.

The only way romance videos would work is by putting together a multi-partnered structure that combines pay TV, home video, book publishing, and domestic and foreign TV. In the eighties, was anyone doing romance video tapes? Yes. Prism Video produced six feature-length romance films, acquired from Comworld. In 1985 the tapes sold for $11.95.

Comworld had limited TV syndication exposure and was one of the first to come out with romance videos. Karl/Lorimar came out with eight romance films from L/A House Productions on a budget of $400,000 each. They were also priced at $11.95 in 1985. To break even, a company has to sell about 60,000 units per title.

Twenty years later, think about adapting to a play the romance DVD video and the downloadable Internet video. What's available to adapt as educational material? Write for various age groups on niche subjects that would appeal to teachers. Follow their rules on what is appropriate for their classrooms. The market also is open for stage and radio/Internet broadcast skits and plays geared to older adults as performers and audiences.

Other media are like open doors to finding a way to put your life story on a disk. Any interview, script, or story can go from print-on-demand published novel or true story book to radio script or stage play. A video can move from a digital high 8 camcorder with a Firewire 1394 cable attached to a personal computer rapidly into the hard disk drive via Windows XP Movie Maker software. Or you can purchase the latest camcorders that record directly onto a mini-disk that looks similar to a small CD or DVD and which can be played directly on your CD or DVD player or saved and played in your computer.

From there it can be saved as a WMV file (a Windows Media file). Then the file can be recorded on a DVD, if long, or a CD if under one hour. Poems can be written, read, and 'burned' to a compact disk (CD) and then mailed out as greeting cards, love letters, or personal histories. Short videos can be emailed.

Romance or life story highlights novels and scripts on audio tape cost less to produce. This market occasionally advertises for romantic novel manuscripts, scripts, and stories in a variety of writer's magazines.

Check out the needs of various magazines for journalists and writers online. If you read a lot of romance genre novels or write in this style, you may want to write your autobiography in this genre, but you'd have to market to publishers who use this genre or biographies in other genres such as factual biography.

If your autobiography is set on events which occurred in your childhood, you might prefer to concentrate on writing appropriate for children's video programming. It's a lot easier to sell to the producers who are basking in the current explosion of children's video programming. Perhaps it's your mission to use the video format to teach children.

Will the script, skit, play, or narrated gift book of a life story do the following?

teach, mentor, motivate, inspire, or inform viewers who can be:
children, teenagers, parents, or 'middle-lifers' on their quests for self-identify or to use in their search for facts: 'middle-lifers' also use life stories or memoirs as guidelines in making their own decisions:

People read other individuals' life's journeys and write introspective journals to gain information in order to make decisions and choices, to transcend past mistakes and learn lessons for the past. People read life stories to learn about foresight, insight, and hindsight in order to avoid pitfalls. Can your diary be dynamic, dramatic, and empowering to others who may be going through similar stages of life? Are your characters charismatic and memorable, likable and strong?

A life story or autobiography when videotaped or filed as a feature-length movie can spring out of a diary or an inner personal journal (which dialogues with the people who impact your life and observes selected, important events).

◆　　　◆　　　◆

"The skill of writing is to create a context in which other people can think."

—Edwin Schlossberg

22

Creative Video Work in Genealogy and Family History Online with Teens

How can you interest teenagers in genealogy and family history if it's perceived as a pursuit of older adults? One of the best ways to promote your creative endeavors is by video podcasting family history or genealogy time capsules online. Video podcasts are age-targeted hubs to launch your creative works in the media before you have pre-sold your creative ideas to your intended audience. There's power in controlling in what shape, how, and when your life's work reaches the public.

Pre-sell your creative work with video podcasts. Launch it in the media before you publish. To persuade the press, create an age-elated hub. This can be a mature adult, parenting, or teen hub. Look at any teen hub from the 1990s, such as Goosehead. There's still room for other shows like Goosehead, and one could feature your unpublished writing, learning, parenting, or merchandising ideas.

Create a similar venture yourself online by first developing the content. You could create content for shows similar to Goosehead or create your own concept. After call, a concept is actually made up of facts built around a foundation or basic message. Think of a concept as a sculpture built step-by-step over a wire frame skeleton.

The idea of a teen hub came about when a 14-year old girl named Ashley Power with her personal Web site caught the attention of Richard Dreyfuss. He made a deal to create content for Goosehead. How did such publicity come to a 14-year olds personal Web site?

Thousands of girls from 11 to 15 daily have personal Web sites and need content. One day actor Richard Dreyfuss's niece appeared in a Goosehead video series. It's quite a leap and rare that the niece of an actor appears in a video series that springs out of a 14-year old girl's Web site. Such rarity is what makes for fame. What part did destiny play? According to media reports, Dreyfuss got in touch with Power and made a deal to create at least two interactive episodes to Goosehead.

What can you do that's interactive? If you're a parent, start with what's familiar to you in parenting. Look at similar sites yourself, and decide what about it made the teen hub or senior citizen life-long learning hubs ripe. How did the concept of a teenage hub move from a 14-year old girl's personal Web site into a video series that caught the eye of a star who writes content for interactive Web?

The episodes, by the way, were called Webisodes. Actually, the technical term is multicasting content as opposed to multimedia that's not always online. Before you test the waters, look at the following sites that use stars to plug products they like. Then think of ways how you can *launch* your unpublished writing in the credible media by *plugging a product* you like and that a star also likes. Look at www.gooshead.com, www.babystyle.com, www.voxxy.com, www. sightsound.com, www.shockwave.com, and www.generationa.com. What did you notice about teen hub sites?

Is there anything similar (based on what you love to do most) that you can do with your sites to produce content or plug a product you like for the age group you want to emphasize? Use your unpublished writing to move your content, be your content, plug your content, or launch someone else's product you use for a fee, and enjoy. That's one other way to launch your unpublished books, booklets, scripts, plays, stories, poems, lyrics, content, or learning material.

Creating Genealogy Video Podcasts: Income Potential

Charge a flat free and/or a retainer for publicity and promotion, such as getting authors on radio and TV programs. You might acquire space on a radio program and ask authors or other people with trendy occupations and interests to be interviewed by you on your own radio show.

Try pod-casting on the Internet as a way to interview people with audio file-based 'radio' shows that people can download to their iPods or other audio devices. What's the current fee? Charge anything from $25 up to have a four to ten-minute radio interview or whatever the market will bear. For half-hour radio interviews, charge double. Don't overcharge authors.

It's better to have a higher volume of clients paying less than be talked about on chat groups as overcharging. You can upload an MP3 audio file and 'pod-cast' the audio on the Internet for less than it costs to buy time on a radio station and charge people to interview them on the air to publicize their books or other items. In promotion of someone's product, never make the language seem as if the author or inventor is talking down to the consumer. You want to make people feel important and positive about their choices. The selling point is to put value on people's decisions and to emphasize commitment to what works well and is healthy in the long run. Help make people feel good about their choices.

If you don't want to compete with the mainstream entertainment industry, there are audiences who want how-to films or videos that were never cinematic entertainment in the first place, but produced direct-to-Web with good multimedia authoring software. Let your unpublished genealogy journalism or other types of family history writing plug, launch, or promote your selected product online, on radio, and on TV. Or package your material with someone else's product. Start a video podcasting site for teenagers or other age groups targeting intergenerational oral history and writing, genealogy, or family history topics.

23

A Molecular Genealogy Revolution (DNA Testing for Family History)

Geneticists today are making inroads in new areas such as phenomics and ancestral genetics. Batsheva Bonné-Tamir, PhD, http://www.tau.ac.il/medicine/USR/bonnétamirb.htm or http://www.tau.ac.il/medicine/ at Tel-Aviv University, Israel, is Head of the National Laboratory for the Genetics of Israeli Populations (with Mia Horowitz) and Director of the Shalom and Varda Yoran Institute for Genome Research Tel-Aviv. She is also on the faculty of the Department of Human Genetics and Molecular Medicine, Sackler School of Medicine.

Dr. Bonné-Tamir states that "One of my most impressive conclusions from the advancement in the last few years and the accumulation of knowledge in the fields of genetics and medicine, is the molecular revolution based on immense sophistication of lab techniques. This is really responsible for the recent increased emphasis on the human-socialanthropological aspects that affect biological diversity."

Bonné-Tamir explains, "At a meeting in 1973, in my paper on Merits and Difficulties in Studies of Middle Eastern Isolates, I said that 'The Middle Eastern isolates have emphasized again the fertile and necessary interrelationship between history and genetics.'"

Do historical events influence genes? "Comparative studies in population genetics are often undertaken in order to attempt reconstruction of historical and migratory movements based on gene frequencies," says Bonné-Tamir. "The Samaritans and Karaites offer opportunities in the opposite direction, for example, to learn the influence of historical events on gene frequencies."

In another paper in 1979 on *Analysis of Genetic Data on Jewish Populations*, Dr. Bonné-Temir wrote that "Our purpose in studying the differences and similarities between various Jewish populations was not to determine whether a Jewish race exists. Nor was it to discover the original genes of 'ancient Hebrews,' or to retrieve genetic characteristics in the historical development of the Jews.

"Rather, it was to evaluate the extent of 'heterogeneity' in the separate populations, to construct a profile of each population as shaped by the genetic data, and to draw inferences about the possible influences of dispersion, migration, and admixture processes on the genetic composition of these populations."

In 1999, Dr. Bonné-Temir organized an international symposium on Genomic Views of Jewish History. "And unfortunately, the many papers presented were never published," says Bonné-Temir.

Molecular Genealogy Research Projects

Certain mtDNA haplogroups and mutations or markers within the haplogroups turn up in research studies of Ashkenazim when scientists look at the maternal lineages. For example, 9.0 of Ashkenazic (Jewish) women have mtDNA haplogroups that follow the Cambride Reference Sequence (CRS) (Anderson et al. 1981).

That means their matrilineal ancestry lines follow the reference sequence that all other mtDNA haplogroup markers are compared with. The CRS shows a specific sequence of mtDNA haplogroup H found in more than 46% of all Europeans and 6% of Middle Eastern peoples. You can view a table of mtDNA sequences titled "Frequently Encountered mtDNA Hapotypes" at Table 3 in the article, "*Founding Mothers of Jewish Communities: Geographically Separated Jewish Groups Were Independently Founded by Very Few Female Ancestors,*" Mark G. Thomas et al, American Journal of Human Genetics, 70:1411-1420, 2002.

The only exception is that the Ashkenazic mtDNA haplogroup maternal ancestral lines, show up at only 2.6% with one mutation away from the CRS 343 creating U3 mtDNA haplogroup instead of the H mtDNA haplogroup. The CRS is H haplogroup.

Where does U3 mtDNA show up at the higher rate of 17%? In Iraqi Jews. Ashkenazi mtDNA shows up at 9.0 percent following the CRS with H mtDNA haplogroup. Yet 27.0% of Moroccan Jews have mtDNA following the CRS. So does more than 46% of all Europeans and 25% of all Middle Eastern people have MtDNA following the CRS. That's haplogroup H of the Cambridge Reference Sequence.

The table in the article mentioned above has many sequences of mtDNA listed. Ashkenazi mtDNA was compared to MtDNA in other Jewish groups—Moroccan, Iraqi, Iranian, Georgian, Bukharan, Yemenite, Ethopian, and Indian. These were compared to non-Jewish Germans, Berbers, Syrians,

Georgian non-Jews, Uzbeks, Yemenites, Ethiopian non-Jews, Hindus, and Israeli Arabs. The percentage of frequencies of HSV-1 mtDNA sequences were listed in the samples from sites 16090-16365.

Looking only at Ashkenazi mtDNA, the mutations 184 and 265T show up in 2.6% of the Ashkenazi mtDNA. Yet in Jews from Bukhara, these same mutations show up in 15.2% of mtDNA.

And 129 and 223 mutations show up in 2.6% of the Ashkenazi mtDNA. Yet in Bukharian Jewish mtDNA, this mutation shows up at 12.1%. The rest of the Ashkenazi mtDNA stands at 9.0% for matching the CRS. That's H haplogroup, the most frequent mtDNA haplogroup found in Europe. Only 1.3% of Ashkenazic mtDNA has one mutation at 274. Yet 20% of Yemenite Jewish mtDNA shows this same mutation at 274.

Be aware that not every Jewish person has been tested for mtDNA or Y-chromosomes. You first have to research how significant samples are in speaking for the majority of any population. They do have scientific credibility, but you must always look at the sample size.

DNA-driven genealogy is about tracing patterns—from patterns in the genes to patterns in the migrations. Where do the women—the founding mothers—of the Eastern European Jewish communities—the Ashkenazim—originate? How do their origins compare with the origins of the founding fathers, the paternal lines?

I asked genetic scientist, Dr. Mark Thomas, Department of Biology, University College London what his latest research findings were on Ashkenazi women as I had read his recent study.*

The article referred to in his letter is titled, *"Founding Mothers of Jewish Communities: Geographically Separated Jewish Groups Were Independently Founded by Very Few Female Ancestors,"* American Journal of Human Genetics. 70:1411-1420, 2002. The study was researched by Dr. Mark G. Thomas, Martin Richards, Michael E. Weale, Antonio Toroni, David B. Goldstein, et al. Here is his reply.

Dear Anne:

Our study did not conclude that they are not related to one another and not related to anyone in the Middle East. Neither did it conclude that they are wholly Slavic.

Our study presented evidence for strong independent female founding events in most Jewish communities. This evidence was

not as strong for Ashkenazi Jews and we proposed that Ashkenazi Jews were made up of a mosaic of different, independently founded communities that has since homogenised.

Because of the evidence for strong independent female founding events, assigning an origin to those founding mothers becomes a very difficult, if not impossible task. There was some suggestion in two communities, Indian Jews and Ethiopian Jews, of a local rather than a Middle Eastern origin for the founding mothers. I have enclosed a PDF version of our paper.

I hope this helps.
Best wishes
Mark

Dr Mark Thomas
Department of Biology
University College London
Web: www.ucl.ac.uk/tcga/

◆   ◆   ◆

DNA Testing for Ancestry

When written records cannot be found, is the next step DNA testing for deep paternal and maternal ancestry? Or further testing of more markers? The Y-chromosome is paternally inherited, and it's a non-recombining portion revealing gene genealogy of any ethnic group. Whether you're interested in human prehistory or your most recent common ancestor, that non-recombining portion of the Y-chromosome will in time show you accurate genetic genealogy.

It's the large stable non-recombining portion of the genome. You have many slowly and rapidly evolving markers. And your ancestry can be read in those markers from your prehistory to current yourself. The fields of DNA-driven genealogy, genomics, and genetic anthropology often come with the prefix 'geno' in front of another word as in "geno-geography" or "geno-journalism."

Men carry their mother's mtDNA but pass on to their sons their Y-chromosome. Women pass on their mtDNA haplogroup only to their daughters. Genomic views of any ethnic group's history are important for further study. Whether you are taking the skeptic's position or the genomic view of your cultural history, biology does have a cultural component that needs to be analyzed scientifically. Finding flaws or benefits in research studies of any kind is the way to find inroads to truths. How else can facts change and knowledge progress?

Molecular genealogy has joined efforts with molecular genetics. How can this information help you in family history research? Ugo A. Perego, MS. Senior Project Administrator, Molecular Genealogy Research Project, Brigham Young University, http://molecular-genealogy.byu.edu, says, "I believe that DNA is the next thing in genealogy—the tool for the 21st century family historians. In the past 20 years, the genealogical world has been revolutionized by the introduction of the Internet.

"An increasing number of people are becoming interested in searching for their ancestors because through emails and websites a large world of family history information is now available to them. The greatest contribution of molecular methods to family history is the fact that in some instances family relationships and blocked genealogies can be extended even in the absence of written records.

"Adoptions, illegitimacies, names that have been changes, migrations, wars, fire, flood, etc. are all situations in which a record may become unavailable. However, no one can change our genetic composition, which we have received by those that came before us.

"Currently, DNA testing is an effective approach to help with strict paternal and maternal lines thanks to the analysis and comparison of the Y chromosome (male line) and mitochondrial DNA (female line) in individuals that have reason to believe the existence of a common paternal or maternal ancestor.

"A large database of genetic and genealogical data is currently been built by the BYU Center for Molecular Genealogy and the **Sorenson Molecular Genealogy Foundation** at: http://smgf.org/. This database will contain thousands of pedigree charts and DNA from people from all over the world. Currently it has already over 35,000 participants in it.

"The purpose of this database is to provide additional knowledge in reconstructing family lines other than the paternal and maternal, by using a large number of autosomal DNA (the DNA found in the non-sex chromosomes).

This research, known as the Molecular Genealogy Research Project is destined to take DNA for genealogists to the next level."

For additional reading, please visit the BYU's Molecular Genealogy Research Project's Web sites, the Sorenson Molecular Genealogy Foundation at: http://smgf.org/, or read an article in PDF file format titled, *Large Scale DNA Variation as an Aid to Reconstruction of Extended Human Pedigrees* at: http://smgf.org/PosterASHG2003.pdf. Another good source of information is the site at Relative

Genetics, a company specializing in Y chromosome analysis for family studies at: http://www.relativegenetics.com. According to The Sorenson Molecular Genealogy Foundation's Web site, "The Sorenson Molecular Genealogy Foundation (SMGF) is a non-profit organization committed to developing the world's foremost database of correlated genetic and genealogical information, and making this information freely available to the public.

"DNA analysis is a powerful new tool for genealogical research. The SMGF database will allow genealogists to use their own genetic profile to identify possible genealogical links. This database is currently the largest of its kind in the world."

For further information on contributing your DNA to the worldwide database, contact the Sorenson Molecular Genealogy Foundation at the address below.

Sorenson Molecular Genealogy Foundation
2511 South West Temple
Salt Lake City, UT 84115
Email: info@smgf.org.
Web site: http://smgf.org/.

What Are Your Genes Doing In That Temporary Container?

Have you ever wondered what your genes are doing in your "temporary container" before they move on and change and where they have traveled during the past 40,000 years or more? When you have your DNA tested, work with the lab and DNA testing company, and ask them to explain to you how the 37+ Y-chromosome markers you had tested as a male or mtDNA as a female help you determine your ancestry or find any matches similar to your DNA in a database. Read the frequently asked questions files of DNA testing companies online. Ask questions by email.

Sons inherit their mtDNA from their own mothers. Then mothers pass mtDNA on to their daughters. Sons also inherit the Y-chromosome from their fathers, but do not pass it to their daughters. Women don't have Y chromosomes.

The mtDNA is passed down from mother to son and mother to daughter through the cytoplasm (the cell contents surrounding the nucleus) in the egg. Only the daughters pass on their mtDNA to their daughters. And sons pass their Y-chromosomes to their sons, but those sons carry the mtDNA of their own mothers.

Even though both sons and daughters are formed from the union of a sperm and an egg, only the daughters will pass their mtDNA (which is the same as their great grandmother's on their maternal side and still further back to the first founder of their mtDNA group. Only daughters will pass the mtDNA on to the next generation.

Each lab has different methods of reporting their results, but you can use DNA test results as a tool for learning family history. Join DNA mailing lists and research or ask questions of the DNA testing firms specializing in genealogy by genetics about how many mutations occur in how many generations.

Do your own research independently of any laboratory that tested your own DNA if you're curious about Y-chromosome DNA tests. Males take Y-chromosome DNA tests to find out paternal ancestry lineages.

Males also can have their mtDNA checked, but women don't have a Y chromosome. So women only can check their maternal lineages with mitochondrial (mtDNA) tests. I also recommend the book titled, *Predictive Medicine for Rookies: Consumer Watchdogs, Reviews, & Genetics Testing Firms Online.* ISBN: 0-595-35146-8, Published: Apr-2005, 402 pages.

24

DNA-Driven Genealogy Reports and Personal History Time Capsules

Did you ever wonder what the next money-making step for entrepreneurs in DNA-driven genealogy is regarding searching records for family history and ancestry? It's about opening a genealogy-driven DNA testing or reporting service. Take your pick: tracking ancestry by DNA for pets or people.

You don't need any science courses or degrees to start or operate this small reporting business. You don't look at anyone's DNA. You only report what the findings regarding ancestry mean in plain language. A laboratory or a university research project partnering with your DNA-driven genealogy reporting service actually does the testing. You package reports to send to clients who have their DNA tested for deep, ancient ancestry or to see whether a group of people with the same surname could be related in the past 600 years or so. You disseminate information in plain language as to how scientists have interpreted your client's Y chromosome, mtDNA, racial percentages, or other DNA-driven genealogy tests for ancestry.

A reporting service can be done online, at home, or in an office. People get tested and receive reports by mail and email, on CDs or in other information packages on the subject of how to interpret their DNA tests for ancestry only. What should you charge per test? About $200 is affordable. You'll have to pay a laboratory to do the testing. Work out your budget with the laboratory.

Laboratories that do the testing can take up to fifty percent of what you make on every test unless they have research grants to test a particular ethnic group and need donors to give DNA for testing. Each lab is different. Shop around for an affordable, reputable laboratory. Your first step would be to ask the genetics and/or molecular anthropology departments of universities who's applying for a grant to do DNA testing. Also check out the oral history libraries which usually are based at universities and ethnic museums. You're bringing together two different groups—genealogists and geneticists.

You'd work with the laboratories that do the testing. Customers want to see online message boards to discuss their DNA test results and find people whose DNA sequences match their own.

So you'd need a Web site with databases of the customers, message boards, and any type of interactive communication system that allows privacy and communication. DNA database material would not show real names or identify the people. So you'd use numbers. Those who want to contact others could use regular email addresses. People want ethnic privacy, but at the same time love to find DNA matches. At this point you might want to work only with dogs, horses, or other pets or farm animals providing a DNA testing service for ancestry or nutrition.

Take your choice as an entrepreneur: sending the DNA of people to laboratories to be tested for ancestry or having the DNA of dogs, horses or other pets and animals sent out to be tested for ancestry and supplying reports to owners regarding ancestry or for information on how to tailor food to the genetic signatures of people or animals. For animals, you'd contact breeders.

For people, your next step is to contact genealogists and genealogy online and print publications. You'd focus on specific ethnic groups as a niche market. The major groups interested in ancestry using DNA testing include Northern European, Ashkenazi, Italian, Greek, Armenian, Eastern European, African, Asian, Latin American, and Middle Eastern.

Many successful entrepreneurs in the DNA testing for ancestry businesses started with a hobby of looking up family history records—genealogy. So if you're a history buff, or if your hobby is family history research, oral history, archaeology, or genealogy, you now can turn to DNA testing.

What you actually sell to customers are DNA test kits and DNA test reports. To promote your business, offer free access to your Web site database with all your clients listed by important DNA sequences. Keep names private and use only assigned numbers or letters to protect the privacy of your clients. Never give private and confidential genetic test information to insurance companies or employers. Clients who want to have their DNA tested for ancestry do not want their names and DNA stored to fall into the "wrong hands." So honor privacy requests. Some people will actually ask you to store DNA for future generations.

If you want to include this service, offer a time capsule. For your clients, you would create a time capsule, which is like a secure scrap book on acid-free paper and on technology that can be transferred in the future when technology changes.

Don't store anything on materials that can't be transferred from one technology to another. For example, have reports on acid-free paper.

You can include a CD or DVD also, but make sure that in the future when the CD players aren't around any longer, the well-preserved report, perhaps laminated or on vellum or other acid-free materials that don't crumble with age can be put into the time capsule. You can include a scrap book with family photos and video on a CD if you wish, or simply offer the DNA test report and comments explaining to the customer what the DNA shows.

Use plain language and no technical terms unless you define them on the same page. Your goal is to help people find other people who match DNA sequences and to use this knowledge to send your customers reports. If no matches can be found, then supply your clients with a thorough report. Keep out any confusing jargon. Show with illustrations how your customer's DNA was tested. In plain language tell them what was done.

Your report will show the results, and tell simply what the results mean. You can offer clients a list of how many people in what countries have their same DNA sequences. Include the present day city or town and the geographic location using longitude and latitude. For example, when I had my mtDNA (maternal lineages) tested, the report included my DNA matches by geographic coordinates. The geographic center is 48.30N 4.65E, Bar sur Aube, France with a deviation of 669.62 miles as done by "Roots for Real," a London company that tests DNA for ancestry. The exact sequences are in the Roots for Real Database (and other mtDNA databases) for my markers.

You're going to ask, with no science background yourself, how will you know what to put in the report? That's the second step. You contact a university laboratory that does DNA testing for outside companies. They will generate all the reports for you. What you do with the report is to promote it by making it look visually appealing. Define any words you think the customer won't understand with simpler words that fully explain what the DNA sequences mean and what the various letters and numbers mean. Any dictionary of genetic terms will give you the meaning in one sentence using plain language. Use short sentences in your reports and plain language.

Your new service targets genealogists who help their own customers find lost relatives. Your secondary market is the general public. Most people taking a DNA test for ancestry want information on where their DNA roamed 20,000 years ago and in the last 10,000 years. DNA testing shows people only where their ancient ancestors camped. However, when sequences with other people match exactly, it could point the way to an ancient common ancestor whose descendants went in a straight line from someone with those sequences who lived 10,000 years ago to a common ancestor who lived only a few generations ago.

Those people may or may not actually be related, but they share the same sequences. The relationship could be back in a straight line 20,000 years or more or only a few centuries. Ancient DNA sequences are spread over a huge area, like mine—from Iceland to Bashkortostan in the Urals. DNA sequences that sprung up only a few generations ago generally are limited to a more narrow geographic area, except for those who lived in isolation in one area for thousands of years, such as the Basques.

You would purchase wholesale DNA kits from laboratory suppliers and send the kits to your customer. The customer takes a painless cheek scraping with a felt or cotton type swab or uses mouthwash put into a small container to obtain DNA that can help accurately determine a relationship with either a 99.9% probability of YES or a 100% certainly that no near term relationship existed.

The DNA sample is sealed and mailed to a laboratory address where it is tested. The laboratory then disposes of the DNA after a report is generated. Then you package the report like a gift card portfolio, a time capsule, or other fancy packaging to look like a gift. You add your promotional material and a thorough explanation of what to expect from the DNA test—the results.

The best way to learn this business is to check out on the Web all the businesses that are doing this successfully. Have your own DNA tested and look at the printout or report of the results. Is it thorough? Does it eliminate jargon? Include in the report materials the client would like to see. Make it look like a press kit. For example, you take a folder such as a report folder. On the outside cover print the name of your company printed and a logo or photograph of something related to DNA that won't frighten away the consumer. Simple graphic art such as a map or globe of the world, a prehistoric statue, for example the Willendorf Venus, or some other symbol is appropriate.

Inside, you'd have maps, charts, and locations for the client to look at. Keep the material visual. Include a CD with the DNA sequences if you can. The explanation would show the customer the steps taken to test the DNA.

Keep that visual with charts and graphs. Don't use small print fonts or scientific terminology to any extent so your customer won't feel your report is over his or her head. Instead use illustrations, geographic maps. Put colorful circles on the cities or geographic locations where that person's DNA is found.

Put a bright color or arrow on the possible geographic area of origin for those DNA sequences. Nobody can pinpoint an exact town for certain, but scientists know where certain DNA sequences are found and where they might have sat out the last Ice Age 20,000 years ago, and survived to pass those same DNA sequences on to their direct descendants, that customer of yours who has those sequences.

In the last decade, businesses have opened offering personality profilers. This decade, since the human genome code was cracked and scientists know a lot more about DNA testing for the courtroom, DNA testing businesses have opened to test DNA for information other than who committed a crime or to prove who's innocent. Applications of DNA testing now are used for finding ancient and not-so-ancient ancestry. DNA testing is not only used for paternity and maternity testing, but for tailoring what you eat to your genetic signature. The new field of pharmacogenetics also tests DNA for markers that allow a client to customize medicine to his or her genetic expression.

You may be an entrepreneur with no science background. That's okay as long as your laboratory contacts are scientists. Your most important contact and contract would be with a DNA testing laboratory. Find out who your competitors contract with as far as testing laboratories. For example, Family Tree DNA at the Web site: http://www.familytreedna.com/faq.html - q1 sends its DNA samples to be tested by the DNA testing laboratories at the University of Arizona.

Bennett Greenspan, President and CEO of Family Tree DNA founded Family Tree in 1999. Greenspan is an entrepreneur and life-long genealogy enthusiast. He successfully turned his family history and ancestry hobby into a full-time vocation running a DNA testing-for-ancestry company. Together with Max Blankfeld, they founded in 1997 GoCollege.com a website for college-bound students which survived the .COM implosion. Max Blankfeld is Greenspan's Vice President of Operations/Marketing. Before entering the business world, Blankfeld was a journalist. After that, he started and managed several successful ventures in the area of public relations as well as consumer goods both in Brazil and the US. Today, the highly successful Family Tree DNA is America's first genealogy-driven DNA testing service.

At the University of Arizona, top DNA research scientists such as geneticist, Mike Hammer, PhD, population geneticist Bruce Walsh, PhD, geneticist Max F. Rothschild, molecular anthropologist, Theodore G. Schurr, and lab manager, Matthew Kaplan along with the rest of the DNA testing team do the testing and analysis. So it's important if you want to open your own DNA for ancestry testing company to contract with a reputable laboratory to do the testing. Find out whether the lab you're going to be dealing with will answer a client's questions in case of problems with a test that might require re-testing. Clients will come to you to answer questions rather than go to the busy laboratory. Most laboratories are either part of a university, a medical school, or are independent DNA testing laboratories run by scientists and their technicians and technologists.

Your business will have a very different focus if you're only dealing with genealogy buffs testing their DNA for ancestry than would a business testing DNA for genetic risk markers in order to tailor a special diet or foods to someone's genetic risk markers. For that more specialized business, you'd have to partner with a nutritionist, scientist, or physician trained in customizing diets to genetic signatures. Many independent laboratories do test genes for the purpose of tailoring diets to genes. The new field is called nutrigenomics. Check out the various Web sites devoted to nutrigenomics if you're interested in this type of DNA testing business. For example, there is Alpha-Genetics at http://www.alpha-genics.com.

According to Dr. Fredric D. Abramson, PhD, S.M., President and CEO of AlphaGenics, Inc., "The key to using diet to manage genes and health lies in managing gene expression (which we call the Expressitype). Knowing your genotype merely tells you a starting point. Genotype is like knowing where the entrance ramps to an interstate can be found. They are important to know, but tell you absolutely nothing about what direction to travel or how the journey will go. That is why Expressitype must be the focus." You can contact AlphaGenics, Inc. at: http://www.alpha-genics.com or write to: Maryland Technology Incubator, 9700 Great Seneca Highway, Rockville, MD 20850.

Why open any kind of a DNA testing business? It's because the entrepreneur is at the forefront of a revolution in our concept of ancestry, diet, and medicines. Genes are tested to reveal how your body metabolizes medicine as well as food, and genes are tested for ancient ancestry or recent relationships such as paternity. Genes are tested for courtroom evidence.

So you have the choice of opening a DNA testing service focusing on diet, ancestry, skin care product matches, or medicine. You can have scientists contract with you to test genes for risk or relationships. Some companies claim to test DNA in order to determine whether the skin care products are right for your genetic signature. It goes beyond the old allergy tests of the eighties.

"Each of us is a unique organism, and for the first time in human history, genetic research is confirming that one diet is not optimum for everyone," says Abramson. Because your genes differ from someone else's, you process food and supplements in a unique way. Your ancestry is unique also.

Do you want to open a business that tunes nutrition to meet the optimum health needs of each person? If so, you need to contract with scientists to do the testing. If you have no science background, it would be an easier first step to open a business that tests DNA only for ancestry and contract with university laboratories who know about genes and ancestry.

Your client would receive a report on only the ancestry. This means the maternal and/or paternal sequences. For a woman it's the mtDNA that's tested. You're testing the maternal lineages. It's ancient and goes back thousands of years. For the man, you can have a lab test the Y-chromosome, the paternal lineages and the mtDNA, the maternal lineages.

What you supply your clients with is a printout report and explanation of the individual's sequences and mtDNA group called the haplogroup and/or the Y-chromosome ancestral genetic markers. For a male, you can test the Y-chromosome and provide those markers, usually 25 markers and the mtDNA. For a woman, you can only test the mtDNA, the maternal line for haplogroup letter and what is called the HVS-1 and HVS-2 sequences. These sequences show the maternal lineages back thousands of years. To get started, look at the Web sites and databases of all the companies that test for ancestry using DNA.

What most of the DNA testing entrepreneurs have in common is that they can do business online. People order the DNA testing kit online. The companies send out a DNA testing kit. The client sends back DNA to a lab to be tested. The process does not involve any blood drawing to test for ancestry. Then the company sends a report directly to the customer about what the DNA test revealed solely in regard to ancient ancestry—maternal or paternal lines.

Reports include the possible geographic location where the DNA sequences originated. Customers usually want to see the name of an actual town, even though towns didn't exist 10,000 years ago when the sequences might have arisen. The whole genome is not tested, only the few ancestral markers, usually 500 base pairs of genes. Testing DNA for ancestry does not have anything to do with testing genes for health risks because only certain genes are tested—genes related to ancestry. And all the testing is done at a laboratory, not at your online business.

If you're interested in a career in genetics counseling and wish to pursue a graduate degree in genetics counseling, that's another career route. For information, contact The American Board of Genetic Counseling. Sometimes social workers with some coursework in biology take a graduate degree in genetic counseling since it combines counseling skills with training in genetics and in interpreting genetics tests for your clients.

The American Board of Genetic Counseling.
9650 Rockville Pike
Bethesda, MD 20814-3998

Phone: (301) 571-1825
FAX: (301) 571-1895
http://www.abgc.net/

Below is a list of several DNA-testing companies. Some of these companies test DNA only for ancestry. Other companies listed below test genes for personalized medicine and nutrigenomics, and some companies test for nutrigenomics, pharmacogenetics, and ancestry.

You'll also find several companies listed that only test the DNA of animals. So you have a choice of testing DNA for a variety of purposes, for testing human DNA only, or for testing animal DNA. And the applications for testing genetic signatures are growing, since this science is still in its infancy in regard to applications of genetic and genomic testing. Below are just a few of the numerous DNA-testing firms that test DNA for ancestry.

◆   ◆   ◆

DNA-Driven Genealogy DNA Testing Companies

Family Tree DNA—Genealogy by Genetics, Ltd.
World Headquarters
1919 North Loop West, Suite 110 Houston, Texas 77008, USA
http://www.familytreeDNA.com/

Roots for Real
http://www.rootsforreal.com
address: PO Box 43708
London W14 8WG UK

Oxford Ancestors
Oxford Ancestors, London,
http://www.oxfordancestors.com/

AncestrybyDNA, DNAPrint genomics, Inc.
900 Cocoanut Ave, Sarasota, FL 34236. USA
http://www.ancestrybydna.com/

GeneTree DNA Testing Center
2495 South West Temple

Salt Lake City, UT 84115
http://www.genetree.com/

Trace Genetics LLC
P.O. Box 2010
Davis, California 95617
info@tracegenetics.com
http://www.tracegenetics.com/aboutus.html

Predictive Genomics for Personalized Medicine including Nutrigenomics

AlphaGenics Inc.
9700 Great Seneca Highway
Rockville, Maryland 20850
info@alpha-genics.com
http://www.alpha-genics.com/index.php

Genovations ™
Great Smokies Diagnostic Laboratory/Genovations™
63 Zillicoa Street
Asheville, NC 28801 USA
http://www.genovations.com/

Centre for Human Nutrigenomics
http://www.nutrigenomics.nl/
According to its Web site, "The Centre for Human NutriGenomics aims at establishing an international centre of expertise combining excellent pre-competitive research and high quality (post)graduate training on the interface of genomics, nutrition and human health."
Nutrigenomics Links: http://nutrigene.4t.com/nutrigen.htm

Bibliographies

Bibliography 1.

Genealogy:

A Bintel Brief: Sixty Years of Letters From the Lower East Side to the Jewish Daily Forward. Metzker, Isaac, ed Doubleday and Co. 1971. Garden City, NY

Climbing Your Family Tree: Online and Offline Genealogy for Kids IRA Wolfman, Tim Robinson (Illustrator), Alex Haley (Introduction)/ Paperback/ Workman Publishing Company, Inc./ October 2001

Complete Beginner's Guide to Genealogy, the Internet, and Your Genealogy Computer Program Karen Clifford/ Paperback/ Genealogical Publishing Company, Incorporated/ February 2001

Complete Idiot's Guide(R) to Online Geneology Rhonda McClure/ Paperback/ Pearson Education/ January 2002

Creating Your Family Heritage Scrapbook : From Ancestors to Grandchildren, Your Complete Resource & Idea Book for Creating a Treasured Heirloom. Nerius, Maria Given, Bill Gardner ISBN: 0761530142 Published by Prima Publishing, Aug 2001

Cyndi's List: A Comprehensive List of 70,000 Genealogy Sites on the Internet (Vol. 1 & 2) Cyndi Howells/ Paperback/ Genealogical Publishing Company, Incorporated/ June 2001.

Discovering Your Female Ancestors: Special strategies for uncovering your hard-to-find information about your female lineage. Carmack, Sharon DeBartolo. Conference Lecture on Audio Tape: Carmack, Sharon DeBartolo.

Folklife and Fieldwork: A Layman's Introduction to Field Techniques. Bartis, Peter. Washington, DC: Library of Congress, 1990.

Genealogy Online for Dummies Matthew L. Helm, April Leigh Helm, April Leigh Helm, Matthew L. Helm/ Paperback/ Wiley, John & Sons, Incorporated/ February 2001

Genealogy Online Elizabeth Powell Crowe/ Paperback/ McGraw-Hill Companies, November 2001

History From Below: How to Uncover and Tell the Story of Your Community, Association, or Union. Brecher, Jeremy. New Haven: Advocate Press/Commonwork Pamphlets, 1988.

My Family Tree Workbook: Genealogy for Beginners Rosemary A. Chorzempa/ Paperback/ Dover Publications, Incorporated/

National Genealogical Society Quarterly 79, no. 3 (September 19991): 183-93

"Numbering Your Genealogy: Sound and Simple Systems." Curran, Joan Ferris.

Oral History and the Law. Neuenschwander, John. Pamphlet Series #1. Albuquerque: Oral History Association, 1993.

Oral History for the Local Historical Society. Baum, Willa K. Nashville: American Association for State and Local History, 1987.

Scrapbook Storytelling: Save Family Stories & Memories with Photos, Journaling & Your Own Creativity Slan, Joanna Campbell, Published by EFG, Incorporated, ISBN: 0963022288 May 1999

"The Silent Woman: Bringing a Name to Life." NE-59. Boston, MA: New England Historic Genealogical Society Sesquicentennial Conference, 1995.

The Source: A Guidebook of American Genealogy Alice Eichholz, Loretto Dennis Szucs (Editor), Sandra Hargreaves Luebking (Editor), Sandra Hargreaves Luebking (Editor)/ Hardcover/ MyFamily.com, Incorporated/ February 1997

To Our Children's Children: Journal of Family Members, Bob Greene, D. G. Fulford 240pp. ISBN: 038549064X Publisher: Doubleday & Company, Incorporated: October 1998.

Transcribing and Editing Oral History. Nashville: American Association for State and Local History, 1991.

Using Oral History in Community History Projects. Buckendorf, Madeline, and Laurie Mercier. Pamphlet Series #4. Albuqueque: Oral History Association, 1992.

Unpuzzling Your Past: The Best-Selling Basic Guide to Genealogy (Expanded, Updated and Revised) Emily Anne Croom, Emily Croom/ Paperback/ F & W Publications, Incorporated/ August 2001

Writing a Woman's Life. Heilbrun, Carolyn G. New York: W.W. Norton, 1988

Your Guide to the Family History Library: How to Access the World's Largest Genealogy Resource Paula Stuart Warren, James W. Warren/ Paperback/ F & W Publications, Incorporated/ August 2001

Your Story: A Guided Interview Through Your Personal and Family History, 2nd ed., 64pp.ISBN: 0966604105 Publisher: Stack Resources, LLC

Bibliography 2.

Genealogy in the Former Ottoman Empire

See: McGowan, Bruce William, 1933- Defter-i mufassal-i liva-i Sirem : an Ottoman revenue survey dating from the reign of Selim II./ Bruce William McGowan.

Ann Arbor, Mich.: University Microfilms, 1967.

See: Bogaziçi University Library Web sites:

http://seyhan.library.boun.edu.tr/search/wN{232}ufus+Defter/
wN{232}ufus+Defter/1,29,29,B/frameset&FF=wN{232}ufus+Defter&9,9,

or http://seyhan.library.boun.edu.tr/search/dTaxation+—+Turkey.
/dtaxation+turkey/-5,-1,0,B/exact&FF=dtaxation+turkey&1,57,

Jurisdictions and localities in Bulgaria:

Michev N. and P. Koledarov. Rechnik na selishchata i selishchnite imena v Bulgariia, 1878-1987 (Dictionary of villages and village names in Bulgaria, 1878-1987), Sofia: Nauka i izkustvo, 1989 (FHL book 949.77 E5m).

See: McGowan, Bruce William, 1933- Defter-i mufassal-i liva-i Sirem : an Otto-man revenue survey dating from the reign of Selim II./ Bruce William McGowan.

Ann Arbor, Mich.: University Microfilms, 1967.

Web sites Research and Genealogy in the Former Ottoman Empire

See: Bogaziçi University Library Web sites:

http://seyhan.library.boun.edu.tr/search/wN{232}ufus+Defter/
wN{232}ufus+Defter/1,29,29,B/frameset&FF=wN{232}ufus+Defter&9,9,

or http://seyhan.library.boun.edu.tr/search/dTaxation+—+Turkey.
/dtaxation+turkey/-5,-1,0,B/exact&FF=dtaxation+turkey&1,57,

◆   ◆   ◆

Bibliography 3.

DNA Testing and Genetics

A Biologist's Guide to Analysis of DNA Microarray Data Steen Knudsen/ Hard-cover/ Wiley, John & Sons, Incorporated/ April 2002

Advances and Opportunities in DNA Testing and Gene Probes Business Com-munications Company Incorporated (Editor)/ Hardcover/ Business Communi-cations/ September 1996

African Exodus, The Origins of Modern Humanity Stringer, Christopher and Robin McKie. Henry Holt And Company 1997

An A to Z of DNA Science: What Scientists Mean when They Talk about Genes and Genomes Jeffre L. Witherly, Galen P. Perry, Darryl L. Leja/ Paperback/ Cold Spring Harbor Laboratory Press/ September 2002

An Introduction to Forensic DNA Analysis Norah Rudin, Keith Inman/ Hard-cover/ CRC Press/ December 2001

Archaeogenetics: DNA and the population prehistory of Europe, Ed. Colin Renfrew & Katie Boyle. McDonald Institute Monographs. Cambridge, UK, Distributed by Oxbow Books UK. In USA: The David Brown Book Company, Oakville, CT. 2000

Cartoon Guide to Genetics Gonick, Larry, With Mark Wheelis: Paperback/ HarperInformation/ July 1991

DNA Detectives, The—Working Against Time, novel, Hart, Anne. Mystery and Suspense Press, iuniverse.com paperback 248 pages at http://www.iuniverse.com or 1-877-823-9235.

DNA for Family Historians (ISBN 0-9539171-0-X). Savin, Alan of Maidenhead, England, is author of the 32-page book. See the Web site: http://www.savin.org/dna/dna-book.html

DNA Microarrays and Gene Expression Pierre Baldi, G. Wesley Hatfield, G. Wesley Hatfield/ Hardcover/ Cambridge University Press/ August 2002

Microarrays for an Integrative Genomics Isaac S. Kohane, Alvin Kho, Atul J. Butte/ Hardcover/ MIT Press/ August 2002

Does It Run in the Family?: A Consumers Guide to DNA Testing for Genetic Disorders Doris Teichler Zallen, Doris Teichler-Zallen, Doris Teichler Zallen/ Hardcover/ Rutgers University Press/ May 1997

Double Helix, The: A Personal Account of the Discovery of the Structure of DNA James D. Watson/ Paperback/ Simon & Schuster Trade Paperbacks/ June 2001

Genes, Peoples, and Languages Luigi Luca Cavalli-Sforza, Mark Seielstad (Translator).

Genetic Witness: Forensic Uses of DNA Tests DIANE Publishing Company (Editor)/ Paperback/ DIANE Publishing Company/ April 1993

History and Geography of Human Genes, The [ABRIDGED] L. Luca Cavalli-Sforza, Paolo Menozzi (Contributor), Alberto Piazza (Contributor).

How to DNA Test Our Family Relationships Terry Carmichael, Alexander Ivanof Kuklin, Ed Grotjan/ Paperback/ Acen Press/ November 2000

Introduction to Genetic Analysis Anthony J. Griffiths, Suzuki, Lewontin, Gelbart, David T. Suzuki, Richard C. Lewontin, Willi Gelbart, Miller, Jeffrey H. Miller/ Hardcover/ W. H. Freeman Company/ February 2000

Jefferson's Children: The Story of One American Family Shannon Lanier, Jane Feldman, Lucian K. Truscott (Introduction)/ Hardcover/ Random House Books for Young Readers/ September 2000

Medical Genetics Lynn B. B. Jorde, Michael J. Bamshad, Raymond L. White, Michael J. Bamshad, John C. Carey, John C. Carey, Raymond L. White, John C. Carey/ Paperback/ Mosby-Year Book, Inc./ July 2000

Molecule Hunt, The: Archaeology and the Search for Ancient DNA Martin Jones/ Hardcover/ Arcade/ April 2002

More Chemistry and Crime: From Marsh Arsenic Test to DNA Profile Richard Saferstein, Samuel M. Gerber (Editor)/ Hardcover/ American Chemical Society/ August 1998

1996, Quest For Perfection—The Drive to Breed Better Human Beings, Maranto, Gina. Scribner, 1996

Our Molecular Future: How Nanotechnology, Robotics, Genetics, and Artificial Intelligence Will Transform Our World Mulhall, Douglas./ Hardcover/ Prometheus Books/ March 2002

Paternity—Disputed, Typing, PCR and DNA Tests: Index of New Information Dexter Z. Franklin/ Hardcover/ Abbe Pub Assn of Washington Dc/ January 1998

Paternity in Primates: Tests and Theories R. D. Martin (Editor), A. F. Dickson (Editor), E. J. Wickings (Editor)/ Hardcover/ Karger, S Publishers/ December 1991

Queen Victoria's Gene: Hemophilia and the Royal Family (Pbk) D. M. Potts, W. T. Potts/ Paperback/ Sutton Publishing, Limited/ June 1999

Redesigning Humans: Our Inevitable Genetic Future Stock, Gregory./ Hardcover/ Houghton Mifflin Company/ April 2002

Rosalind Franklin: The Dark Lady of DNA, Brenda Maddox/ Hardcover/ HarperCollins Publishers/ October 2002

Schaum's Outline Of Genetics Susan Elrod, William D. Stansfield/ Paperback/ McGraw-Hill Companies, The/ December 2001

Seven Daughters of Eve, The: The Science That Reveals Our Genetic Ancestry. Sykes, Bryan. ISBN: 0393323145 Publisher: Norton, W. W. & Company, Inc. May 2002

Stedman's OB-GYN & Genetics Words Ellen Atwood (Editor), Stedmans/ Paperback/ Lippincott Williams & Wilkins/ December 2000

◆   ◆   ◆

Middle East Genealogy Books

Before Taliban: Genealogies of the Afghan Jihad
by David B. Edwards (Paperback—April 2002)

Nationalism and the Genealogical Imagination: Oral History and Textual Authority in Tribal Jordan (Comparative Studies on Muslim Societies ; 23)
by Andrew Shryock (Paperback—February 1997)

Old Bohemian and Moravian Jewish Cemeteries
by Arno Parik, et al

Al-Sabah: Genealogy and History of Kuwait's Ruling Family, 1752-1986 (Middle East Cultures Series, No 13)
by Alan Rush

Genealogies of Conflict: Class, Identity, and State in Palestine/Israel and South Africa
by Ran Greenstein

History of Seyd Said, Sultan of Muscat
by Shaik Mansur, Robin Bidewell (Introduction) (Hardcover—1984)

Amarna Personal Names (American Schools of Oriental Research Dissertation, Vol 9)
by Richard S. Hess (Hardcover—October 1996)

Soberanos de leyenda
by Antonio García Jiménez

◆   ◆   ◆

Iran Genealogy-Related Books

Another Sea, Another Shore: Stories of Iranian Migration
by Shouleh Vatanabadi, et all (2003)

Funny in Farsi: A Memoir of Growing Up Iranian in America
by Firoozeh Dumas (2003)

Wedding Song: Memoirs of an Iranian Jewish Woman
by Farideh Goldin (2003)

Exiled Memories: Stories of the Iranian Diaspora
by Zohreh Sullivan (2001)

Journey from the Land of No : A Girlhood Caught in Revolutionary Iran
by Roya Hakakian (2004)

Inside Iran: Women's Lives
by Jane Mary Howard (2002)

◆   ◆   ◆

Books, Audios, and Videos by Anne Hart

Also See: Articles, Excerpts, & Video/Audio Links
Web links at http://www.newswriting.net

Instructional Videos and Audios at:
http://www.newswriting.net/writingvideos.htm

List of Anne Hart's published paperback books currently in print

http://www.newswriting.net
http://annehart.tripod.com

Audio Book of MP3 audio Creative Writing and Personal History Journalism Lectures

ISBN 1-59971-232-6; BAR CODE/ISBN: 9781599712321, Email: newswriting@hotmail.com for audio book information.

Video Lectures: 7 Video Lectures on personal history journalism also are available at http:// www.hollyflicks.com.

About the Author

Anne Hart has written more than 65 published books, including non-fiction, plays, and novels. Hart currently is an independent journalist writing for numerous magazines. She holds a graduate degree and is a member of the Association of Journalists and Authors and Mensa. Hart also has taught university-level courses in journalism and creative writing. She specializes in writing books and articles on genealogy, journalism, life story writing, self-help, documentary production, folklore, and social history.

Index

978-0-595-38698-7
0-595-38698-9

Printed in the United States
141515LV00001B/451/A

9 780595 386987